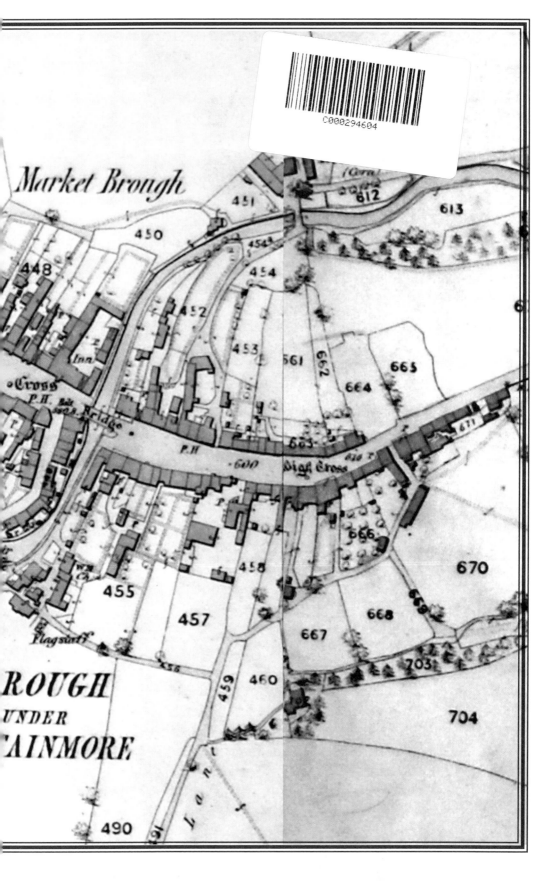

The Story of Brough-under-Stainmore

Margaret E. Gowling

HAYLOFT PUBLISHING LTD
STAINMORE

First published by Hayloft 2011

Hayloft Publishing Ltd, South Stainmore, Kirkby Stephen,
Cumbria, CA17 4DJ

tel: 07971 352473
email: books@hayloft.eu
web: www.hayloft.eu

ISBN 1 904524 79 6

CAP data for this title are available from the British Library

Designed, printed and bound in the EU

Papers used by Hayloft are natural, recyclable products made from wood grown in
sustainable forest. The manufacturing processes conform to the environmental
regulations of the country of origin.

Endpapers - first Ordnance Survey map, Brough, surveyed 1858.
Jacket photograph © Peter Koronka

To dare.

To Jack and Lucy, and to Sam and Imogen.

M Gadle.

18.6. 2011

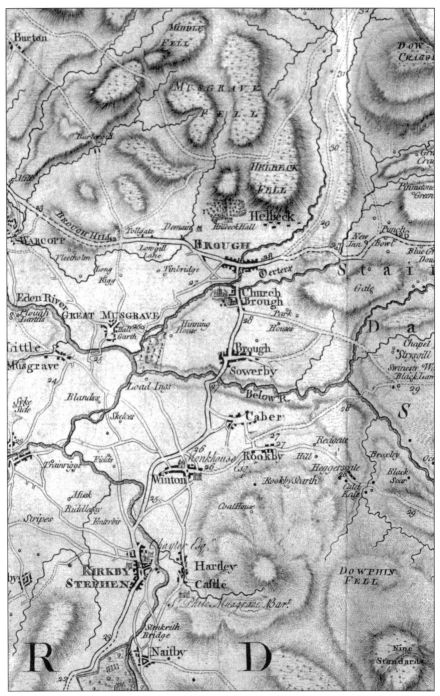

Map 1: T. Jefferys, Map of Westmorland, 1770.

Contents

Maps, Tables and Appendices

Place names and personal names change their spelling frequently. In most cases the original spelling of surnames as found in the documents is used to avoid any misinterpretation of the text. In the case of places where the varied spellings appear often in the same document, the common one is used, for example, Helbeck for Hillbeck, Hilbeck and Hellbeck and Brough Sowerby for Burgh Sowerby, or Soureby.

Foreword

Not by hearsay but by ancient records. John Denton.[1]

THE castle at Brough-under-Stainmore has been a landmark for travellers crossing Cumbria for centuries, yet little is known about other aspects of life there. The archaeology, architecture and aristocracy of the castle have all been covered in well researched books and articles. In addition its nineteenth century history has recently been covered in an excellent study of the Upper Eden Valley. Little, however, has been done on the lives of the ordinary villagers. This is an attempt to fill that gap.

This book does not claim to be a comprehensive history of Brough. It is based on local documents, and the survival of these is erratic and patchy. Yet enough remain to give glimpses of life which the official histories omit. How else would one know about the fate of Agnes, wife of Adam, or about the attack on the king's tax collector, or even what happened when Cuthbert Cumpston shot a hare? Is it possible to use the surnames of the 1380 Poll tax to distinguish occupations? Why did one tenant pay his rent in cumin? How did the cotton mill at Yosgill get its workers, and where did the miners of nineteenth century Stainmore go?

Situated on the edge of Stainmore where the uplands join the lowlands of the Eden Valley, its people had to cope with difficulties presented not only by natural features, such as the landscape and climate, but also with the human factors. For much of its early history, Brough lay within a border region, of the Roman Empire, and later of the Norman possessions. Then for centuries it was within a buffer zone between Scotland and England, which was rarely at peace. It lay on the edge of Northern England, well away from the centre of monarchical and administrative power. Even when the political position stabilised following the Union of Scotland and England, Brough could not take advantage of the developments taking place in Northern England, for once again it lay at a distance from main sources of power, which by this time were economic ones based on large reserves of coal, and iron ore. Its early building of a turnpike road was no substitute for mineral wealth or access to a deep water port. Again it was life on the edge.

Note 1: F. Haverfield, 'Cotton Iulius F. VI', CW2, 11 (1911), 369-70.

Samuel and Nathaniel Buck's engraving of the south-east view of Brough Castle, 26 March 1739.

As the sources used are discontinuous, this cannot be a seamless narrative, but the book is divided up into various periods, depending on what is available. Most of the work relies on documents held in the Cumbrian Record Offices, and my thanks go to Richard Hall, Peter Eyre and David Bowcock, and all the staff at the Kendal and Carlisle Record Offices who have been so willing to search their holdings. Chiefly I must thank the owners of the documents who have allowed me to quote from them. These include Lord Hothfield, the Dean and Chapter of Carlisle Cathedral, the Lowther Estate, and E. and E. A. Heelis of Appleby. Another splendid holding is at Kendal Library and I appreciate the help of Jackie Fay, the Local History librarian there.

In addition, Paul Booth and Dr Simon Harris of the History Department at the University of Liverpool, made some very helpful comments on the interpretations of some of the Medieval documents, while Dr David Williams and Mrs Marion Williams commented on an early draft of the first sections of the book, checked the geological details and were ever on hand to sort out computer problems. Dr Marie-Ann Ha helped with the initial planning of the work and kept a watching brief on the nutritional standards of each period; the subject I hope, of a future study. Both she and Sam Ha gave invaluable advice at the proof reading stage of the book.

Local people have been very helpful in lending material and searching their memories. These include John Walton, Alan Bell, Pat Smith and Ann Birkbeck, Thomas Raine of Brough Sowerby mill, Joyce Scott of Sowerby Park and Maureen Scott, late of Hollins. Thanks to Jon and Sue Atkins for the loan of the copy of the Buck engraving of Brough Castle, to Keith Morgan for helping with the re-framing, to David Yeadell for the drawings, to Cumbria Record office for permission to use among other things, the Brough Market charter and Mr Chris Dent of Swindale Grange, not only for lending his collection of first edition Ordnance maps, but for showing me the site at High Mill. A number of enthusiasts have walked the district with me looking at old water courses, and park boundaries. These include, Harry Hawkins, Dr Stephen Walker, Sir Martin Holdgate, Dawn Robertson, Isobel Derry and Ann Sandell. I am deeply grateful to everyone else who has helped in all sorts of ways to make this book possible.

A book as wide ranging in period as this must be heavily reliant on the work of other authors. My debt to the archaeologists and to those earlier writers whose research was document-based is profound. These are acknowledged in the text.

My husband John, prefers not to be named as a second author, but he has done an incredible amount of the work, for which I am very grateful. As a member of the Medieval Latin group based at the University of Liverpool, and then working under Dr Angus Winchester at Lancaster, he is responsible for transcribing the Poll tax and the fifteenth century manorial account. He is responsible for the chapters on the turnpike, the mining and Yosgill Mill. He has also indexed the book.

My greatest thanks must go to our publisher and editor, Dawn Robertson of Hayloft Publishing Ltd. Without her enthusiasm, knowledge and skills, nothing would have been achieved. All remaining errors are my own.

Margaret Gowling,
January 2011

CHAPTER 1

Introduction

*Brough-under-Stainmore is one of those grand localities where the
majestic continuity of British History dominates our imagination.* [2]

THIS splendid quotation forms the introduction to the last history to be published about Brough. This is not an example of flowery Victorian literature,
but the beginning of a serious academic study by Dr W. D. Simpson in
1946. It would appear that a reappraisal of the development of Brough is
needed. In more prosaic terms, Brough-under-Stainmore can be described
as a small settlement in the North Pennines, now known chiefly for its
ruined castle, which stands on a steep hillside overlooking the main route
through the Stainmore Gap. A medieval church, tucked away in the corner
of the green, and a few mounds, are the only other visible signs of its past
importance. Yet it was once the site of a Roman fort, later a Medieval
stronghold and then an early market centre.

By Tudor times, its fortunes had waned. Neglected by absentee manorial lords, it lost its market rights and became, to quote Sir Daniel Fleming:
"a decayed town — little more than a village,"[3] connected to the world only
by a "very exceeding poore thoroughfare to Burgh." A brief period of
revival in the eighteenth century followed the building of the first turnpike
in the area. This stimulated the development of the coaching trade and also
mining on Stainmore. This in turn led to investment in two new, but short-
lived enterprises as mills for cotton and dyestuffs were established.
However, when the railways were built in the nineteenth century, the lines
focused on Kirkby Stephen, five miles to the south, and Brough was left
without a rail link. To add to its problems, the long established droving
trade, which had, for centuries, brought people to the village, took to the
rails.

An unnamed traveller in August 1880 summed up the situation —
"Brough-on-Stainmore, that picturesque and extensive, but now greatly
decayed, market town."[4]

Note 2: Simpson, W D, *Brough-under-Stainmore: the castle and the church*, TCWAA, NS
XIII, 1946, pg126
Note 3: Fleming, D. ed. Duckett, *Description of the Countie of Westmorland AD1671*,
Kendal, 1871.
Note 4: Report of CWAA members' excursion to the Upper Eden Valley in 1879, TCWAA,
1st series, Kendal, 1881, p63.

Today Brough has a population of just under 300 households, divided between Church Brough around the castle, Market Brough along the main street, and Helbeck on the hillside.[5] Half a mile away is Brough Sowerby with another 55 households. Because of boundary changes, Stainmore (with 106 households) has not been included in the Brough figures.[6] Added together, these still make it less than half the size of Kirkby Stephen. It has no market, and no fair, and the main road by-passes the village. While this situation can attract commuters and retired people, there is not enough dynamic activity to sustain the services needed by a working population. It is in danger of becoming fossilised.

The changing fortunes of Brough are intriguing, and well worth a study. Important though its castle may have been, its presence alone could not halt the post-Medieval decline of the adjacent village. In this respect, it was certainly not unique for, like others in the district, such as Bowes, Appleby and Brougham, the limitations of its defensive position caused problems. In the case of Brough, the site was not the difficulty for, to the east of the castle and less than five minutes walk away, there was gently sloping land. The location, however, was a different matter. Politically, it was remote from the centres of power in England, as it was situated in the troubled Border zone of Northern England and Scotland which remained in turmoil until the reign of James I.

Even when peace was restored, its development was hindered by its remoteness. It was far inland and cut off to the north and east by the bleak, mountainous country of the North Pennines. The Stainmore Gap, one of the few passes through this area, was frequently hazardous. The Eden Valley to the south and west of Brough, presented other problems in that it was wide but marshy and equally difficult to negotiate. The climate added to the difficulties as the growing season was short, winters were severe and the rainfall heavy. In most of the parish, arable farming was limited to marginal land and there were few other resources to exploit.

However, another factor does need to be considered, and that is the human element. Brough was just one of a string of castles and manors which, from the thirteenth century, was owned by the Clifford family. Brough came very low in the hierarchy, and had little of the investment which Appleby, Brougham and Skipton shared. Yet Kirkby Stephen, a later market centre and without a resident lord had managed to develop a much wider range of activities, during the seventeenth century, and it was able to provide more of the services required in the coaching period and later, welcomed the railway companies.

Note 5: Cumbria County Council, policy document, 2008.
Note 6: ibid.

What lay behind these different attitudes? Did the problems lie in the social organisation of Brough or were the difficulties related more to the barren landscape of a large part of its parish?

This work will try to shed light on the social and economic development of Brough from around the beginning of the fourteenth century, for this is the period of the earliest surviving documentary evidence. However, to put this medieval scene into context, it is necessary to examine the Roman settlement and for this, the published work of a number of archaeological surveys have been used. For the later periods, reference has been made to original documents wherever possible.

Previous research on Brough has tended to concentrate on its development as a defensive site in Roman and Medieval times. Without the archaeologists little would be known of the early period. Apart from reports published in the 1950s by Prof. Eric Birley, the only other recent work was in 1972 by Manchester University Archaeological department, led by Dr. M. J. Jones. The possible routes of a Roman road across Stainmore into Brough were examined and also the area just outside the fort, which revealed an extra-mural settlement containing a Roman bathhouse and cemetery and early medieval housing. It has led to the hypothesis that there may have been continuous settlement in Church Brough since Roman times.

This work by archaeologists and historians has concentrated on the Roman period, in particular the fort, and then the nearby stone foundations of the Medieval period. Obviously these leave visible remains and are also better documented. However, a village history concentrating on these relics is inevitably biased towards the ruling classes and to the political scene while the normal occupation of the area is ignored. The more extensive documentation which has survived from the late Tudor period needs to be studied as this seems to have been a crucial period in the development of the village economy, a period which saw the decline of the market but the rise of long distance through-trade. The annual cattle fair however, retained its importance until the railways developed.

General histories of the area have covered Brough. One of the earliest, and one which is still valuable, is that of Nicolson and Burn, *History and Antiquities of the Counties of Westmorland and Cumberland*, published in 1777. It made use of rare documents collected a century earlier by Thomas Machell; some of these have now disappeared. The emphasis was on landownership and church property. Other writers, like Ferguson, have re-worked the same information. Many general histories such as those found in the nineteenth century directories of Westmorland, have relied on dubious sources.

The most systematic description of Brough is to be found in an article by Dr W. D. Simpson published by the Cumberland and Westmorland Antiquarian and Archaeological Society (CWAAS) in 1946.[7] His emphasis was on the history of the castle and the church for which he used both archaeological and documentary evidence. Some revision is needed in light of the more recent finds, but most of his work is still relevant. He was, for example, the first to point to the planned layout of Church Brough, a suggestion which Professor M. Beresford took up in his massive study of English new towns of the Middle Ages.[8]

One problem for researchers is the lack of original documents; villages had fewer needs for records than towns. Some may have been lost or destroyed, for many documents which should have been kept in the parish chest are missing. For the Medieval period there are occasional references in the Bishops' registers and in the State papers there are a number of Inquisitions Post Mortems (IPM). These describe the estates on the death of the lord of the manor. In addition, there are the poll taxes for 1379-80. Brough is particularly fortunate in having one set of steward's accounts for 1425 which at present, are being transcribed and translated. Then in the Elizabethan period, personal details of villagers appear in the Parish Registers which begin in 1559, and in the first surviving manor rental which dates from 1604. From then on, there are scattered papers, of tithes, churchwardens' accounts, and poor law accounts. There are also wills and inventories. Manor court records and Quarter Sessions records have survived from the end of the seventeenth century. By the end of the following century, the records are more numerous, and include many of the documents of at least one Turnpike Trust, and details of the leases of coal mines. The nineteenth century is well covered and it is the later censuses from 1851 onwards which are the most valuable.

This history will, of necessity, be somewhat disjointed for it is reliant on the chance survival of documents and there are many gaps, especially in the Medieval period. However, these sources do throw new light on the life of the villagers, which is an aspect ignored by previous histories.

Note 7: Simpson, op.cit.
Note 8: Beresford, M. W. *New Towns in the Middle Ages,* London: Lutterworth, (1967)

CHAPTER 2

Brough, as seen by early map makers

THROUGHOUT its history, Brough has been known by a variety of spellings, both on maps and in documents. The name Brough, or Burgus subtus Staynesmore,[9] (and its variations of Burc, Bourghe, or Burgh) originally meant a fortified settlement, a post-Roman name for the Roman fort of Verteris. In time, two villages grew up, one called Burgh Supra or sometimes Over Burgh, which is today Church Brough. The other was Nether or Lower Burgh, now Market Brough. Even the place names dictionary gets the two muddled, for it suggests that the southern village was Nether, or Inferior.[10] Manor accounts however, are clear that this was not so and by 1604 what is today Market Brough was called Nether Brough. Further discussion will be found in a later chapter. Helbeck, (or Hillbeck, in polite times) lay to the north of Brough. Brough Sowerby lay to the south, separated by ill-drained land (the sour land) from Church Brough. Although the Blenkinsops had held Helbeck before the Cliffords arrived on the scene, both Helbeck and Brough Sowerby were sub-tenancies of the Cliffords from at least the late thirteenth century but organised as different manors.

Brough was established before Westmorland was named. The first documented mention of the Barony of Westmeringland was in 1175, when it was not as extensive as the later county. When this was established, the northern part became known as the Bottom of Westmorland and this was later divided into West ward and East ward; the latter was centred on Appleby by the seventeenth century, if not earlier.[11]

When discussing the location of Brough it is useful to look at how it was depicted in the early maps. No estate map for Brough or any other locally made plans have been found before the nineteenth century tithe and enclosure awards were made. The earliest published map of Westmorland in any detail is that of Saxton which Speed later copied.[12] Made at the end of the sixteenth century, this delightful map shows Burgh castle, but its village is insignificant compared with Appleby and Kirkby Stephen and similar in size to Great Musgrave. The parks of Hartley Castle and Wharton are

Note 9: Smith, A. H., ed. *Place names of Westmorland*, XLII, EPNS CUP (1967).
Note 10: Ibid, 2, p63.
Note 11: Phillips, C., Ferguson, C., and Wareham, A., *Westmorland Hearth Tax*, British Record Society and CWAAS, (2009)
Note 12: Saxton, C., Maps from 1576, Speed, J. maps from 1610 (see next page)

Map 2: A section from Christopher Saxton's map of Westmorland, 1576, with later additions.

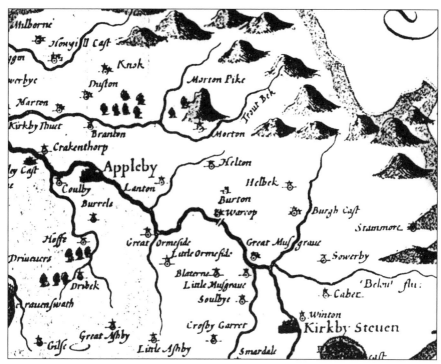

Map 3: A section from John Speed's map of the county in 1610.

shown to be of greater importance. The uplands, depicted as pictograms, lie well to the north, far beyond Helbeck, while Stainmore is a lowland area with the hills rising only on the Yorkshire border. The Swindale Beck is clearly shown, flowing southwards from the northern hills to join the Belah and the Eden at Great Musgrave. There are no roads marked, as the purpose of the map was to show the ancient buildings and the residences of the gentry. A number of later map publishers used the Saxton map as a base.

It was not until 1770 that a newly surveyed large-scale map was produced for the area. This was published by Jefferys, and it is very different from the older maps.[13] The hills are hachured and stand out clearly, with Helbeck Fell and Stainmore surrounding Brough on the north and east. Both these fells are clearly part of a major upland, with steep slopes and flat, but rocky hill tops. The Swindale and Augill becks flow through dramatic incised valleys from the north to a confluence in Church Brough before joining the Eden. The Belah (called Below) has entered the Eden at Load Ings.

The Eden Valley is flat enough from then on to allow the river to meander westwards through its generally marshy flood plain, which is interrupted

Note 13: Jefferys, T., *Historic Map of Westmorland, 1770, fac,.*CWAAS, 2001 (see page 4)

Map 4: Part of Morden's map of Westmorland, 1695. This shows the main road.

in places by small hills and steep river banks. Clearly marked, and labelled as the Roman or Military Way, is the main east to west road through Brough. By 1770, this had been turnpiked, and tollgates and some inns are shown. It is joined at Brough by a main road from the south via Orton, Ash Fell, and Kirkby Stephen. A smaller road out of Brough goes north into Teesdale and another one leads into the Musgrave Fells, but there is none shown between Helbeck and Market Brough. There are tracks to the south east, to the settlements of South Stainmore, and another, through Kaber, towards Tan Hill where coal pits are marked.

With the publication of the first edition of the large scale Ordnance Survey[14] maps [OS] the details of the Brough area become clearer. The survey was carried out in the late 1850s and the sheets published in December 1860. These, for the first time, showed the height of the land, the details of the river beds, field boundaries, and some types of vegetation, as well as the position of the larger mines and quarries, and important buildings. They revealed a lot of detail which the early mapmakers had been unable to measure. In addition, because of its mineral potential, the local geology had been surveyed by mineral prospecting companies before the first official maps were produced by the British Institute of Geological Surveys, which began work in 1835.

Two major landscapes are clearly shown on these maps. To the north and east, uplands dominate. To the south and west lies the lower area of the Eden Valley. Brough is sited on the lower slopes of the uplands, which are part of the Pennine escarpment, at the junction with the Eden lowlands. North of Brough, the Musgrave and Hillbeck (Helbeck) High Fells rise to over 1,900 feet and beyond at Burton Fell, the height is 2,399 feet. Mount Ida, which on a clear day dominates the view northwards from the village, is 1,474 feet. To the east of the Middleton road lies Stainmore, an area which stretches to the county boundary on the east, and southwards towards Kaber. It rises to over 1,800 feet at Iron Band, and even the route through the Stainmore Gap reaches 1,436 feet at the county boundary.

The uplands form part of the main watershed of England and the landscape has been deeply dissected by numerous streams. The Swindale and the Augill flow southwards to the Eden while the Argill joins the Belah, which collect the waters from the south and east before entering the Eden. Their river beds are shown with waterfalls, and rapids which are separated by sections of meanders with gravel deposits and small islands. These features are the result not only of a varied geology, but also of a highly fluctuating regime of precipitation.

Note 14: 25 inch, first ed. Ordnance Survey Sheet 16.16/16.15. Surveyed 1858, published 1860. Second ed. part re-surveyed 1897, pub. 1898.

The map shows that the uplands form a series of escarpments facing south west, with numerous steep sided cliffs, screes and exposed rock faces. The fell tops are flatter with wide deposits of marshy ground, separating bare rock fields. The main rock types are hinted at in some of the map details: Grindstone Hill, stone quarries, lime kilns, shake holes, and mines. This is an area of old hard rocks, mainly Carboniferous in age, consisting of limestone, with a variety of sandstones, varying from the coarse, block-like millstone grits, to the finely bedded sandstones and shales, which were used for roofing and known locally as slates. There are also small pockets of coal measures. Lead and other minerals were found in small scattered pipes or veins in the limestone areas.

Separating the uplands from the lowlands are a series of faults and the Eden valley is on younger, softer rocks, which overlie the older Carboniferous ones. These are the characteristic red rocks of the Penrith sandstone and shales, with some harder bands of St Bees sandstone. In places cliffs have been formed, as by the side of Brough church, but the landscape is generally one of rolling hills, about 580 to 600 feet high.

The whole landscape was modified during the Ice Ages. The last ice moved from the north west, across the Shap area, then across Brough and over into the eastern uplands towards the Vale of York. It left deep glacial troughs, and large lakes of melt water. On the higher land which was not covered by ice, the severe frosts shattered the exposed rocks and left broken boulders and screes. The lower areas, however, were covered with boulder clay, which was of thick mounds of unconsolidated, unsorted sands, gravel and other rock debris, now known to have been formed underneath moving ice. Often these deposits were left in small rounded hills, known as drumlins, which were separated by ill-drained hollows. These cover a large part of the Eden valley around Brough and Brough Sowerby.

In addition, in the post-glacial period, the Eden took over a wide open valley, part of which had been a lake bed, much of it covered in boulder clay and lake silts. The map shows the river meandering through a wide flood plain, with small islands along its braided channel. Even the smaller streams such as the Swindale and the Augill Beck, could undercut their banks and change their courses in time of flood once they had reached the lowlands. It was as the result of this type of erosion that, in the late eighteenth century, artefacts dating from Roman times, were revealed at the base of the hill on which the fort had been built. These highlighted the importance of the Roman occupation which will be discussed in the next chapter.

CHAPTER 3

The Roman period: the fort of Verteris

THE name Brough, as discussed in the previous chapter, is a fairly common place name in Northern England, and derives from the Old English term used for a fortification or a fortified dwelling. In this case, the fortification was a Roman one called *Verteris,* which, when it was built some time in the first century AD, was situated at a strategic point on the northern frontier of the Roman empire,

Verteris is the earliest recorded structure in Brough.[15] It stands at the western end of the Stainmore Gap, on a steep hillside, with the Swindale Beck at its foot flowing through marshy ground. To the south and west, the land slopes away more gently to the Eden Valley, but to the north there is the wild upland of the Pennines. The Stainmore Gap was an east-west pass in this upland, through which the Romans built first a road and then a series of fortlets from Greta Bridge, via Bowes and Maiden Castle to Brough and Kirkby Thore. These probably date from Agricola's time, (77-83AD).[16] Between the fortlets were marching camps and signal stations. Near to Brough there were additional small four-post towers, surrounded by circular ditches. Using their modern names, these were at the Punch Bowl, Augill Bridge, and on what is today Appleby Golf course. It is thought that these were extra signalling stations, needed because of the poor visibility in the area.

The Stainmore Gap was an important route for troop movements and food supplies, linking York with Carlisle. At Kirkby Thore, there was a smaller route northwards, the Maiden Way, and near *Brocavum,* (Brougham) a southern link to the Lune Valley. Brough itself, may have been at the junction of a route to the south, via the Eden and the Lune Valleys, but until there are more excavations, this can only be conjecture. Professor E. Birley for example, in 1954, suggested that Brough could have been a nodal point where routes through the lowlands, via Ravenstonedale from Low Borrow Bridge, (near Tebay) and through Mallerstang from Bainbridge, converged with the main Stainmore route. He maintained that the fort at Brough faced south to control, as he put it, "the unruly inhabitants" of Mallerstang and the hill country around. He also thought that,

---

Note 15: Royal Commission on Historical Monuments. *An inventory of the Historical Monuments in Westmorland*, HMSO, (1936)
Note 16: Shotter, D., *Romans and Britons in North West England*, NWCRS (2004)

close to Brough, the more fertile areas of the Eden valley would be occupied by native groups of farmers and metal workers.[17] He concludes that the relatively large British population continued to prove a serious security problem throughout the Roman occupation.

The fort is built on a steep, north-facing hillside overlooking the Swindale Beck. This hill is referred to as an escarpment, a band of solid rock, in the archaeological reports as late as 1989. Yet its surface reveals a different character. The hillsides are subject to soil creep, (small land slips) and the erosion surfaces along the beck show a lot of unconsolidated material. According to the geological survey, this hill is a drumlin, a pile of easily eroded morainic deposits left by the ice-sheets, with patches of fluvio-glacial gravels nearby left by the melt waters.[18] The Swindale Beck at its foot, is quite small (except when in spate), but even so, it has undercut the hillside, with the result that a large number of finds have been discovered by chance. The most numerous of these were lead seals, many of which the local blacksmiths melted down and sold as solder to the tinkers. Archaeologists have since discovered that the Swindale cut into a waste heap dating from Roman times. Among the finds were weapons (spear and lance heads), ornaments, (brooches, beads of glass, amber and brass), horse-trappings, pottery and domestic implements (spoons, keys, needles and the like).

The finds from the river bed gave some clues to the site before major excavations were undertaken. One of the most interesting examinations was that of the lead seals by Professor Ian Richmond. His conclusions, in an article written in 1936 are still thought-provoking.[19] These seals, dated as third century, were of 67% lead and 23% tin. They were used to seal goods in transit. Most were official seals with the name of the military unit on: a few were private seals. The greatest number of them, (46) registered the marks of the Thracian cohort VII, suggesting that they had special responsibilities. The seals were all broken: in other words, they had been on in-coming goods. They were used on bulky valuable items, all of which needed elaborate controls. Some items were metal, and all had been transported over considerable distances. Part of the trade could have been in lead from the Alston lead mines, which were being worked at this time.

Richmond suggested that this represented the movement of objects from at least three places, and that at the Brough headquarters, the goods were

---

Note 17: Birley, E., Roman Fort at Brough, *TCWAA,* 1959, p45-50.
Note 18: Burgess, I. G. and Holliday, D. W*., Geology of the country around Brough under Stainmore,* Insitute of Geological Sciences, HMSO (1979), p92.
Note 19: Richmond, I. A., Roman leaden seals from Brough-under-Stainmore, T*CWAA, NS XXXVI,* p104-125, (1936).

either unpacked for storage or sent on. He therefore speculates that all this movement needed the complex control which only an official from the Imperial Finance department could manage. The fort would need to be an administrative centre, housing scribes, accountants and other officials, as well as combat troops.

According to his theory, the Thracians and other seal makers would be based at the source of the trade. Later writers like Birley, however, have taken these references to mean that the VII cohort was based at Brough, with the other six or seven cohorts as represented by seals, occupying the site at other times during the third century.[20] A quarter of a Thracians cohort was usually mounted, and this would tie up well with the horse equipment found near the site.

The authorities are all agreed that the seals represent evidence of long term use of the site, and this meant that a variety of army units with men from all over the empire, occupied it over the ages. There was, for example, a tombstone found at the fort, with an inscription in Greek. It is in memory of Hermes, a sixteen-year-old boy from Syria.

The fort at Verteris was partly excavated in the 1920s and then by Professor Eric Birley in 1954. The conclusions were that it covered about 1.2 hectares and could have housed 500 men. The fort cannot be accurately dated, but it is thought to have been occupied from the late first century until the late fourth century AD.[21] An inscribed stone of 197AD shows that this frontier zone was not easy to control, for it commemorates the rebuilding of the fort after its destruction by native tribes.

Later archaeologists explored the area outside the fort when it was planned to re-align the Brough to Kirkby Stephen road in 1971. Manchester University students under Dr M. J. Jones, were helped by Kirkby Stephen School staff and students. The first report was published in 1977 and a later one in 1989.[22] A major discovery was the existence of a Romano-British cemetery, associated with the occupation of the fort and lying 300 metres to the east. Over 50 cremation urns were discovered, mainly by Mr R. Downing of the Grammar School: two were in lead caskets, and others had pottery shards nearby.

Other important finds were in the area between the fort and the cemetery. The *vicus* or extra mural settlement lay there, close to the road leading eastwards from the fort. Here pits, post-holes, relics of wattle and daub walls, some stone hearths and charcoal remains were found, all suggesting

---

Note 20: Birley. op.cit. p49
Note 21: Verterae in older accounts.
Note 22: Jones, M. J. et al, Archaeological work at Brough-under-Stainmore, *TCWAA,*
1977, p17 and 1989, p143.

small houses or workshops. One or two characteristic Roman features about the fillings of the post-holes were noted, but otherwise, there is no certainty about the age. The same remains could equally well be those of medieval buildings. However, Jones has suggested that these may be Roman strip houses, end on to the small street.

Also found in the *vicus* is a structure which has been identified as the bathhouse. There was at least one warm room as well as the baths, and the hypocaust, in which one piece of coal was lying. This has been identified as coming from the Tan Hill coal seam, but there is no way of knowing when the coal got there. For safety's sake the baths and the blacksmiths' workshops and other dangerous trades were normally located outside the fort. Finds of intricate bronze ornaments, some of Irish design, have been found in the area. There were also two German-made (sic) quern stones for grinding corn.

The extra-mural villages were important service centres for the garrisons and this one was probably occupied, as others were, by native Britons and old soldiers who were normally given land when they retired. In times of peace the Roman roads were trade routes, and a typical layout of a Roman fort would have had a market place just in front of the gates. The 1972 excavations tried to locate the course of the road into Brough. The route over Stainmore was known but the last stretch into the fort had been lost, probably when the main turnpike was made in the mid-eighteenth century. The results are still inconclusive. Most favoured is the southerly one which later became the old coal road, now Leacett Lane, because it would have come straight into the southern side of the fort. The other suggestions are routes through Forest Farm, either north of the Augill Beck or straight into the present day Market Brough.[23]

Much still needs to be excavated and many questions still remain to be answered. The main conclusion is that there is evidence of a pre-conquest civilian settlement outside the fort, which survived for three centuries. Whether this settlement continued right through the period from the Roman withdrawal until the Normans arrived has yet to be proved.

Note 23: Jones, M. J.et al., *TCWAA*. op.cit, 1989.

CHAPTER 4

The Post-Roman period

WHAT happened to Brough in the post-Roman period? Archaeological surveys have found little that can be accurately dated, and there are no known surviving local documents. One possibility is a study of place names; these can be used to give some idea of the sequence of development in the Upper Eden Valley. This is a highly specialised subject and the information for this chapter is based on the Westmorland volume of the English Place Name Society, (EPNS), and on the work of Professor C. Phythian-Adams.[24]

At the time of the Roman occupation, there were probably older British settlements in the region, as the names of the rivers Eden, Lune, and Kent, and possibly that of Mallerstang, pre-date the Roman period. There may have been others, but like some of the Roman names, few now remain. Even the name of the fort *Verteris* was displaced and down-graded. It became *Burh*, which, although it is Old English for a fort, seems to mean one of secondary importance. *Ceaster* was the term used for the forts such as Muncaster and Papcastle, which continued to be active for longer.

One puzzle of the post-Roman period is the kingdom of Rheged. Did it exist, and if so was it just the area around the Solway Basin, or did it spread across Westmorland into Yorkshire? Phythian-Adams points out that only one precise reference to its location has been found and that is to Urien of Rheged, who was named as Prince of Catterick.[25] On the other hand, historians have associated Urien's residence, *Llwfenydd,* with the river Lyvennet in Westmorland. This is a problem which hopefully academics can sort out in years to come.

Place names can help with later periods as new settlers brought their own distinctive languages. From the early seventh century, groups of Anglians from what is now Germany, moved into the Eden Valley, naming such places as Hilton, Murton and Dufton. The suffix *ton* is Old English for homestead. These settlements are on the lower slopes of the hills facing south, and on reasonably good sites for the area, thus suggesting that the incomers faced little local opposition. According to the EPNS, although similar name endings are to be found in the Lower Kent and Lower Lune valleys, the total is very small for the size of the area. A century or so later,

---

Note 24: Smith, A. H., *Westmorland Place Names*, op. cit.
Note 25: Phythian-Adams, C., *Land of the Cumbrians, a study in British Provincial Origins, AD 400-1170,* p49, Scolar Press, (1996).

some solid evidence of the conversion of the Anglians to Christianity has been found. There are remains of carved stone crosses, and one, at Kirkby Stephen has been dated at some time in the second half of the eighth century. Yet the name Kirkby, meaning the farmstead[s] with a church, is not an Anglian place-name. A later influx of settlers probably renamed it, for Kirkby is a Scandinavian name. Similar changes possibly took place elsewhere, for more Scandinavian names than Anglian ones have survived.

Does this mean then, that the old Anglian villages were wiped out by the Viking hordes of legend? Modern research has shown that, for Cumbria, the war-like invasion by these people is a myth. Although place names indicate that Scandinavian incomers moved into the area, possibly at the beginning of the tenth century, the main point to emphasise is that they came not from the east but from the west. They came from Ireland, Scotland, and the Isle of Man, where they had settled two generations earlier, when poor harvests had driven them from their homelands. They moved in small groups in search of farm land. A few artefacts have been found fairly near to Brough, at Ormside, and Orton, while at Kirkby Stephen there is a small hog-back tomb stone, possibly dating from the tenth century, and also the Loki stone. This is part of a carved cross shaft, tentatively dated around the ninth or tenth century, which reflects Norse design and legend.[26]

One other find, which came from archaeological digs locally, is a small medallion in the shape of a fish.[27] This has been noted as a dolphin, dating from the Roman period. There is, however, a sketch of a similar one to be found in St Ninian's Church, Simonsburn, in Northumberland. As the fish was a symbol used by the early Christians, this is the more likely explanation.

Place names help to give a clearer picture of the Scandinavian settlement pattern. Appleby and a number of local villages have names ending in *by*, (Waitby, Kirkby, Soulby) the word for a farmstead in both Norse and Danish. This could mean that the invaders came in either from the Danelaw around York, or from the west coast. However, experts have shown that many of the place names in Cumbria have Norse, rather than Danish elements, and in addition, there are Irish components to some names. Even more telling is that in the remoter uplands, there are names demonstrating the later changes which occurred in the Norse language. This supports the theory that these people moved in from the west coast, along the Eden valley and then onto Stainmore. Typical are *Stein*, stoney, (Stainmore); *Gil*, a

Note 26: Bailey, R. and Cramp, R., *Corpus of Anglo-Saxon stone sculptures in Anglo-Saxon and pre-Norman Stones,* OUP, vol 2, (1988).

Note 27: This is the logo used by the Upper Eden History Society, found in a nearby parish. Information from Chris Irwin.

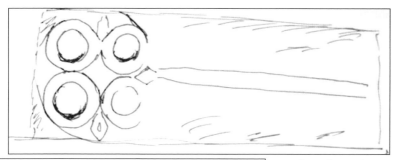

Medieval and Roman stones found in Brough, now in the walls of the south porch of St. Michael's Church, Brough. Drawings by kind permission of David Yeadell.

ravine, (Gaisgill, Howgill); *Skali,* a summer pasture (Scales); *Cragge*, a crag; *Bekkr*, a beck; *dalr,* a dale; *gate,* a road, and *Cros,* a cross, (Crosby).[28] Although much of this argument is conjectural, nevertheless the survival of so many Scandinavian names is significant.

In his book the *Land of the Cumbrians,* Phythian-Adams argues that post-Roman Brough lost its former importance and became part of a buffer zone based on an Anglian settlement at the place which later became known as Kirkby Stephen. He makes the point that during the Norse period, this was an international boundary between the Danelaw and other subject territories, and the kingdom of Cumbria.[29] During the tenth century, there was a kingdom of Cumbria, but although three of its kings can be named as Owain, Dunmail and Malcolm, its extent is not known. It possibly included not only parts of modern Cumbria but also the

Note 28: Smith, A. H., op. cit.
Note 29: Phythian-Adams C., op.cit. p112.

lands north of the Solway Firth.

Knowledge of the history of this period is hedged by uncertainties. Legend records a a few notable events. In 954AD, for example, Eric Bloodaxe, the last Norwegian king based at York, was killed in a skirmish, around Rere (Rey) Cross on Stainmore, (in Old Norse *Rere* means a boundary stone). Another example is of an early eleventh century battle won by Malcolm II, king of the Cumbrians, over Uhtred, Earl of Northumbria. Phythian-Adams locates this battle at Brough-under-Stainmore, which may explain the origin of Battle Hill at Brough.

The relationship between the Scottish kingdoms and Cumbria is not clear. In 971AD Kenneth II of Scotland ravaged Westmorland as far as Rere Cross, and yet two years later, he and Malcolm, King of the Cumbrians, made a united appeal to Edgar, King of the English. Perhaps, as one authority suggests, this was an attempt to get recognition for a newly enlarged kingdom of Cumbria.[30]

The history of this period still needs to be untangled and all that can be said is that at the time of the Norman conquest, it is not clear if the Brough area of the Upper Eden was part of a Scottish lordship, or under some other overlord.

Note 30: Smyth A. P., *Warlords and Holy Men* quoted by Phythian-Adams, p120.

CHAPTER 5

Border Turmoil and the Norman Castle

THERE is a great gap in our knowledge of the period of Brough's history, not only for the centuries immediately following the Roman withdrawal, but also for the early Norman period. This may never be filled as the artefacts of the ordinary households rarely survive. Even the details of the building of the castle by the early Normans are uncertain and it is necessary for this account to rely on the specialist architectural historians of English Heritage, who now maintain the site.[31]

When the Normans conquered England, the north-western part, including the Eden Valley, remained in turmoil, with part of it under the overlordship of the Scottish Crown. Once again, it had become a troubled and disputed frontier zone. It was therefore never included in the Domesday Book. Although William Rufus subdued and settled the area around Carlisle by building a castle and defences there, the rest of the frontier between Scotland and England needed pacifying. The first castle built by the Normans at Brough may have been erected in his reign. It occupied the northern part of the old Roman fort site, and was probably a wooden keep, on stone foundations, surrounded by newly dug ditches and ramparts.

Once again the Stainmore Gap needed to be guarded as well as the routes over the hills from Scotland. It was an important Crown stronghold in a lawless age, and it survived because strong men like Hugh de Morville in the mid-twelfth century, served it as constables. In 1174, a large Scottish army, under King William marched in from the west, took Appleby, and moved on to Brough. There the Scots set the keep alight, and the spirited, though hopeless, defence by just six English knights, became a legend. To quote a contemporary poem by Jordan Fantosme, they were, "evermore shouting 'You shall be vanquished'." As the tower did not burn completely it has been suggested that it was of masonry.[32] Records show that by the end of the reign of Henry II in 1189, Brough had a large stone-built castle with an outer bailey, and within a very short time, it had had to be rebuilt and strengthened twice.

In the early thirteenth century, it was no longer practical for the Crown to have direct control of northern castles so these, with their lands, were

---

Note 31: Charleton, J., *Brough Castle,* English Heritage, no date. Simpson, W. D. op. cit. Holdgate, M., *The Story of Appleby in Westmorland*, Hayloft, Kirkby Stephen, (2006), p48ff. Note 32: Charlton, J., *Brough Castle.*

allocated to loyal followers in return for Border service. Brough was given to Robert de Vipont (Veteripont), in 1203/4. He and his family had a number of other castles in Cumbria, and Brough appears to have been occupied only in times of trouble, so that by 1245 "the castle was decayed and rotten".[33] However, in the late thirteenth century it was enlarged, to include a gatehouse and domestic buildings so that it could be permanently occupied, but early deaths of the owners and incompetent administrators in the periods of wardships of the heirs, led to further decay. Some stability came at the beginning of the fourteenth century when the Cliffords, by intermarriage, took over the estate. The castle was again enlarged to provide both defensive and residential accommodation and both Edward the first and Edward the second stayed there on their way to their Scottish campaigns.

The Border troubles provoked by Edward I put the castle back into the war zone. Not only were there armies tramping through the area, but the king's demand for food was a problem for the already impoverished farming communities. The Scottish raids increased in intensity. In 1314, and again in 1319, their armies devastated large parts of the Eden Valley. They burnt the town of Brough, trampled the crops, "and carried off an immense booty of beasts, horses and oxen, about 500."[34] Robert de Clifford was killed at the battle of Bannockburn, and, rather than leave his widow to cope, the Crown temporarily took back the property. A knight, Robert de Welle was ordered to supply fifteen men at arms fully mailed and mounted, and twenty hobelars (light lancers) mounted on hobbies (fell ponies), of which the king would pay for ten of each.[35] Once again, the Stainmore Gap was crucial.

Despite periods of truce and negotiations, the area was never really at peace. In 1333, the State papers record that, "all wishing to leave the counties of Cumberland and Westmorland with their goods and animals are to be allowed through the king's forests with the use of pastures there." In 1337, the entry in the register of Bishop John de Kirkby stated, "The clergy are well nigh ruined by the fury of the Scots," and again in 1339, "the bishop's own sheep had almost totally perished in the enemy raids," yet another in 1343 shows how the English took advantage of the chaos for "many disturbers - feigning to be Scots - come daily - imprisoning men, taking ransoms and killing."[36]

Note 33: Simpson, op.cit. p235.

Note 34: Todd, J. ed., *Lanercost Cartulary*, TCWAA (Record,) xi (1997). Also Fraser, E. M., ed. *Northern Petitions*, Surtees Society, 194 (1981), p121.

Note 35: Curwen, J. F., *Later Records of North Westmorland*, CWAA (Record) viii, (Kendal 1932). Hubelars (soldiers) and hobbies (small horses or ponies) are probably Norman-French words.

Note 36: Storey, R. L., ed. *Register of John de Kirkby*, Canterbury and York Society, (1993)

There were further serious attacks in the middle of the fourteenth century and Pendragon Castle, in the upper Eden valley, was burnt in 1341.[37] After a short period of peace, the threat of attacks became more marked but the Cliffords were engaged elsewhere and it was necessary in 1383 for a Sheriff's commission to command stone cutters, masons and other labourers to repair certain castles of Roger de Clifford, "as a refuge for the king's subjects."[38] Appleby was burnt down in 1388, but Brough seems to have been spared, although a 1424 inquisition shows that Brough Castle was deserted and derelict: its lords had abandoned it for other parts of their estates and for other wars.[39]

Defence of the border lands was not the only problem of fourteenth century Westmorland. Other more persistent difficulties were present throughout the century. Dr Angus Winchester's study entitled *The Harvest of the Hills* suggests that there were periods of harvest failure and famine, of sheep murrain, and other livestock diseases. "People prefer full barns to eternal bliss," reported the rector of Crosby Garrett in 1332 when he failed to collect his tithes.[40] Most serious of all was the Black Death of 1348-9, which re-occurred in the Eden Valley in 1352/3 and 1362. In 1352 the vice-sheriff for Cumberland reported that the king's lands in Carlisle were, "gone to waste for lack of labourers," and the tax demands were rendered void "depressed by the mortal pestilence."[41] Appleby borough, in one of its many petitions in the 1380s stated that, "the impoverishment of the town by pestilence - has forced merchants to take themselves to other markets."[42]

It is generally thought that a third of the population died in England. There are no figures for the Eden Valley, but the Bishop of Carlisle proved fifty wills in 1362, instead of the normal three or four a year. While this might be due to the greater efficiency of the probate service, there are other indications of a mortality crisis. Eleven nuncupative wills were made at Thursby in August 1362, and the rectors or vicars of Kirkby Stephen, Morland, Brougham, Kirkby Thore, Musgrave, Edenhall and Ousby all died in that month.[43] The following year, the bishop, in what appears to be a

---

Note 37: Perriman, D. and Robinson, J., *Medieval Fortified Buildings of Cumbria*, CWAA (Extra) 1998, p300.

Note 38: Simpson, op.cit. p223, CPR 1381-5, p344.

Note 39: See Chapter 4

Note 40: Storey, R. L. ed., John de Kirkby register, op.cit. 1332.

Note 41: Storey, R. L.ed., Register of Bishop Gilbert Welton, Canterbury and York Society, (1999), introduction.

Note 42: *Calendar Inquisitions Miscellaneous, [CIM], Richard 1377-88 vol.14*, HMSO (1957), and in Northern Petitions, op.cit.

Note 43: Storey R. L. ed. op. cit. Introduction and register of Gilbert Welton. Storey estimates that possibly 20% of the incumbents died in the 1361 outbreak.

panic measure, petitioned the pope for permission to ordain forty new candidates, many of whom were under the canonical age.[44]

About this time the State intervened. In an effort to control the economy, statutes controlling wages and living standards were passed by Edward III, and his successors. How far these were obeyed is unknown, but they are indicators of what was to be considered "normal" for the average villager, and they set the standards by which manor rents may be judged. The following tables give some idea of what was expected.

TABLE 1: Some State Regulations in the Fourteenth century
First the wages had to be regulated:

STATUTE OF ARTIFICERS	1352 (25 Edw. III)
Carters, ploughmen, shepherds, swineherds	All to be paid by the year
Haymaking	1*d.* a day without meat or drink
Mower of meadows	5*d.* a day
Reapers of corn	2*d.* a day
Master carpenter	3*d.* a day
Other carpenters	2*d.* a day
Master freemason	4*d.* a day
Their servants	1½*d.* a day
Tilers, plaisterers	3*d.* a day

Then the holidays were controlled, by a Statute of 25 Edw. III [1361][45]

'No labourer, servant or artificer shall take wages on festival days. Idleness will be punished by two years return to slavery.'

Later, more wage regulations were needed.

Note 44: Ibid, 1363
Note 45: *Calendar State Papers, [CSP],* 34 Ed. III, HMSO.

TABLE 2: Wage Regulations, 1389

WAGE REGULATIONS: MAXIMUM	1389 (12 Rich. II)
Bailiff for husbandry	13s 4d a year and his clothing
Master Hine	10s a year
Shepherd	10s a year
Oxherd, swineherd, cow herd	6s a year
Driver of the plough	7s a year

Meanwhile some wage earners were showing off their wealth so in 1364 more laws were passed. These were the Sumptuary Laws against extravagance:

> *Carters, ploughmen, drivers of the plough. oxherds, shepherds,* and all other people not having 40 shillings worth of goods shall wear no cloth but blanket and russet wool of 12 pence and shall wear girdles of linen.
>
> *Wives and daughters* shall wear no vail of silk but only yarn made within the realm nor no manner of fur - but only lamb, conie, cattle and fox.

Recreation was seen to be too popular and in need of control too. Therefore in 1389, [12 Rich. II] the following regulations were made:[46]

> Servants and artificers shall leave all playing at tennis or football or other games called coites, dice, casting of stones, - and shall wear no buckles, swords nor daggers, but they shall have bows and arrows and use the same on Sundays and holidays.

Brough people were probably not as concerned with rich clothing and other outward show as townspeople, but the restrictions on wages would be annoying. Given a severe shortage of labour, the manor bailiff would need to decide whether to ignore the regulations and so get the land worked, or let it fall derelict.

Note 46: *Calendar State Papers: 12 Richard II*, HMSO

Samuel Sparrow engraving of Brough Castle published by Samuel Hooper in 'The Antiquities of England and Wales', 1775. .

The fate of the ordinary villager during the hazards of the fourteenth century was not recorded but the effects as seen by the manorial accounts suggest that a large portion of the work force suffered. Why else should the Bishop of Carlisle, Thomas Appleby, issue a mandate in 1369 for processions and prayers, "to turn aside God's wrath for there have been two pestilences... and drought and floods"? A few fragmentary views of the life in Brough can be gained from contemporary documents and these will be discussed in the next chapter.

CHAPTER 6

Brough at the start of the 14th century

THE first survey of Brough with details of the village was in 1314-5, in the inquisition following the death of Robert de Clifford, (IPM).[47] This showed the state of the manor in the immediate aftermath of some severe Scottish raids, but before the Black Death. The fortunes of the settlement were closely tied to those of the castle so that when the castle was occupied, trade flourished, but when it was unoccupied by the lords, an income was still required. This meant that the land had to be worked either as demesne land or in some other form by locally based labour, under the supervision of the steward.

A nucleated village had therefore developed once again outside the castle ramparts in the area of the Roman *vicus*. This is the present day Church Brough, but in the early tax returns it was *Burgh Supra*. Today, all that remains visible of this early village are the castle ruins, the church and a series of long crofts stretching back from the village green. There is a base of an old market cross on the green and the relics of another medieval one now in the churchyard, but moved from present-day Market Brough. St Michael's Church lies hidden behind one side of the green.

The 1315 survey assessed the total wealth of the manor as £49 15*s.* 7*d.* In addition there was Brough Sowerby, worked as a separate manor, worth £11 15*s.* 7*d.* The IPM shows that the castle with its herbage was worth half a mark (6*s.* 8*d*). It had two parks, Castle Park and Sowerby Park. These were enclosed areas generally used for the keeping of deer, for rabbit warrens and for preserved fisheries. In the adjacent village there were ten tofts, (each a house and garth) worth 6*d* each, plus a number of free tenants who may or may not have had houses there. There was a bake-house, the only one recorded between Brough and the far end of Mallerstang, and "one watermill burnt," but still worth £6 13*s.* 4*d.* The accompanying farmland was varied and included plough lands and meadow and 200 acres of demesne land which had originally been reserved for the support of the lord, and worked by the services of the villeins.

The 1315 survey shows that there was a second village, labelled Lower

---

Note 47: Nicolson, J. & Burn, R., [N&B] *The History and Antiquities of the Counties of Westmorland and Cumberland*, London (1777), p.278 ff. Also *CIPM 8 EdII. 1314-15*, HMSO. This work relies on the inquisition for Robert de Clifford, dated as 8 Ed II. This covers the regnal year from July 1314 to July 1315.

Brough with Stainmore. Here there were more houses, for there were 24 and a half tofts "which are burnt" but still worth 12d, twice the value of those in Church Brough. Even more revealing are the numbers of vaccaries, or large scale cattle farms on Stainmore. There were "ten vaccaries burned," worth 10s each and five vaccaries not burned, worth a total of £20. This was damage inflicted by the Scots, and seems to have been mainly on the route through Lower Brough, and on the more accessible sites on Stainmore.

Somewhere in Brough there was a tavern, for a court case in 1256, gives details, "Agnes wife of Adam, son of Benedict was found killed between Helbeck and Burgh. The jurors say that Adam, the husband of the aforesaid, killed her as they came from the tavern in Brough."[48]

Archaeology has added to the details of the new settlement which had grown up to the north of the original one.[49] Although much of the east to west Roman road across Stainmore seems to have become the 'Great Highway' of Medieval times, the exception was the stretch near Brough. This had been re-aligned to a less marshy site, north of the Swindale Beck, perhaps at some time in the twelfth century, possibly when Sowerby Park was laid out. In Market Brough it was joined by a well marked route southwards to Kirkby Stephen and beyond. When the rivers were bridged is not clear, but by the fourteenth century, money was being left in wills to repair one at Brough and one at Brough Sowerby.[50] A ribbon of housing grew along the track to the new road and then a linear village seems to have been laid out, in a planned fashion, along the main road.

In the modern landscape some of the parallel plots reaching to back lanes on both sides of the main road can still be seen. This evidence is reinforced by the tallage (tax) accounts of the late twelfth century, which add one important detail. They list the inhabitants as *burgesses*. Therefore this new village might have been an attempt by the lord to build a new borough as a market centre on the main road. The tax returns confirm that there were two villages, and that only one had *burgesses*. Confusion lies in deciding which one they lived in. To Simpson, it is Church Brough, which shows "an unmistakable, if incomplete attempt to lay out a town in dependence upon a castle."[51] But Beresford, using the 1196 tallage returns to support his theory, identifies the new village as the borough. In that year the burgesses of

---

Note 48: Curwen Records, op.cit. p.135, 1256 Assize roll.
Note 49: Jones, M. J. op.cit. 1989.
Note 50: Storey, R. L. *Register of Bishop Thomas Appleby 1365-95*, Canterbury & York Society, (2006).
Note 51: Simpson, op.cit. 1946. Beresford, M. W., *New Towns of the Middle Ages*, Lutterworth, (1967), p502-3.

Brough paid 18s in tax while the *villata*, (that is traditional demesne tenants), of Brough Superior paid 9s. Maybe there were two planned settlements: a manorial village near the castle and a borough along the main road.

What was borough status and why was it important? The authority on this subject was Maurice Beresford, whose book, the *New Towns of the Middle Ages,* published in 1967, is still regarded as the definitive text.[52] In general the founding of boroughs in the twelfth and thirteenth centuries was done by the feudal lords as a way to increase their revenue. Higher rents could be charged for *burgage* plots, (as borough holdings were called) than for agricultural land, and craftsmen would be encouraged to set up businesses where the rents were paid in money, and without the disruptions of customary services. No smith, having heated his furnace, wanted to be called for three days boon work in the hay fields. A weekly market allowing goods to be sold regularly was an additional benefit for the craftsman while the lord had another source of income from the *stallage*, the tolls. The inhabitants were freemen: free to move out of the town, and free to transfer the ownership of their plots.

These new towns were set out by the lord along a main trading route, with space for a market, and parallel plots of land laid out evenly stretching back from houses built along the road.

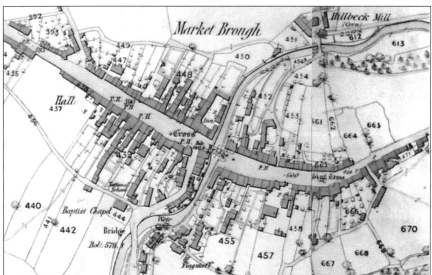

Map 5: The 19th century OS map shows very clearly that Market Brough was laid out as a likely market along a main road. On the north side of the road particularly the long burgage plots behind the houses, which face on to the street, are distinct. There are some on the south side also.

Note 52: Maurice Beresford, ibid.

It has long been thought that Brough was a Medieval seigniorial borough, but no firm documentary evidence of this has been found. There is no record of a borough charter, but, as Beresford points out, that is not unusual if the borough were founded by the lord and not the crown.[53] Given the juxtaposition of the castle, the church and the village with what look like burgage plots around a market square, the lay-out of Church Brough has long been regarded by historians as a planned settlement. Yet a second and more successful attempt seems to have been made later, for Market Brough too has visible burgage plots, indicative of borough status. This move may have been caused by the changes in the road alignments already mentioned.

Brough could have been a seigniorial borough, for there was no legal requirement for the lord to register his foundation. The assumption has been that Brough was given borough status at an early date, but that it failed to develop, and had to cede importance to Appleby, a chartered royal borough, and to Kirkby Stephen, which, although it was not a borough, was an important ecclesiastical centre. New evidence has come to light from transcriptions of two documents being prepared for later chapters in this book. Although the new evidence is not conclusive it contains information which strongly points to borough status for Brough.

Before looking at this evidence there are two things to consider. First, the two communities of Brough were dealt with in formal documents as one unit for administrative purposes, but their different origins are revealed in the way that their tenancies were assessed: customary dues as opposed to money rents. They were, however, both part of one manor and were one unit. Secondly it needs to be remembered that the name of Brough and the word for borough are very similar in medieval Latin. The oldest documented name for the settlement is Burc, [probably old Norse,] which eventually became Brough.[54]

Poll Tax returns of 1379[55]
In medieval terms the villages were both described, depending on the document, as *Vill* or *Villata,* both terms meaning 'township' or 'settlement'. The first document, the Poll Tax of 1379 is dealt with further in chapter 7. It contains two administrators' summary sheets, which list *Vill, Villata* along with other places. In describing Brough they differ very slightly, but both suggest borough status. One document, for example, listing Brough, uses the expression *De Vill et burgo de Staynesmore.* The second has *De Villata*

Note 53: Beresford, op.cit., p381, p502-3; Tait, J. *The Medieval English Borough,* Manchester University Press, (1936, reprint 1999).
Note 54: Smith, A. H. op.cit.
Note 55: PRO E/179/195/18 and E/179/195/19.

de burgo de Staynesmore. In each case for the word *burgo* (from the medi-aeval Latin word *burgus, burgum,*)[56] the lower case is used, whereas all other place names start with capital letters. Therefore it is likely that in this context *burgus* meant 'borough'. It was not the usual place name Brough but an indication of status. Government officials had to be precise, so if the monarch's tax gatherers listed it as a borough then that word had some sig-nificance. They had recorded Appleby as *Baronia*, Barony, not as *Vill* or *Villata.*

The Steward's Account
The second document, the 1425/6 steward's account, (see chapter 8), while not stating that Brough was a borough, makes references to matters which were relevant only to boroughs. At the beginning it refers to *liberi tenentes*, - free tenants - likely then only to be found in boroughs. Later on, dealing with *Nethirburgh*, now Market Brough, it mentions the *furnus,* sometimes *fornus,* meaning 'oven' in the sense of a communal bread baking oven for the use of the tenants. This probably means 'the lord's oven', designated by him as the only legal one in the new community. (There was also the old bakehouse in Church Brough). This is emphasised further on, where the oven is referred to as being demised (leased out) to two local men.

Other features of boroughs can be found. There were money rents of 12d for the burgage plots, typical of borough rents elsewhere, and the ten-ants listed would be called burgesses. Unlike the tenants of Church Brough, they paid none of the traditional dues like the reke silver (the ancient fuel toll) and the constable's rent was paid in money and not in oats. The refer-ence to *burgagii,* or burgage plots, distinguished from the *tofts* of Church Brough, is significant. 'Burgages' were a feature of boroughs, not of other type of settlement, and the burgages mentioned were in Market Brough, where they were still to be found as late as 1604, listed in the Clifford Rental.[57]

Despite the lack of a charter, circumstantial and visual evidence points to a planned new borough which was laid out on the new site north of the older settlement of Church Brough at some time before the end of the twelfth century. It can now be argued that Brough was a borough, and, with Appleby, one of only two in the East Ward of Westmorland. Initially Brough's trade flourished, and its market was chartered in the reign of Edward III, but as a borough it failed. It was not alone in its failure - Wavermouth on the Solway, and Warenmouth in Northumberland among

---

Note 56: This means a borough or fortified town. Brough was not regarded as a fortified town as it had no walls.
Note 57: CRO[K] WD/Hoth. Box 34. Manor Rental.

many others, decayed. The over enthusiastic founding of towns by their lords could not be sustained by the trade of the period.

Brough Market (Appendix III)

Brough might not have had a borough charter, but it did have a market charter. This merely formalised the customary arrangements because it is clear from other sources that markets and fairs had been common long before that date. In 1200, Lower Brough paid 25 marks for a Sunday market and a two day fair at the feast of St John the Baptist.[58] Lower Brough was identified as Nether Brough in both the 1315 IPM and later manor records.[59] By 1200, the newer village had outgrown the older and had taken over the markets and fairs. The location of the market had changed at some time. Because it had originally been on the green in the older village the market tolls continued to be returned in the manorial accounts with the traditional fees of the castle.[60] By the beginning of the fourteenth century, if not earlier, Brough fairs were regular events, for in 1315 the annual tolls from the fairs were valued at 10s.[61]

The first extant market charter, granted to the Clifford family in 1331, confirmed a customary market and fixed the fair on St Matthew's day in Nether Brough. Apart from the fair in 1200 already mentioned, there is other evidence of a customary fair before a charter had been obtained. Simpson quotes a bond registered in 1281 in Boston, Lincolnshire, for a debt owed by Sir Robert de Clifford to an Appleby merchant. This debt of £17 was for wool bought at Boston market, which was to be paid, "at the next market at Burgh-under-Steynesmor on St Matthew's day forthcoming."[62]

There is indirect evidence of long distance trade in some of the local court cases. In 1378, "Agnes wife of Thomas del Garth of Winton, with John Oxenthwaite, her attorney and his executors sued William de Gerstane of York draper, and Richard de Gerstane, merchant of Beverley for £50 which was owed."[63] There was a similar court case that same year between another local widow, Mary Warcoppe, against two merchants of York, John de Aldborough, who, she alleged, owed her £20 and John de Escryk, for an another debt, (which is illegible). Yet another case of debt recovery involved a plaintiff called Nicholas Scot, who, despite the turmoil of the

---

Note 58: Pipe Rolls p178 ff. Beresford, op.cit. p502.
Note 59: In the 1604 manorial rental there were still burgesses listed.
Note 60: IPM Robert de Clifford, 1315.
Note 61: Ibid.
Note 62: Simpson, op.cit. p228.
Note 63: Agnes was the widow of Thomas del Garth.

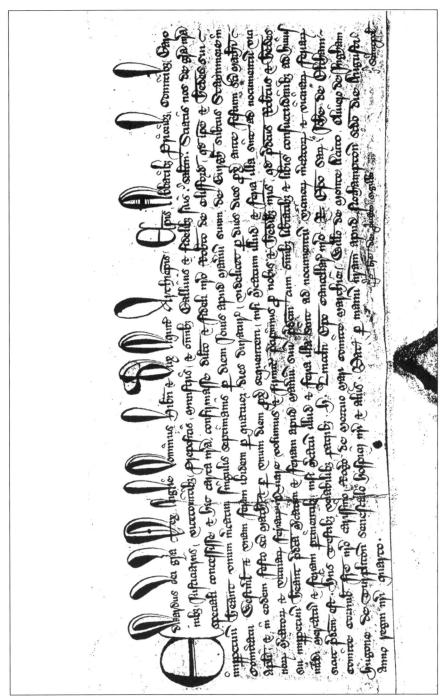

Brough's Market Charter - translation Appendix III, CRO(K) WD/Hoth.

The old Market Cross, with kind permission of John Walton.

times, may have been involved in cross border trade, either with or without an official license.[64]

Another long distance traveller was Richard le Nappare of Northants. "In September 1315, he stole three oxen price 30s in Brough-under-Stainmore, - and he was hanged." Richard, a cloth worker, had travelled a long distance, and surely only the most optimistic of thieves would expect to get away with three slow moving beasts, unless Brough Fair was in progress.[65] Another later piece of evidence shows that in 1382 William de Laton willed that his nine horses pastured in Greystoke Park should be sold at the next Brough Fair, so even in that unsettled period, it was expected that a fair would be held.[66] Scattered though these examples are, when taken together, they suggest that Brough was developing as a market centre in the fourteenth century.

Church lands
There was, however, a second strand to the land-holding within the village which the manorial accounts do not touch, and this is the land owned by the church, which was surveyed in the 1340s, again just before the plague. Church and manor overlapped but their boundaries were not contiguous,

Note 64: Curwen, op.cit. p136-7 [De Banco Rolls 472].
Note 65: Calendar Close Rolls, 1315-18, HMSO, p.356.
Note 66: Storey R. L., ed., Register Thomas de Appleby, 1363-95, op.cit.

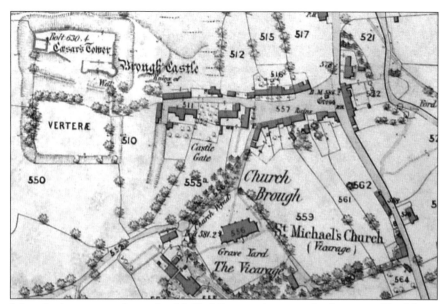

Map 6: An extract from the 1860 OS map showing the layout of buildings around the village green.

and for years Brough Church was a chapelry within the parish of Kirkby Stephen.[67]

It was thought by Simpson that the church was an integral part of a seignorial village. It may have been, but it appears to have some characteristics which pre-date the setting up of the manor. There are some Norman features, the nave is mid-twelfth century, and the chancel a little later, built at a time when St Mary's Priory, York, owned the rights. This was before the castle had been granted to the Viponts, although they may have added the north aisle in the fourteenth century.

Brough was part of Kirkby Stephen parish, probably until the fourteenth century, and so along with Kirkby, it had been given as part of the foundation endowment of St Mary's Abbey, York, in 1090 by Ivo de Talebois. There is no evidence that he did anything else in the parish. This was before the Diocese of Carlisle was founded, but once that had been established a long running series of disputes broke out between the prior and the bishop. When an agreement was reached in 1292, it merely paved the way for fresh claims, between the crown and the Cliffords, although by this time Brough was probably a parish in its own right, for this would explain a writ of 1332.

Note 67: N&B, p464, and Bishop's registers, 1223-38 in a grant to St Mary's Abbey, York, the chapel of Brough on the death of Thomas Boek shall be annexed to the church of Kirkby Stephen.

In it, the Crown ordered the bishop-elect to admit a suitable person to the church at Brough-under-Stainmore on the king's presentation which, it was stated, he had removed from Robert de Clifford.[68]

The matter was settled in 1344 when Pope Clement VI gave the rectorial rights to Queen's Hall, (later Queen's College), Oxford. At this time the holdings of the church were valued at £53 16s. 7d., a nine-fold increase in value from 1318 and making it a little more valuable than the lordship of Brough, which was valued at just under £50. The church holdings included a manse, a big grange and the chaplain's messuage. The glebe land included two acres of land adjoining the manse, lands and tenements in Helbeck, and meadows.[69]

But Queen's Hall did not get everything. The grange was excluded and so was, "the enclosed place with houses built by Robert de Eglesfeld, lately rector." The most likely site is where today a regular set of buildings with crofts still exist, on the south side of the green at Church Brough. These back on to the churchyard, and seem to be an early planned expansion of the village, built when economic confidence was high.[70] For the parishioners, there were problems with absentee clergy. Eglesfield, for example, was either in Oxford at the college he was helping to found or at court where he was chaplain to the Queen. The vicars put in to work the parish fell short of the desired standards, as the bishop fully realised. One such was probably John de Sancto Ned.[71]

> *In 1346 John de Sancto Ned, clerk, was accused of the theft of 10s.8d from William King of Aldborough on Staynmore. He was arrested and imprisoned, then delivered to the archdeacon and the vicar of St Lawrence, Appleby. At the consistory court a jury found him guilty.*

Church and Manor in the fourteenth century

A summary of the situation in the fourteenth century shows that there were two Brough villages. Church Brough was organised as a manorial centre, around the castle demesne lands, and Market Brough was a planned borough with burgesses.

In the former, the manor rents of the *villata* were paid by customary services, in the latter the *burgesses* paid money rents. There were 200 acres

---

Note 68: Storey, R. L. ed., op.cit. *Kirkby Register,* July 1323. *Calendar of State Papers* [CSP] *HIII, 1223-38,* HMSO, St Mary's Abbey granted Brough chapel on the death of Thomas Boek to Kirkby Stephen.
Note 69: Storey, R. L. ed., *Kirkby Register* 753/754.
Note 70: CCR 1315-18, and Simpson p241.
Note 71: Storey, R. L. ed., *Kirkby register.* Consistory court details: 1346, 819. He was accused of theft 2/2/1345, and recorded in Gaol delivery book 17/3/1346.

Old postcard of Church Brough, courtesy of John Walton.

of demesne land in Church Brough worked by the tenants, apart from 22 acres of it which had been leased out at 9d per acre in 1315. The twenty oxgangs of ploughland were valuable, bringing in 80 shillings, but the parks were more important, and worth 100 shillings. The parks were kept as ever-ready larders for the arrival of the lord, as in 1315, the Brough constable was ordered to send six bucks from Brough Park to feed the garrison at Carlisle. The parks were constant temptations to poachers. In 1316 the keeper of the Clifford lands, Bartholemew de Badlesmere complained that the parks had been broken into and deer removed, and throughout the century, there were other cases. Typical were the complaints in 1368 that the fisheries had been robbed, and in 1376 that the warren had lost its hares, coneys, pheasants and partridges.[72]

Nether Brough, the larger settlement, had no demesne services to perform and the burgesses paid a money rent. There was no mention of common fields but the villages did have common rights up on Stainmore. However, traditional methods of farming seem to have been changing as four closes of new improvement plus an agistment (that is land let out for grazing), were leased to three freeholders, Adam de Caberg, Nicholas de Musgrave and Geoffrey Teasdal, (sic). They paid a total of 115 shillings for enclosed land, which could be improved at their expense. Better crops and more controlled stock breeding then became a possibility.

Note 72: Simpson, op.cit., p241.

Commercial farming on a larger scale was present too. The fifteen vaccaries of the 1315 IPM were large enclosed farms under the supervision of the steward. All fifteen were named in the 1422 IPM, and most can be traced today. They were isolated farms, off the main highway out of Brough, to the east, and later taking over more remote marginal land in the interior of Stainmore. They were, in effect, stages in the colonisation of the waste, in an area at a distance from the manorial centre. This concentration of vaccaries appears elsewhere in the Clifford holdings in Westmorland. For instance, eleven have been identified in Mallerstang. This type of farming seems to have been a planned response by Brough manor to the difficult terrain around Stainmore.

There are no details of the Stainmore vaccaries but research by Eric Foster and colleagues on the vaccaries of a part of Lancashire reveal some details of this type of farming, which was carried out in a similar type of environment. Their transcriptions are of the accounts for the vaccaries in Rossendale, Pendle and Trawden, which were part of the Earl of Lincoln's estates, from 1277 to 1278. These show that in Rossendale, the numbers of cows varied from between 25 and 30 per farm and in Pendle and Trawden the numbers were higher, up to 45 or more. The numbers of yearlings were generally below twenty as were the numbers of calves. The steward had to account for the beasts and the hides, with full details of losses from murrain and strangulation by wolves. Despite the number of cows, this set of accounts makes no mention of butter or cheese - maybe there was another set of accounts for them. However, these records infer that the wealth of the vaccaries lay in the breeding programme, with few beasts kept for fattening.[73]

The Clifford papers give the impression that cattle were the most important part of the farming economy, which will surprise anyone knowing the present day landscape. Where are the sheep which can use the marginal land? They were certainly around. In 1314, Hugh de Burgo (the vicar of Brough) lost 199 sheep, worth £10 - (they were) "driven away by several men. They were found in Kirkby Stephen and his men assaulted."[74]

The ecclesiastical valuation of 1344, made when the church lands were to be handed to Queen's Hall, also shows another aspect of the economy. The survey covered Helbeck and Brough Sowerby as well as the two Broughs. It shows a wide range of produce. The most valuable tithes were from the arable land, with cereals amounting to a third of the total value,

---

Note 73: Eric Foster ed. and members of the Ranulf Higden Society, *The Accounts of Henry de Lacy, Earl of Lincoln, 1277-78.* I am very grateful for the chance to use this work, to be published soon. Mallerstang vaccaries, Dr. Angus Winchester, personal communication.
Note 74: Curwen Records, op.cit., CPR Ed II, 2 p241

The Norman door arch and, inset, details, from St. Michael's Church, Brough, drawing by David Yeadell, with many thanks.

and accompanied by much smaller quantities of hemp and flax. Hay (the only crop to be tithed on Stainmore) yielded just over £3 5s. The mills (two in Brough, one in Helbeck, and one in Brough Sowerby) yielded just over 21 shillings (Table 3).

However, lambs and wool were the second most valuable source of tithes, yielding £10. Cattle products, including calves, as well as butter and cheese, together with poultry and piglets were worth less than the hay. These records probably show the products of the fields and garths of the villagers, whereas the manor records emphasise the commercial side of the farming. One other item of interest is the value of the income from the rector's demesne lands (the glebe). This was £3 7s. 6d. yearly; a high income when the contemporary wage rates are considered: a local mason earned 3d. a day and haymakers, one penny a day.

The wealth of the church was considerable, and, apart from the castle garrison, the clergy were the only group for which horses are mentioned. The vicar of Brough was left two young horses in 1362 by John de Bowes, vicar of Kirkby Stephen and in 1380 the vicar of Appleby brought a case against John Wilkinson of Brough Sowerby, accusing him of killing two of his mares valued at £6 at Brough.[75] The ordinary tenant, almost certainly used oxen for ploughing, or ploughed by hand.

Note 75: Storey, R. L., ed., Register of Bishop Gilbert Welton. op.cit., p.501. Curwen, J., op.cit., Records Trinity 1380 De Banco Roll 479 [378].

TABLE 3: Inquest into the Value of Brough Church, 21 April 1344	
Tithe of great and lesser sheaves	£11.6s.8d
Tithe of sheaves of Brough Sowerby	£ 6
Tithe of sheaves of Hillbeck	£ 4
Tithe of lambs and wool whole parish	£10
Tithe of calves and chickens	24s.1d
Tithe of cheese and butter	20s.9d
Tithe of hay on Stainmore	38s
Tithe of hay in remainder of parish	27s.2d
Tithes of geese in whole parish	2s
Tithes of piglets	20d
For mortuaries sold [best beasts left to church]	22s. 6d
Flax and Hemp	7s
Tithe of Eggs	6d
Rents from rectors demesne lands	£ 3. 7s. 6d
Tithes for mill[s] at Brough	14s
Tithes for Sowerby and Helbeck mills	7s. 3d
[There were other oblations, fees, etc. From the Register of Bishop John de Kirkby, 753.]	

How important was Brough in the Upper Eden Valley?

Both the church valuation and the Clifford IPM were taken in the first half of the fourteenth century. There are some surviving tax lists from this period, of the Lay Subsidies in the State papers. Unfortunately for Brough, the 1332 tax list is illegible and the 1334 subsidy could not be collected in the area, because of poverty. The 1336 list is therefore, the earliest source to illustrate the relative importance of Brough in the Upper Eden Valley. This was a tax on individuals owning more than ten shillings worth of moveable goods, (the value of a cow). Household goods and food were exempt. It shows that Brough (including Brough Sowerby and Helbeck) paid £6, almost double that of Kirkby Stephen, another Clifford manor, but which, at that time, had no market charter.[76]

Both parts of Appleby, on the other hand, together paid £4 18s. 6½d., significantly less than the Brough area. In 1336, therefore, Brough was probably somewhat more wealthy, or larger, than Appleby. Appleby being a royal borough, however, was taxed at a tenth, but Brough, possibly as a

---

Note 76: Glascock, R. G., *Lay subsidy of 1334,* Records of Economic and Social History, OUP 1975. Fraser, C. M.,*Cumberland and Westmorland Lay Subsidies for 1332,* TCWAA (1966) p 131-58.

seignorial borough of lower status, had been taxed at a lower rate of one fifteenth. As will be seen later, the situation was similar, in 1379. This suggests that in the fourteenth century, Appleby suffered more than Brough because of Scottish depredation and the outbreaks of plague. Westmorland was excused a number of later subsidies when there were problems with the Scots, but sometimes the matter was taken into local hands as in 1352, when John de Colleby, the Westmorland tax collector, was assaulted by Roger de Layburn on his way to Helbeck. (Roger) "felled him to the ground, imprisoned him until he made a fine of 60*s.* for his deliverance and stole from him £10 in tax and two marks of his own."[77]

However, the Poll Taxes taken around 1380 set a new standard in tax collection, for the king's officials who were responsible for the collection, noted the name of each individual and the tax paid. Even more interesting is the fact that Brough heads the list for the Eden valley assessments. The significance of this will be considered in the next chapter.

Note 77: *Calendar Patent Rolls, 1350-4,* p273, HMSO.

CHAPTER 7

The 1379 Brough Poll Tax:
surnames and occupations

ALTHOUGH it is not possible to create an accurate profile of Brough and its immediate environs in the late fourteenth century it is possible to make some crude estimates of population and occupation, using taxation documents. In addition some personal names can be read in these documents, enabling us to have a limited idea of individual people. We can also, to an extent, learn what trades were carried on. However, there are severe limitations to this. Transcription of the texts can be difficult, and is subject to error. Assumptions based on surnames about trades at this period can never be definite, as names were fluid; some surnames were established, others were not. What can be calculated reasonably firmly is the population, as the tax returns used, although not always legible, give a fairly good idea of the numbers of people taxed. Allowing for certain variables, such as evasion, untaxed children, and so on, it seems that Church Brough, with Market Brough, Helbeck and Brough Sowerby had a population of 250 or so tax-paying adults at least, to which must be added an unknown number of children. There would probably also be some untaxed paupers and beggars.

Financial crises in the late fourteenth century compelled the government frequently to raise money urgently, and in 1377, 1379 and 1381 it imposed special poll taxes. Some of the Westmorland tax records have been found in the National Archives although parts are somewhat faded and not always easily read.[78] The documents seen are thought to be from the 1379 tax.

Some are nominative lists, in that they contain personal names, and others are summaries of the amounts raised for the whole of the Westmorland East Ward. Both are of considerable interest. First, Brough is placed at the top in the summary list rather than Appleby and may have been the base from which the tax collectors worked, perhaps because it was a better route and administrative centre than Appleby, or perhaps the castle was more secure. The settlement was presumably then a place of relative importance.

Once again, it shows that more tax was raised in Brough, with Stainmore than elsewhere in the Ward, implying that Brough had a greater population than any other place in the Ward. The amount becomes even more impressive if Brough Sowerby and Helbeck are added in. The table below shows

---

Note 78: PRO, National Archives E/179/195/17, E/179/195/18, E/179/195/19.

the figures for several places in the Eden Valley. Even Appleby and Kirkby Stephen produced less. It should not be assumed that Brough was wealthier or significantly more important than other places, but it was probably larger.

TABLE 4: Places in the Eden Valley listed in the Poll Tax, with amounts raised.

Latin name used in the text	Modern version	Amount (as in text)
Vill et Burgus cum Stannesmore	Township and borough with Stainmore	XLs
Hellebeck	Hellbeck	Xs
Soureby iuxta Burgh	Brough Sowerby	Xs
Cabergh	Kaber	Vs Viijd
Wynton	Winton	XXiijs iiijd
Kirkeby Stephan cum Mallerstang	Kirkby Stephen with Mallerstang	XXXiijs iiijd
Querton	Wharton	Xs
Smerdall	Smardale	Vs
Nateby	Nateby	Xs
Wateby	Waitby	Vijs Vjd
Souleby	Soulby	XXvs
Herceley	Hartley	Xs
Musgrave Magna	Great Musgrave	illegible
Musgrave Parva	Little Musgrave	Vjs Viijd
Warthecop	Warcop	XXs
Sandeford	Sandford	Xvs
Newbiggyng	Newbiggin	Xs
Soureby Temple	Temple Sowerby	Xiijs iiijd
Kirkebythore	Kirkby Thore	XXXvs
Baronia de Appeby	Appleby with Bongate	Xixs + obolus
Crakanthorpe	Crackenthorpe	Xiiijs

A further point of interest, as discussed in the previous chapter is, that if the transcription is correct, Brough is described as *Vill et Burgus cum Stannysmore*, i.e. the 'township and borough with Stainmore.'

The Poll Tax lists will be found in Appendix IV, but first an explanation is needed. It has not been possible to transcribe all the names from the nominative lists because of their poor condition, but as many as possible are given for Brough, Brough Sowerby and Helbeck. The list for Nether Brough is very faded and the figures for tax paid are difficult to read. Brough itself was, for the purposes of this tax, divided into two parts: *Vill et Burgus cum Stainmore*. Reference to monetary values are given in Appendix II.

The figures have to be read with caution as some people, who were either unwilling or unable to pay, may have absented themselves on taxation day, and the village officials responsible for identifying the taxpayers may have connived at this.[79] Paupers and beggars were excluded, as well as children under the age of fifteen. Accurate estimates of actual population are therefore impossible, but the numbers recorded can be used as a basis of comparison to judge the relative size of the adult population in the different settlements.

The tax payable per head was four old pence, that is one groat for single taxpayers, and one groat for married couples. Craftsmen, designated *art.* (artificers) seem to have paid sixpence.[80] Wealthier persons, such as the Blenkinsops at Helbeck, classified as "Esquier" paid a much higher rate, at half a mark. The two Broughs and Brough Sowerby seem not, at this time, to have any wealthy residents.

Surnames were only just coming into use in this part of Westmorland in the 1370s and 80s. The Poll Tax lists show a variety of names, some may have been temporary, some more firmly attached to family groups. What should also be remembered is that surnames around this time were still fluid; a son might not bear his father's name. For example, if *John son of Adam del Milne*, eventually had a son, this son might be called *Johnson*.

There were several types of name used. One group was based on family connections: *Wilkinson, Jakson, Thomson, Symonson* and the like. In one or two cases the connection was a daughter: *Alice Addydoghter, Johanna Shephirddoghter, and Emma Sabdoghter*. Another type of surname indicated where the person came from: *de Tybay, de Dene, de Bolton, de Dent, de Staynemore and de Pennston*. More of these location names can be found

---

Note 79: Fenwick, Carolyn C., *The Poll Taxes of 1377, 1379 and 1381*, Oxford, (1998), Vol. 1 xxiii-iv.

Note 80: In the Lancashire Poll taxes, some lists include details of craft workers. Those of Brough do not.

in Nether Brough than in Church Brough. These suggest a fair amount of movement between villages.

There is a third type of surname which needs to be examined and these are the ones that refer to occupations. Carolyn Fenwick, an authority on the Poll Tax, suggests that occupational titles might well be given, in the absence of a surname, to distinguish individuals.[81] Some of these may well have stuck thereafter, but not necessarily.

Although it may be rash to assume occupations from the surnames in these lists, it can be argued that there must be some reason for these particular terms to be used to identify people. Either these were their occupations or they were those of their family, thus giving a clue to the work in the district.

In Nether Brough, Church Brough, Helbeck and Brough Sowerby 251 people were taxed. Nether Brough had the largest work force, with 110 taxable adults, of which five were listed as artificers, and in some cases the surnames of the latter may be a clue to the type of trade. Church Brough was smaller; there were 72 taxable adults, but there were eight artificers. Clergy were excluded from this particular tax. Seventeen of Helbeck's population can be counted but only nine of these are legible. Brough Sowerby had 42 taxable inhabitants which included one artificer.

The Nether Brough population included the miller, *William att Milne*. He may have been at Low Mill as that site today is just inside the township boundary. There were two *Baksters* or bakers. Other distinctive surnames included a *Webster* or weaver, and two *Colyers* who might be coal miners or charcoal burners. There was also a *Colyer* in nearby Helbeck. Two, possibly three smiths, are mentioned, one of whom, *William Smyth, artificer,* employed two servants, Thomas and Anna. There is a shepherd and there are a number of servants: *Margaria, Joanna, Elena and Alice. Thomas Thomasman Robynson* may have been a man servant.

Although Church Brough had fewer taxable adults, there seems to have been a larger number of craftsmen. There is one unidentified artificer whose surname gives no clues but there were also three *Wallers,* a *Mason*, a *Wryght,* and three *Smyths.* Although there was no miller listed, there were two *Baksters* and a *Cock* (cook). These names suggest that the castle, as the centre of the manorial administration, and currently being used as the base for the tax collection, continued to provide local employment. Richard *Clark* was near the top of the Church Brough tax list. There was a *Forester,* possibly in charge of the parks, and in Brough Sowerby there were *Wachers,* again possibly connected with the deer parks.

Note 81: Fenwick, Carolyn C., op.cit.

Was the one *Shephird* in Nether Brough distinctive in some way? Was he perhaps the lord's flock-master? There are suggestions of a woollen production. There were several *Websters*, (weavers). *John Webster* of Brough was classed as an artificer and in Helbeck there was a *Walker* (fuller).[82] In Brough Sowerby there was a *Thomas Barker*, a name which had connections with the tanning industry. There was evidence of a trader; Thomas *Chapman* (a pedlar) is named along with his wife and servant. A number of servants, mainly women were taxed. In some cases they were employees, for example, *Mapota*, servant of *John del Bakhous*. Although the vicar was not taxable, he had two male servants who were. Wives were taxed with their husbands and there is no indication of their work.

Shepherds were common in Brough Sowerby, with possibly two generations represented. There was Johanna *Shephirddoghter* and Thomas *Shepherdson,* William *Shephird* and Agnes *Shephird.* One puzzle is why there seem to be no cattle-based surnames.

While it must be accepted that evidence from names cannot prove anything, at least it can be said that the various types of occupations so named were likely to have been known within the district. A few more definite records of the area survive for the first quarter of the fifteenth century, and the next chapter will examine the changes which were taking place.

Note 82: A doubtful reading because of legibility, but could the *Tose*r of Helbeck perhaps be one who separated the strands in the first stages of wool preparation, or a wool teaser i.e. one who finished cloth?

CHAPTER 8

The fifteenth century:
the effect of the Black Death

FROM 1389 to 1424, there were at least five inquisitions dealing with the Clifford lands in Westmorland. Two deaths close together, first of the lord, John de Clifford in 1422 and then his mother, Elizabeth, in 1424, allow a more complete assessment of the estates including the dower-land, than before.

An earlier inquisition, in 1389-90 had found that the Lord Roger held the same number of tofts as in the 1315 list, and the number of freeholders had increased to nine.[83] The vaccaries now numbered 29. There may have been some subdivision, but the inquisition is too general for details. Certainly the area they covered had extended to Redgate, and Heggerscales, and in the north, to Hazel Bank. But, "much has been destroyed by the Scots." When Maud, his widow died in 1403, there was a similar comment about the Scots, and the only vaccary, which had retained its value of 70s was Heggerscales, which was well away from the main road. The others were worth only 100 shillings together.

The details in the Lady Elizabeth's inquisition in 1424 were more specific. The castle was derelict, and the castle park had been let out for 10s (50p), whereas a century earlier, the value had been 100s for two parks. The rents for the demesne were down to 3d an acre for the arable, and 6d an acre for the meadow, that is a third and a half of the 1315 value respectively. As the village arable was listed in oxgangs in 1315, and in bovates a century later, comparison is difficult.

There were twenty cottages "totally wasted", with a possible nine others (number unclear) each worth 12d yearly, and in Church Brough, the messuages were "in great part lying waste for lack of tenants" with the effect that reke silver, (or rike silver) a tax paid by cottagers[84] for fuel, was down.[85] The watermill was worth 26s.8d, a fifth of the value of the burnt mill of

Note 83: Calendar of Inquisitons Post Mortem, [CIPM]: 13 RII, for Roger Clifford; 4 HIV for Maud, widow of Roger de Clifford, (May 1403); 15R II for Thomas Clifford; 10 Hen V for John de Clifford, May 1422; Lady Elizabeth, 2 Henry VI (taken March 1424). For Lady Elizabeth, widow of Thomas and mother of John de Clifford, [CIPM 1-5 Henry VI ed K. Parkin, Boydell].
Note 84: IPM 13 RII Reke silver paid on 56 messuages and 6 bovates. Roger de Clifford.
Note 85: IPM 2 Hen VI

1315, but the 25 tofts let to free tenants were still occupied, along with ten acres on Sowerbymore, farmed severally, (that is in common) which was valued at six shillings.

There is a section of the inquisition detailing additional payments, separate from rents lists: "Magna Burgh and Parva Burgh, bovates and lands, for which free tenants pay 10*s*." This could relate to past services which have been commuted: a change at which the eighteenth century writers Nicolson and Burn hint.[86]

There were ten vaccaries, on Stainmore which were occupied but worth on average only 6s.8d each, again that is less than the burnt ones of 1315. The pasture and woodland lying beyond these farms, at a penny an acre, had yet to be improved. At Redgate Close, Rookeby, a mine of sea-coal, worth 13*s*. 4*d*. was no longer worked and there was no income from it: in fact, there was still 4*s*. 3*d*. owing for it. However, the fees from fairs and markets at 20 shillings were higher than previously. Brough Sowerby was valued at 66*s*. 8*d*. and had one free tenant William de Bernes who had accumulated two messuages and twelve acres of arable paying only 7*d*. yearly.

It should be noted, however, that not all the Brough estates feature in Lady Elizabeth's IPM. Ten or more vaccaries and the "olde park," which had belonged to John, her son, had not been included; this may also be true of some of his other holdings, which may have been part of his widow's dower or part of the wardship deal made with the Nevilles of Raby Castle. The discrepancies over the number of vaccaries listed in the various documents are mainly a matter of terminology. Sometimes Old Park and Sowerby Park were included along with Redgate and others in the south.

In all, this is a depressing picture of an area from which agriculture had retreated. The value of the demesne lands was down, probably because the services of customary tenants were no longer available. Many cottages were unoccupied and the vaccaries, originally worked on the lord's terms, could not afford the necessary amount of waged labour.

The picture is relieved only by the list of freeholders which shows that de Bernes was not the only free tenant to take advantage of the situation. Thomas Smyth, Thomas de Oxenthwayte and Thomas de Tulverdofe were also able to acquire land and each had sizeable holdings. The table on the following page is taken from the *Inquistion Post-Mortem* of Elizabeth de Clifford, 1424.

Note 86: Commuted to money rents, N&B, p579.

TABLE 5: Brough Free Tenants, 1424

Tenant	House etc.	Farm land	Yearly rent
Thomas de Oxenthwayte	Messuage	8 acres arable	3s
John de Soureby	Messuage	4 acres arable	14d
Thomas de Tulverdofe	Two messuages	2 bovates	4s.3d
William Spencer	Messuage	2 bovates	2d
Thomas de Derby	Messuage and a cottage	4 acres arable	8d
Thomas Smyth and Alice his wife in her right	Three messuages	24 acres arable	12s.7d and a cradle when the lady of the manor gives birth
Thomas Bucle	Tenement and adjacent croft	3 acres arable	2s.3½d
Agnes Huchunsondoghter		3 acres arable	15¼d
Richard Musgrave	Licence for mill at Musgrave		12d
In Brough Sowerby William de Bernes	Two messuages	12 acres arable	7 pence

The Steward's Account

The accounts of Robert Crag, the steward, for Brough, in 1425 show more details of the economy, and the adaptations that were being made at that time. As far as is known only one major manor account survives for Brough in the Hothfield collection of the Clifford Medieval records.[87] This covered the twelve months period from November 1425 to November 1426, and was written entirely in Medieval Latin. Most of it is in good condition and easily transcribable, but parts of it are worn or damaged and can only be partially read: much of the section dealing with Stainmore is impossible to decipher. The document consists of two sheets of parchment, written on both faces, and amounts to 259 lines.

Nearly all is in one hand writing, but there are occasional different hands, possibly of persons using the document later for notes. It deals mainly with Brough, Brough Sowerby and Stainmore, but has brief

---

Note 87: CRO(K) WD/Hoth, Box 45

accounts for other manors lower down the Eden valley. Nothing is said about Helbeck. Possibly it was written by Richard Drax, who is referred to towards the end as a 'cleric', but about whom nothing else is known. Read together with the other contemporary documents and records cited here it helps to build up a picture of the community, but, being drawn up for a special purpose, it deals with somewhat different matters.

In this chapter modern place names are generally used but, usually, the 1425 spelling is given italicised in brackets, e.g. Upper Brough (*Overburgh*). Brough itself was written as *Burgh subtus Staynmore*, sometimes *Staynesmore*, i.e. Brough-under-Stainmore. Family names are given as written, but it should be noted that different spellings were occasionally used for a single name. First names are given in their modern English forms. Some of the personal and place names are still recognisable, but others have obviously changed in the intervening period. Although the document includes places in the Clifford estates outside Brough, this chapter refers to them only when this may help put a Brough matter in a wider context. Upper and Lower Brough (*Netherburgh*) were treated as one manor, Brough Sowerby (*Soureby iuxta Burgh*) being treated separately, although there seem to be cases where this distinction was not rigidly followed. Appendix V gives the names of such local people as are mentioned, and Appendix VI gives place names. Each appendix gives both the modern and the old versions of names. Rents, where quoted, are for one financial year, from Saint Martin in the winter (Martinmas) to the following Martinmas.

The account suggests three main developments, which follow on from what was happening before. First, the manor had still not fully recovered from the hardships, e.g. disease, depopulation, and warfare of the preceding century; second, large areas of the former demesne land were being enclosed; third, 'new' men were becoming significant. It seems clear that the manor was increasingly taking rents rather than having the land worked directly. John, the last Lord Clifford, had recently died and the management of the estate had been handed to the Nevilles at Raby Castle, presumably in wardship for the young heir.

The first point, the economic depression, is demonstrated by the references to rental returns being reduced. One example, which recurs frequently, is, "*De firma unius acre dimidie prati dominicalis… que solebat reddere per annum ijs vjd. Et de firma herbagij vocati Sourebymore que solebat reddere per annum xiijs iiijd...*" Translated this is, "The letting of half an acre of demesne meadow... which used to return two shillings and sixpence a year. And the letting of the pasturage called Sowerby moor which used to return thirteen shillings and fourpence per year..."

Another example refers to an eel fishery near the Sowerby vaccary, for which apparently no tenant could be found. However, it was still being worked as is shown by a later mention, presumably the demesne was working it. Again, the forge, formerly let to Stephen Smyth, was apparently derelict and could not be let. Another case was that of the cottage formerly tenanted by a woman, Mapota Calshird. This was 'decayed' and apparently unlet, as was the cottage of Adam Lambard. Either depopulation meant less demand or there had been insufficient economic recovery after the problems of the preceding century.

The free rents for tenements in Upper and Lower Brough together amounted to one pound, six shillings, ten pence and two farthings for the year. The rent for 100 acres of former demesne land in Lower Brough, being let at eighteen pence per acre, was nine pounds, whereas earlier it had been worth eleven pounds, at 22 pence per acre. This was a significant drop. Eighteen bovates of land, probably in Upper Brough, previously worth five pounds eight shillings, now brought in four pounds, ten shillings. Both the eel fishery, which had been worth ten shillings, and the Brough fishery, had no takers, and remained as demesne holdings. On the other hand the Brough Sowerby fishery had been let to a consortium. One possibility is that the ordinary people were now able to beat down prices, but this can only be speculation. Fortunately for the manor, the autumn fair at Brough accounted for five pounds eighteen shillings and three pence, net. No amount was given for previous fairs, so a comparison cannot be made. It is possible perhaps, that the fair might have attracted distant traders with special commodities, as Thomas Smyth of Brough paid his rent, not in cash, but as half a pound of cumin. The document does not show how or where he obtained the spice.

Nevertheless, there is clear evidence that the manor was adapting to changing conditions by enclosing and improving land, especially at Brough Sowerby and on Stainmore, where there are references to '*foreland*' and '*approviamenta*' ('improvements' or possibly 'enclosure'). This was rented to private individuals, who could then farm outside the manorial traditions and concentrate, for example, on controlling the quality of their livestock in their own closes.

On the second point, 75 acres of demesne land on Sowerbymoor (*Sourebymore*) had been enclosed by the late Lady Clifford. Part of this had been let to Thomas Skayfe and his colleagues, while another close there called Wateflatt,[88] had also been recently enclosed by Lady Clifford. The remaining land forming part of Wateflatt had not been enclosed and was let separately. A close at Brough Castle, presumably an enclosure to separate

---

Note 88: This may mean 'Water Marsh', but this is only speculation.

it from other demesne land near the castle, was let. Other terms used, e.g. *parcella terre* ('a parcel of land'), *clausum herbagij*, ('a close of herbage'), suggest either actual enclosure or defined and limited pieces of land. Not all of the land available was in fact being let and remained, "in the hands of the Lord." The document implies that the process of enclosure had been going on for some years, and was possibly accelerating, although still incomplete.

What the document does show is that 'new men' were emerging as agricultural entrepreneurs, taking over the working of land from the demesne. Some seem to have been operating alone, Thomas Bukles being an example; others worked in groups, *Johannes Wardale et sui socij,* (John Wardale and his associates) had rented part of the new enclosure in Over Brough, while Thomas Skayfe and his associates had taken over much of Sowerbymoor. William Spenser and his associates were working unenclosed land at Sowerbymoor, indicating that this land was now in at least two parts. Developments at Brough Sowerby concerning the fishery there and at least one vaccary show that individuals were working together, as at Brough.

The document shows that the new men were willing to pay high rents. At a time when the average shepherd and farm labourer earned between six and ten shillings a year, the Scaife family paid over five pounds rental per annum, and the Buckles, over eight pounds. The Spensers and Cumstons were paying three pounds or just over, the Wardales four pounds five shillings, while John Lethemann/Ladyman, and the two Glentons were each paying around one pound ten shillings. These amounts have to be compared with the more common and much lower rents being paid by, say, Mapota Calshird, paying two shillings and Robert Douglass paying one penny.

It is impossible from this document to find out how well these 'new men' coped, in either the short or the long term. Many of the surnames can be found nearly two centuries later in the 1604 rental and some can still be found in the Brough area or not far away in the Eden Valley. The Bukles (Buckles) family survived and produced at least one famous name, Cuthbert Buckle, founder of Stainmore School. The Scaife family, to use the modern spelling, seems to have been very enterprising in 1425, and to have become significant locally, well before its famous seventeenth century representative. Some of these new men were becoming local administrators, for example, one Skaife was *prepositus,* steward, of Brough Sowerby. Obviously the enterprising men were taking advantage of the economic changes occurring, but we do not know what became of the poorer or less enterprising people.

It is reasonable to surmise that direct demesne farming had become unprofitable for the Clifford estate, and that more could be gained from letting the land to tenants who may have been more energetic as well as better market oriented. The document does not tell us what agricultural activity was actually carried out on such lands. Some of the new holdings, particularly towards Stainmore, must have been devoted to livestock, presumably cattle and sheep. Sowerbymoor, perhaps between Brough Sowerby and Over Brough, may also have been primarily used for cattle, but there are hints of pig farming. A word, *Grismenland* (the land of the pig men), which cannot be located, implies organised work with pigs, as does another reference to a pig house in Over Brough, although the building, whatever it was, had not been let.

Given the nature of the land and the probable small population density it is possible that cattle-raising for meat was the main activity, rather than dairy farming. If the export of cheese and butter was worthwhile there is nothing here to demonstrate it. There is no reference in this account to sheep farming, although wool must have been needed locally.

It was outside the scope of the accounts to list the products of the farms. However, there is indirect evidence of cereal growing for there were corn mills, a barley kiln and the Constable's rent which was paid in oats. There was a water-powered corn mill, within the castle close, let to Thomas Bukles, which he seems either to have sub-let to John Maltby and Thomas Ubank, or worked with them. There was no other mention of a corn mill within Brough, although one is mentioned possibly on Stainmore and one in Brough Sowerby.[89] It appears that cereals for bread were produced locally. A further reference to John Letheman renting a barley kiln in Lower Brough implies both barley growing and ale production, although on what scale is unknown.

The other clue is a separate rental return for oats which was in two parts, first in money at four shillings ten pence for four quarters seven bushels, then secondly, three and a half bushels in kind. These were probably the constable's dues, from the two Broughs, as they were still being recorded as such in the 1604 rental. Other food supplies include the eel fishery near Brough Sowerby, already mentioned, and the fishery apparently at Brough Sowerby, let to a consortium led by Robert Cumston. There were also fishing rights on the Swindale, near the castle, but again there is no detail.

The document mentions coal mining, or, rather, the absence of it. There seems to have been some local coal mining at an earlier stage, and there certainly was afterwards, but there seems to have been none going on locally in this year. The same is true of lead mining. One detail which can be read

Note 89: There was a mill at Oxenthwaite, which was part of Stainmore in the later accounts.

is that the lead mine 'there' (location not specified) was not expected to produce a return during the current year.

On Stainmore, the record shows that the vaccaries were valuable for they gave a total return of twenty five pounds eighteen shillings. It is unfortunate that, due to damage, much of the Stainmore section cannot be read, even under UV light, and therefore few vaccaries can be identified in this document. Despite these problems, it appears that there was other income from Stainmore, apart from the vaccaries, for an additional net sum of sixteen pounds eighteen shillings and one penny was collected. In addition, *cheminage*, Latin *cheminagium*, thought to be middle English *Way Penny*, which was a type of toll to be paid for using roads or tracks, brought in one pound six shillings eight pence, much less than previously.

Brough Sowerby returned eighteen pounds ten shillings and threepence for the year, about half of the value of the two Broughs. The water mill paid thirty three shillings and fourpence. More idea of the value of land there can be found in Appendix V in which the holdings of named individuals are given.

The total receipts for Upper and Lower Brough were £40 8*s.* 7*d.* After deductions for decay, and expenses, £38 14*s.* was sent to Raby.

Finally a completely unrelated, but very human, item. Thomas Smyth, as part of his rent, was expected to provide a cradle, when the Lady Clifford was expecting a child. None was required in this year.

Surnames in this account
Many personal and place names are given in the document, and these are listed in Appendices V and VI. Some names of officials within the Clifford estates are excluded from the list as they may not be local Brough people. Where possible details of the place or activity within Brough linked to an individual is given. The names should be compared with those identified in the 1379 Poll Tax.

Family names here are generally clear from the text but spellings for any one name, as already said, can vary, and transcription can also be difficult. There are three versions of the Buckles name but it is likely they were all from one family, possibly an extended one. In some cases, e.g. the Glentons, presumably father and son, there was a standard spelling, but it is not always clear which one was meant, although usually the account distinguished between them.

Many family names, in addition to those due to a person's place of origin, could be linked to an occupation or to a physical characteristic. The Wardales in this list may have originated from Weardale and John Scardale may have come from a place of that name. At some time, however, John and Thomas Walker may have had a fuller in the family; a forebear of John Whithede may have had white or very fair hair, but all this is speculation. The 1379 Poll tax returns for Brough, insofar as they can be read with any certainty, show many different names from the Steward's account 45 years later, and many of the occupational names of the former have disappeared. This may mean that there had been population movement, but it could also mean that people changed their surnames. Also there were many gaps in the Poll Tax readings, and possibly the 1425/6 names were amongst those not transcribed.

It has to be accepted that we cannot estimate the population of the manor at this date from the names available, as the surnames identified almost certainly only cover a small part of the total population. It is likely that the poorest or the most insignificant are omitted because they could not afford to pay rents and scratched a living as hired labourers. Others may have been craftsmen or even traders. There is virtually no reference to blacksmiths, carpenters or masons here, although they may have had dual roles as craftsmen and small farmers, and there would have been craftsmen of some sort in the community. No mention is made of coal miners or of mining in this account, although mining was carried on at Redgate and possibly elsewhere both before and shortly after this account.

There are about 40 surnames listed of people likely to be local to Brough, and of these over half can be traced in later records, such as the parish registers and the cotton mill records of the late eighteenth century. If those later names are descendants of the early fifteenth century families there may have been a reasonably high degree of family stability locally. Some names, such as Buckle and Scaife, are almost certainly from the early families, and their histories are well documented,[90] but others, such as Sanderson, Robinson and Smith cannot be so definitely linked. The Wardale name, however, may be that of one family throughout. This does not mean that a whole family remained settled in Brough all the time. Individuals went away, some as far as London, some not so far.

Place names

Place names are more difficult, as many are illegible, but can still be of interest. Obvious places like Upper Brough, Lower Brough and Brough Sowerby are clear enough. Some names have disappeared from later records as field names and land usage changed over time. *Blechefeld,* which appears in two different spellings, seems to have been on Stainmore, and may mean a field for bleaching textiles or a black field. It can not be

---

Note 90: Nicolson and Burn (1777) refer to the Buckle family, p.575. For the Scaife history see the Scaife Study Group records.

traced now. The modern Heggerscales was written as *Egilscale* and is recognisable, as is Redgate Close, written as *Redegateclose*.

Conclusion

For very few manors in fifteenth century Westmorland were there inquisitions and almost contemporary stewards' accounts, as are found at Brough. In some cases it is hard to reconcile the Brough valuations, for example of the vaccaries, and the number of unoccupied houses, but in others, they complement each other. The main conclusions are the same for both.

First and most obvious is that by the 1420s, the area was one of waste and decay. Where the inquisitions generalise, with phrases like, "much destroyed by the Scots," the steward, who had to make up the losses he could not account for, was much more specific.[91] He named the previous tenants of unoccupied holdings, and gave the previous rents, and locations.

"Decay" was listed carefully. There were derelict pig-houses, cattle sheds, and the forge of Stephen Smyth. The fishery on the Swindale, possibly the one in the lord's deer park mentioned in the late fourteenth century poaching case, could not be let, nor could the eel traps at Sowerby. Two cottages were decayed, some land on Sowerbymoor was unlet, the turbary remained unleased, and neither the lead mine nor the coal mine was being worked. The steward had £1 16*s*. 5*d*. in unpaid rents for which he pleaded to be excused.

Secondly, there had been a change in the type of landholding. When the Cliffords took over the estate at the beginning of the fourteenth century, much of the land had been classified as demesne and farmed for the lord, though there was a sign of change, for even then the most profitable rents came from closes of new improvement, rented out at 115 shillings, and one farthing. By the following century, the acreage under demesne had decreased, with at least three large closes carved out of it and let out for money rents to groups.

In 1424-26, land was let to free tenants at lower rents than previously, as in the 100 acres of demesne, bringing in 18*d*. an acre, which had once brought in 22*d*. an acre. In the Lady Elizabeth's IPM, the most valuable demesne land brought in 6*d*. an acre. The bovates which, in her time were worth 20*d*. each, were worth three times that amount in the account. Could this really have happened in two years? The water mill also seems to have increased in value, until it is seen that its figure includes, among other things, the common oven and that there seems to be another mill and kiln in Nether Brough, which may have been part of the wardship estate of

---

Note 91: CIPM, 13RII, Lady Elizabeth Clifford

John's son, and so not in the Lady Elizabeth's inquisiton. Here there is a problem for the modern interpreter, for the values given in the inquisitions and in the Steward's accounts are difficult to reconcile. The Steward is likely to be the more accurate as he had to justify every penny he could or could not collect; the local people called before the king's representatives to give the IPM values had no such concern,[92] although they wished to emphasise the amount of decay, in the hope, perhaps, of being spared the next round of taxes. However, it is clear from both accounts that the 100 acres in Nether Brough, and the pasture land had lost their value. So too had the arable land, the bovates, one of which remained unlet.[93] The value of the vaccaries, at £25 was higher than that given in the inquisitions of 1422 and 1424, but it is not clear whether these covered the same land as before.

Some freeholders had been able to take advantage of the unlet land and had begun to accumulate tenancies. Thomas Buckle, the steward of Brough Sowerby, with holdings there, had leased the Castle park and the mill, a tenement and an adjacent croft. Thomas and Alice Smyth had three messuages and 24 acres of land. House rents in Church Brough seem to have risen to those of Market Brough, possibly because the old labour services had been commuted and although some had been returned to the lord, presumably on the death of the tenant, at least three of these had been re-let and brought in eleven shillings. In addition, the barley kiln had been let and a water corn-mill, which had been undemised, (unleased) had been let from the February of 1426. Maybe there was an improvement in the economy, for the market tolls were nearly £6 in profit.[94] Even so, the total collected from the estate by the steward was about three quarters of the valuation of the same lands in 1315.[95]

After this document there is a long gap in the source material for Brough. It is not until the Tudor period that a fuller picture emerges.

Note 92: Dr Angus Winchester, personal communication.
Note 93: IPM Elizabeth 2 HVI, 1424, p305-6. This gives 22 Bovates worth each 20d.
Note 94: £5.18s 4d in profit plus 21d stallage made £6. [Fairs were worth 10s in 1315.]
Note 95: In 1315 the value had been £ 49.18s.4½d.

CHAPTER 9

Change or Decay: Tudor and Stuart periods

To Bowes, a very exceding poore thorowfayre, and on - to Burgh on Stane
More, [and]Appleby a poore village. Ther is an old castel on the side of
Edon Water cawlled Burgh[96]

THIS is John Leland's[97] description of Brough on his tour through England
and Wales in the reign of Henry VIII. By his London standards, this was a
poor, undeveloped region. Yet remote though it might be from the political
centre of power, Westmorland felt the effect of the changes of the early
Tudor period, and with disastrous results for some individuals. The
changes, either directly or indirectly instigated by central government,
affected the lives of ordinary villagers for they covered important issues,
such as tenants' rights, farming practices, church worship and land prices.
Some of these caused unrest at village level, but some became part of coun-
ty-wide mass protest. In the largest of these, the Pilgrimage of Grace,
Westmorland men were part of a general rising which had spread across the
other northern counties. This was a religious and economic protest which
had serious repercussions in the Upper Eden valley with the vicar of
Brough, one of the leaders, ending up in the Tower of London.

But first it is necessary to set the scene, looking initially at the regional
importance of the village and then at the changing significance of the features which had governed its early growth. A diocesan survey in 1563
reported 140 households in Brough, making it less than half the size of
Kirkby Stephen which had 300 households while both parts of Appleby
together had 237 households.[98] This must have been in each case, the whole
parish, and probably included a bit of inspired guesswork for the rural
parts.[99] The Stainmore part of Brough manor, however, spread into Kirkby
Stephen parish. Other sources suggest that Stainmore and Brough Sowerby

---

Note 96: *Fro the castel is a vill[age] cawled Burgh[am]? and there is a great pilgrim[age]*
to... This is in another part of the manuscript and could be either Brough or Brougham.
Brough did have pilgrims to the holy well, N&B.

Note 97: Leland, *Itinerary in England and Wales, 1539-1545*, vol 5 p.47, 147, in reign of
Henry VIIIth, Fac. by Centaur Press, London, 1964.

Note 98: B. L. Harley manuscript, now published by Dyer P & Palliser D. M., eds. *Diocesan*
Population returns 1563 and 1601, OUP (2005).

Note 99: B. L. Harl. 594, quoted Appleby, A. B., *Famine in Tudor and Stuart England*,
Liverpool University Press, (1978).

probably had a greater number of households than the combined total for Church and Market Brough.

Seventeenth century surveys give a little more detail but each had its own agenda. The manor rentals do not cover the very poor who had neither land nor cottage, and the Protestation returns were for males over the age of eighteen only. They do, however, show that Market Brough was larger than Church Brough and that the Stainmore population was larger still.

The Hearth Taxes of 1674 are of more use, as they listed householders and the most recent publication of these returns includes those householders who were exempt as well as those who paid.[100] In the parish of Brough, Helbeck, and Stainmore, there were 282 households. Again these show that Market Brough was substantially larger than Church Brough, with 58 households in the former and 36 in the latter. Helbeck had twelve households, Brough Sowerby had 48, and Stainmore had 128 households, (but the problem is knowing which part of Stainmore was counted).[101] At least it can be seen that there was some degree of migration. Over the three decades from 1641, nearly 40 per cent of the householders had moved, either between villages or in from elsewhere. Some moves were politically motivated. There were five households of Blenkinsops in Market Brough. This family had lost their home, Helbeck Hall during the civil war, and it was still occupied by Major Scaife.

Parish Registers[102]

Tax lists are not an accurate measure of population, but there is another source. The Brough parish registers survive with only a few gaps, from 1559. They can be used to illustrate the general trends but because there were many surnames and Christian names in common, family reconstruction is almost impossible over any length of time. Also some of the neighbouring parish registers have been lost, so there is no way to measure the amount of mobility between the villages.

Until the 1590s, the parish registers for Brough, show a growing population with roughly twice as many baptisms as burials. However, this trend was punctured by dramatic variations in the death rates, for there was little protection from natural or man-made hazards. In 1597, 71 people, five of whom were strangers, were buried at Brough. This was more than twice the annual average of burial rate throughout the 1570s. In the 1590s two

---

Note 100: Phillips, C. et al op. cit.
Note 101: East Stainmore was part of Brough manor and so was the part of South Stainmore which included Heggerscales but there was also Middle and South Stainmore.
Note 102: Brierley, H. ed., *Registers of Brough-under-Stainmore*, H. Titus Wilson, Kendal 1923. The originals are in CRO[K].

schoolmasters died in quick succession, and at least two families, the Whartons and the Hodgsons, were, according to the registers, wiped out by the plague. A third school master arrived in 1596. Within a decade, five out of his eight children were dead.

TABLE 6: Plague in Brough

1597 Died of plague.

Isbell d. of Abraam Wharton of the plague	10 Nov.
Francis, s of George Nattrass	22 Nov.
Mychaell s of Abraam Wharton	28 |Nov.
Thomas s. of Abraham Wharton	30 Nov.
Abraam Wharton and his daughter, his mother and his made [maid]	
	1 Dec.

1598

Annas Hodgeson, widow, of the plague	6 Julie
Grace wife of Thomas Waller	7 Julie
Ann d. of John Jackson sen.	17 Julie
Jenet d. of John Hodgeson	17 Julie
Elizabeth wife of John Hodgeson	25 Julie
John son of John Hodgeson	29 Julie
Henry Hodgeson	30 Julie
Janet Hodgeson, widow	3 Aug.
Jaine d. of John Hodgeson	8 Aug.

Both families had young children:-
Abram Wharton married Margaret Simpson in July 1582. Their children were:

Annas	baptised	Nov. 1582
Isbell		1584
Thomas		1586 - buried 1587
Mychaell		1588
Thomas		1591

John Hodgeson married Elizabeth Hodgeson in 1594. Their children were:

Jenet	baptised	1595
John		1598

There is no record of Jaine's baptism
(Spelling as in original)   CRO(K) WPR 23A/1G

In 1623, the total of deaths was higher still, at 110. There were only two marriages that year, and the following year showed a mere nineteen baptisms compared with 50 a year later when the situation was more normal. Research by Andrew Appleby suggests that many of these deaths, like those in other Cumbrian villages, were due to starvation, or at the very least, malnutrition and disease. These were the results of a series of poor harvests in areas already at the limit of subsistence farming.[103] For all villagers, there was the ever present expectation of death: in infancy, in child-bed and from illnesses compounded by malnutrition.

The records show that short-lived marriages, with many births, were often followed by a number of hasty re-marriages, in an attempt to provide step-mothers for a single parent family. Ysobell Brunscall, for example and Henry Cumpston married in 1568. They had six children baptised, two of whom died in infancy, and then Ysobell herself died in childbirth in 1587, but after a fairly long marriage of nineteen years. Within a year, Henry had married Agnes Hodgson. She was childless when she died in 1590 and a few months later Henry married Ann Wardell: they had no children and Henry died in 1606.

Another example is Anthonye Appleby who farmed at Sowerby Park. He married Elizabeth Jackson in 1582, and when she died childless in 1591 he remarried later that year. There were two daughters before his second wife died in 1597. The following year, Anthonye married Janet Jackson and by 1600 they had had two children. Finally a third example, with a happier ending, possibly because the bride came from a well off family and the husband had a large isolated farm on Stainmore. Hew Patrigg married Grace Ubank in 1617. By 1630 they had had nine children, of whom two died as infants.

Later in the seventeenth century there were fewer years of crisis. Research by Appleby makes the point that after 1623, there were less problems in Westmorland in time of dearth. There were fewer people tied to the land, better farming practices leading to higher yields, more opportunities of alternative employment and better transport systems for distributing food.[104]

But how accessible was Brough? Sir Daniel Fleming, writing in 1671, was not impressed. His description includes phrases like "a great but no good road, - the worst hard road in England," - "from Bowes to Brough taking six hours," but at least by then, there was a regular communication, "the post passing twice a week."[105]

Note 103: Appleby A. B., op.cit., Chap. 8.
Note 104: Appleby A., op.cit., p.188.
Note 105: N&B, p.577.

By the end of the seventeenth century, the Brough villages were still small with little sign of growth, for as Fleming continues, "here was but a little town placed at the foot of Stainmore. Now the town is decayed and become a small village."

Why the decay? What had happened to this town with its ancient castle, its church and its manor which was part of the Clifford holdings?

By Tudor times a stronghold on a defensible site was an out-dated concept; it was useless against the new military techniques of the period. When the castle was accidentally burnt down at Christmas in 1521, it was left in ruins. It was over a century and a quarter before it was rebuilt by Lady Anne Clifford in 1659-62. For her, it was a medieval symbol of power, and she restored the tower and keep, as well as building a large number of residential and service rooms, which included a brewery and a kitchen. She also had the nearby mill, which she described as "old and decayed," taken down and rebuilt in the summer of 1661.[106] Four years later, another fire destroyed the furnishings in the tower, but the Earl of Thanet, when he inherited the estate, had no intention of living there. Instead, he stripped much of the stonework and used it to rebuild Appleby Castle. The site was further plundered for its stone, as local villagers rebuilt their own houses and, over a century later in the 1790s, the manorial mill. A major structural collapse of part of the keep about the same time was never repaired. The castle had become a romantic ruin.

The church property seems to have been better cared for. The building shows evidence of alterations during the sixteenth and seventeenth centuries.[107] The tower was built around 1513 by the Blenkinsop family, and Lady Anne Clifford added a number of improvements in her time. The nave was re-roofed and a number of new windows put in. The church remained the property of Queen's College, although the tithes had been farmed (rented) out. However, there had been trouble. In 1506, John Brunskill, a local man, had endowed a chantry chapel, dedicated to St Mary and St Gabriel. This was not in the church but a separate institution. It was connected with the holy well of St Winifred, which lay at the eastern end of Market Brough.[108] Brunskill provided two beds, either for travellers or for the sick, and two priests were appointed. Apart from their main functions of singing and praying for the souls of the benefactors of the chapel, one was to teach

Note 106: Clifford, D. J., ed., *Diaries Lady Anne Clifford*, Sutton, (2003), p.155, and CRO[K] WD/Hoth/10, vol 3, [Also WD/Cat acc 5694] *Great Booke of Record - of Lady Anne.*

Note 107: RCHM op. cit. p49 ff.

Note 108: N&B. vol 1, p464 f., p575. There are different figures for the valuation in 1546. See *Survey of 1546 Cumberland and Westmorland Chantries; Brough,* p147 TCWAA, 1964.

singing and the other to teach grammar. Mr Rasebeck, the vicar of Brough raised objections to the foundation as it was under Shap Abbey and so out of his control. He took the matter to the bishop, and then to the archbishop. The latter judged him to be "an abandoned wretch" so he then, to quote Nicolson and Burn: *"set up a cross, and lighted up candles in the church at mid day time - caused the bells to be rung and cursed with bell book and candle all those who should receive any oblations."* His efforts were rewarded; he was allowed twenty shillings a year.

The chantry did not survive for long, but in its place a school was established, financed by its endowments. A 1546 survey shows that one of the chantry masters, John de Bek, had continued to teach there.[109] This was a "fregrammar schole - of the foundation of John Brunscall - to saye divine service and to teach scholars to wryte." It therefore pre-dates Kirkby Stephen Grammar School. It was endowed with a mansion and garth in which the master lived and a little chapel in Gypgarthe.[110] It was financed by the rents from fifteen tenements. These included some five local burgages, but also one at Barnard Castle, and another at Yanwath. In all its yearly income was £7 11*s*. 4*d*. In the 1590s when two schoolmasters died in quick succession, a third, a young man, from Temple Sowerby took over. He can be traced back to that village through the parish registers, and in his father's will, there is a codicil dated 1579, stating:

> "I give to my son John Gowling the summe of tenne pounds of good and lawful money of england to be paid to him over and above his child's portion towardses his funding at the scole provided that he shall not have yt but to maynten (maintain) him at his books only."*(sic)*[111]

After his stint as school master in Brough, he may have gone to work for the Lowthers, as he can be traced to Askham and Penrith, and an important document transferring the Whitehaven estate from Sir John Lowther to his brother Christopher Lowther, was witnessed by a John Gowling, in 1638.

A second school was established nearby on Stainmore at the end of the century. In 1594 in the will of Christopher Buckle, an annuity of £8 a year was left for a school master to teach the children to read, write and cast accounts, whereupon the inhabitants built a school house, which was to serve as a chapel on Sundays. One proviso was that on Easter day the congregation had to go to Brough Church for the service. Later, in 1699, the Earl of Thanet, having had to repair the building, enclosed the waste land of

---

Note 109: Translations give John de Bek the title of Sir. This is a mis-translation of the Latin *Dom,* abbrev. *dominus*, meaning master.
Note 110: The chapel was later demolished.
Note 111: CRO[C] D&C wills and inventories.

The church of St. Michael's, Brough.

Slapestones and gave it as an endowment. Within a short time, there were disputes over the holding and although a court case found in favour of the curate, he had to put up with "gates broken down, cattle maimed" - before he got his rights.[112]

Brough Church, because it belonged to Queen's College, Oxford, was not directly affected by the dissolution of the monasteries, but the religious policies of the king sparked off unsettling rumours which spread quickly throughout Westmorland. It was said that some churches would be closed, and their valuables removed, while fees for marriages and burials would be raised. At the same time there were many changes in landownership. The monastic land had come on to the market, and new landlords like Thomas Wharton in Kirkby Stephen, enclosed land which had been previously farmed in common, and then demanded high entry fines from new tenants. Villagers got their revenge. There are incidents recorded of the new hedges torn down, as on John Warcoppe's land at Smardale. An "assembly of twenty four men" cut down the improvements of John Sharpe, steward at Orton, and those of John Pekerryng of Crosby.[113] In July 1535, at Burgh, (Brough) Westmorland, Sir Edward Musgrave and Christopher Wharton were bound over to keep the peace, after one of the Musgrave servants had

---

Note 112: N&B 574 ff., p275 Brough School, p575 Stainmore.
Note 113: Brewer J. E., Gairdner J., Brodie R. H., eds. *Calendar of Letters and Papers, Foreign and Domestic of the Reign of Henry VIII*, vol 8&9: 1008, 1030 1046, HMSO

been killed in a local deer hunting dispute. A letter to the king from John Appleby mentioned unlawful assemblies of men in harness with bows and bills to the number of 200, throughout the northern counties in 1535.[114]

These risings were part of the period of uncertainty as innovations in farming and land holding were compounded by bad harvests and the usual border troubles. The troubles were made worse by the inadequacies of the Lord Warden of the Western March, Thomas Clifford.[115] The closing of the small monasteries in 1536 left gaps in the care of the sick, in education, and in other social services. A second problem was the disappearance of the monastic sheep farms which had attracted merchants into the area through whom the local farmers could sell their wool.[116]

The Pilgrimage of Grace
Historians continue to argue the causes behind the unrest of the 1530s, but Harrison, in his study of the risings in the Lake Counties, maintains that it was the religious factors which were the most important in Westmorland. The protest movement, known as the Pilgrimage of Grace affected Lincolnshire and Yorkshire as well as the Lake Counties.

The troubles began in Lincolnshire, spreading quickly to York and into the Craven area, thus affecting Dentdale. At one stage, Robert Aske, the leader of the commoners, or pilgrims (as the local villagers were known) claimed that he had collected 30,000 men. In Westmorland the rising began, on 15 October 1536, when the vicar, (in some accounts the curate) of Kirkby Stephen 'forgot' to proclaim the holy day of St Luke. This omission was seen as a major threat to the main sheep fair of the year. The congregation held the vicar until he did their bidding, but as John Breay writes, "this was the spark which ignited the whole of the Eden valley."[117]

The next day, vast numbers met on Sandford Moor where they chose their captains. Christopher Blenkinsop, the Stainmore bailiff was chosen for Brough, and Robert Thomson, the vicar of Brough was elected the chaplain. The following days the rebels made for Wharton Hall and then to Lammerside to enlist Sir Thomas Wharton. He had fled so his son was taken instead. That week there was a grand march down the Eden Valley to Penrith. Continuing to Carlisle, the rebels found a stronger opposition there than had been expected. They disbanded after they had stated their aims, and then, on hearing the king's proclamation against unlawful assemblies

Note 114: ibid 1030.
Note 115: Harrison, S. M., *Pilgrimage of Grace in the Lake Counties 1536-7*, p28, Royal Historical Society, London (1981).
Note 116: Breay, J., *Light in the Dales*, Canterbury Press, Norwich, p10, (1996).
Note 117: Breay, J., op.cit. p9.

read out, they returned home.

This was not the end. The Duke of Norfolk, the king's representative, ordered Sir Thomas Clifford to sort out the rebels on his own lands, and at New Year, 1537, the latter unwisely took some of his Border moss troopers into Kirkby Stephen. Old rivalries die hard and, unable to capture the leaders of the rioters, they plundered the town, before being chased away by the local people. This provoked a second rising in February 1537. Before setting off again for Carlisle, a preparatory service was held in Penrith Church, at which Christopher Blenkinsop ordered the vicar of Brough to pray for the Pope. By this stage in the reign of Henry VIII, such an action was treason.

Six thousand men from the Eden Valley and Cockermouth are said to have marched on Carlisle. This time they could not breach its defences, and were themselves surrounded. The Duke of Norfolk arrived, martial law was imposed and the rebels surrendered. Seventy four men, including Christopher Blenkinsop were hanged. Twenty three of these came from Kirkby Stephen parish. The vicar of Brough died in the Tower of London. By 2 March, Wharton reported that the Borders were quiet.[118] The memory of this terrible ending seems to have restrained further significant protest by the commoners for the next two centuries. There was, apart from landowners like the Scaifes and the Wallers, little active involvement in the seventeenth century civil wars at Brough, and the Kaber Rigg Plot of 1663 had, at the most, thirty protesters, nearly all from outside the parish.

Medieval Brough had changed. The derelict castle and the transfer of the chantry into a school had caused little alarm. But the perceived threats to the church, coupled with the contemporary farming changes had led to a violent although short-lived reaction. What happened then to the other medieval institution, the manor and its customs?

The Manor

Almost all the area of Brough, with the exception of Helbeck which was under the Blenkinsops, was controlled by the Clifford family as tenants in chief of the crown. There was a manor survey, taken in 1604, when there were serious worries about the solvency of George Clifford, the third Earl of Cumberland. This, combined with the manor rental book for the same year, shows that the villages remained small, with Market Brough having 50 tenants and Church Brough 32.

Two main factors affected the community: first there seems to have been some pressure on the land, possibly due to population growth and secondly, with the burnt out castle, there was no resident lord. The manorial lands

Note 118: Breay, J. op.cit, p15, also Moorhouse, G., *Pilgrimage of Grace*, Weidenfeld and Nicolson, (2002).

were let out, and some individuals, like John Rudd and Robert Leigh were able to build up considerable holdings.

The Castle Park and its '*herbage*' had been subdivided and let out in six sections, with John Rudd, holding the bulk. The demesne arable and meadow were let too. In addition, Sowerby (Soureby) Moor, which in 1424 had three tenants, now had 21 tenants and Sowerby Park had ten. The vaccaries on Stainmore had been split between 74 tenants, and those around Heggerscales had also been subdivided. Brough Sowerby had grown; there were 38 tenants. New Hall though, remained intact and was let for £13 11s. 7d., but with a remission of 40 shillings allowed for the provision of hay for the deer. This may have been the remnant of the medieval deer park.[119]

Farm land had been extended and improved: Lancelot Waller rented newly improved wasteland with a cottage, Thomas Jackson had improved land and Elizabeth Atkins leased "a greatly improved garth." Other improvements are mentioned at Augill side, at Dumma Crag and at Thorney Scale. Some tenants held several parcels of land. John Smith, for example, had a toft, an oxgang of land, a cottage and a garth, for which he paid 6s. 10d. John Jackson had two oxgangs, two acres of demesne, meadow, arable in Sowerby and common rights. He had set up a house on the common "all builded upon the waste," with stones taken from the castle.[120]

New houses had been built in Church Brough by John Rudd and William Blyth, and four other houses, probably new additions, appear in a separate list from the old rental for that same village. There were still four holdings listed as burgages in the Nether Brough rentals.[121]

A few relics of the manorial tenure survived. There was a common kiln, and bakehouse. Mill dues were still collected (now worth £12) as was the ancient rekesilver toll and the constable's dues, (some paid in oats, others at the commuted rate of 8d). There was common land for both communities rented on East Stainmore.[122] The survey shows that there was still a weekly market, worth 24s. 5d. and a fair held at the feast of St Matthew. A note in the rental states that "there is now no fair nor market here (in Over Burgh) but all is in Nether Brough."[123]

Little is known about Helbeck manor which was owned by the Blenkinsops, until the mid seventeenth century. Although one member of

Note 119: CRO[K] WD/Hoth box 34, East Stainmore survey. CRO[C], DLons Li/1/28 Letter of Lady Anne Clifford re New Hall, "My cosin William Middleton shall have the rent of £15 half yearly for two years as a gift from me." (sic)
Note 120: CRO[K], WD/Hoth, Box 34, D1 Manor survey, p147.
Note 121: Anthony Salkeld, Thomas Varey and Lancelot Johnson, in Market or Nether Brough, held burgages, remnants of the old planned borough.
Note 122: Originally it had been let in blocks worth a mark each.
Note 123: CRO[K] WD/Hoth Box 34, D1 survey, D2 Rental, Location of market, p49.

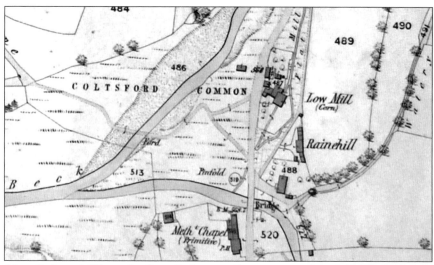

Map 7: Low Mill on the first Ordnance Survey map, dated 1860.

the family had been hanged for his part in the sixteenth century risings, the family continued to be staunchly catholic and the 1641 Protestation returns (taken as an oath of loyalty to the church and crown) show that not only family members but also their tenants and servants were papists. During the Civil Wars, when Charles I was fighting the Parliamentarians, the estates, first of the recusants, and then from 1643, of the Royalists, were sequestrated. However, when Parliament needed more money, these families were allowed to compound for them, in other words, pay for the use of their land. There are no records of the Blenkinsops doing this but later, in the Interregnum, in April 1650, Francis Blenkinsop presented the Committee of Compounding with a certificate stating that Robert Wardell, Major Arthur Scaife and his brother Lancelot Scaife farmed (that is rented out) Helbeck demesne, along with Graistone Flat Close, to Richard Foster and his son.[124] John Thomson, in a later petition to the committee commented that, they (the Scaifes) farmed Helbeck at "small rates" and "by the sword."[125]

This was part of a larger dispute within the local Commonwealth party. The Scaifes had attempted to take over much of the sequestrated land around Kirkby and John Thomson, (Thompson) a wealthy merchant of Kirkby Stephen and a puritan, was protesting at the way in which they had got Hartley Castle. This is dramatically described in the minutes of the

Note 124: State Papers 1643-60, Green, M. A. E., *Calendar of Committee of Compounding 1650.* [CCC] HMSO, [1889-92], p196, 12.
Note 125: Ibid p585, June 1650-51, 3024, Re: Thomas Blenkinsop. William Mason had a contract for six years for Mr Blenkinsop's land. He gave a bond of £500 for the lease to the Compounding committee. But John Fallowfield, one of the commissioners took the land.

committee for Compounding, where the commissioner in charge, begged for help, "to free the state of these contests - or me from this service." His minutes recounted what happened. On the 29 January, 1650, the day published for "letting the domain lately belonging to Sir Philip Musgrave," (whose lands had been sequestrated) - "divers people repaired thither - a candle was lighted and set up," by the agent Robert Wardell, saying that who bid the most while it burned should farm (rent) the domain for the following year. Several people bid, and the highest by John Thomson, of Kirkby Stephen, was accepted.

Then in came Major Arthur Scaife, with his men. He claimed that as he had rented it under the old committee, it was his and he would defend his rights with his horse troops, saying that anyone who wanted it needed, "a longer sword than (me) - thereby so to win it," and Thomas Buster, the Major's trumpeter, threatened to "run his sword through the guts of anyone else who brought horses in."[126] - John Thomson, whose bid of £153 had originally been accepted, petitioned against the Scaife's behaviour. The result was that yet another of their followers demanded a meeting with Thomson in Gramskey, [Gramsceugh] "by 8 o'clock tomorrow with back swords."[127] It was obviously not easy to oppose the Scaifes and the Blenkinsops did not get Helbeck back after the Restoration.[128] When Arthur Scaife died in 1692, he was still in possession of the Hall which he left along with land in Waitby and Warcop Tower, and by 1678, Thomas Blenkinsopp esquire, and his family were claiming poor relief.[129]

No other estate in Brough parish was forfeited and there were no serious engagements in the immediate area.[130] This was a predominantly Parliamentarian area with small scattered groups of Royalists under Sir Philip Musgrave, Sir Thomas Sandford, and Sir John Lowther. After the execution of the king and with the ever-present threat of a renewed conflict led by his son, local parliamentary committees were set up to examine the strength of the "enemy." The reports of these proceedings make uncomfortable reading, with the parliamentary supporters competing with each other to show how loyal they had been, while accusing their neighbours of aiding the enemy. Thomas Ewbank of Stainmore described how, in 1648 when he had been at Raby Castle (a parliamentary stronghold), he ventured into

---

Note 126: CCC, 1650, op.cit. p196, /12.
Note 127: CCC, p196, vol G, CCL.
Note 128: According to N&B, they sold the estate to the Scaifes, but there is no way to prove this now, p580.
Note 129: CRO[K], WQ/O/3, Magistrates order book 1675.
Note 130: CCC, VII G, cclvii, p547, 1648, Thomas Waller of Ewbank was listed for sequestration, but no further action reported.

Barney castle, where he overheard plans by the royalists to raise 3,000 men to march on Durham, and so he himself had led the leader back over the border.

Robert Wardell and the Wallers reported on a plot centred on Gaythorn, Asby, in 1648, while others told how, as servants at Howgill Castle, they had been forced to help defend Howgill Castle with twenty muskets brought from Newcastle. John Bonkin of Keiber, (Kaber) accused a neighbour, Thomas Halliday, of collecting several men to fight for the king, on the promise of 12d a day while threatening those who would not help.[131] This atmosphere of distrust and dislike cannot easily have been dispelled after the Restoration, and some of the later incidents on Stainmore may possibly be related to the rivalries of this time.

Lady Anne and the disputes over tenants' rights
This account is mainly based on the detailed research, published by John Breay in his book, *The Light in the Dales*.[132]

When the Civil Wars had ended, Brough tenants were faced with other problems which were related not only to the ownership of their manor, but also to the terms of their own tenancies. These dated back to the beginning of the century. George Clifford, the third Earl of Cumberland, who was the holder of the Clifford estates in the last quarter of the sixteenth century, had preferred life in London or on the high seas and had shown little interest in his estates. When he died in 1605, he left massive debts and a legal tangle over the inheritance of his estate. According to his will, his brother Francis and his male heirs would occupy the lands. His wife, Margaret, and his daughter, Lady Anne Clifford, refused to accept this and spent the next ten years battling through the courts. Neither would accept the verdicts against them nor the money offered.

In the end, in 1616, King James made an award: the Earl Francis was to hold the Clifford lands but to make a payment of £17,000 to Lady Anne, taken from the income of the northern estates. The tenants were to continue to hold at their ancient rents and the dropping fine (on change of the tenant) was to be *7d*. This amount caused hardship for the new earl who had to sell some of his property to raise the money. It was even harder for his tenants.

The evidence comes from depositions made by three Brough tenants in

---

Note 131: Royal Composition papers. The Royalists of Westmorland, transcription by Winder, F.A., in *Westmorland Notebook,* vol 1, part v, p197-208, Kendal, (1889). This is more detailed than the one published by HMSO which is CCC, vol G CCLVI, p521 for questioning of suspects.
Note 132: Breay, J. op.cit, p149f.

1650 for a later, but related, court case against the estate. According to Thomas Johnson of Stainmore, for example, the award impoverished the area, for the demands were excessive. The rent for his tenement was 16s.10d, (so he seems to have had a substantial holding), and although he paid twenty pounds towards the award, that was not enough and his beasts and sheep were taken. It was worse for others. Twenty tenants, he said, were utterly beggared: several were imprisoned, and two, Lancelot Johnson and Christopher Carter, died in prison. Two other Brough men confirmed these tragedies of 1616.

Thomas Laidman, aged 60 in 1650, named sixteen people who were unable to pay, even after they had sold up. There were also 27 tenants on Stainmore and another eighteen at Brough Sowerby who "went a-begging or died." Lancelot Blenkinsop of Helbeck, aged 66 in 1650, named men like John Rudd, Henry Rudd, Robert Wardell, Matthew Smith, Anthony Appleby and William Waller, who had had to sell all or part of their holdings. Even allowing for a certain amount of righteous indignation and exaggeration, these accounts cannot hide the horrors of the period, although it must also be remembered that this was a time of poor harvests, of famine, sickness, and civil unrest.

When Lady Anne eventually inherited the lands after the death of Earl Henry in 1643, she still could not reach Westmorland because of the unsettled situation during the Civil Wars. At least her estates were not forfeited as her husband served on the Council of State. When she managed to get there in 1649, she found herself embroiled in a number of disputes with her tenants. The tenants paid customary rents, set up in the reign of Henry II. There were also dropping fines taken at the change of ownership and general fines on the change of the lord. The only way the lord could improve his income to compensate for inflation, was to raise the fines, or if new land was improved, then rack rents could be charged. Her first manorial courts, the first for a long period, were intended to deal with admissions and alienations only. They brought to light a number of problems, and those courts of the Upper Eden Valley were, to quote John Breay, "particularly stormy."[133]

There were six years of rent arrears to be collected and those who could not pay had their beasts distrained. Lady Anne added to the burden by raising the dropping and general fines too suddenly. In the past these had been twice the annual rent: they were to be raised to eight times the rents. Brough tenants maintained that they were willing to pay all their arrears, but not all at once. They pleaded poverty: they had had to provide the passing

Note 133: Breay, J. op.cit, p149.

armies with food and draught animals, their land had been wasted, and then the new government had introduced heavy taxes to Cumberland and Westmorland. They claimed that their rents should be reduced by the amount they were paying for their monthly taxes.

Their case was taken to Chancery, (hence the depositions quoted earlier), and over the next few years to several other courts. Lady Anne won at the Appleby Assizes in 1654, yet opposition continued, and the tenants were sued again and again, climaxing with the Court of Common Pleas at Westminster in 1656. Once more Lady Anne won, but by default as the tenants refused to plead. James Waller (Walker) of Nether Brough lost his tenement and house, when he refused to attend a London court. His land was soon re-let on new conditions to John Salkeld. The rest of the tenants were sued again at a later court and lost.[134] The law suits cost each side £4,000, and the results for the tenants were bankruptcy and poverty. As Lady Anne wrote in her diary, "by that means, I altered the tenure of this land which was the principal thing I was at in my suites in law with my Westmerland tenants."(sic)[135]

Lady Anne had similar problems with the Mallerstang tenants. Like Stainmore this was an area of difficult farming and the estate's rising demands were more than its economy could bear. It can be argued, however, that Lady Anne put much back into the area, by using local craftsmen and supplies for her restoration work. The rebuilding of a number of castles, among them Pendragon and Brough, and the restoration of churches, including that of Brough, proclaimed her own power and wealth. She compensated the villagers by rebuilding both the mill at Brough and the communal oven. In many ways, her demands were reasonable; the old rents took no account of inflation and other changes. The problems were that the tenants had already paid much towards her £17,000 portion, and that they had been unprepared for the extra local taxation of the Commonwealth period. It was hard for them to raise cash suddenly in this area of marginal farming. All that was needed was a slower introduction of the changes and a more sympathetic approach. Instead the tenants had to fight for survival and had little chance to invest in the larger scale economic activities of the late seventeenth century. The next section will look at the economy.

Note 134: Breay, J. op.cit, p160.
Note 135: Clifford, D. J. H., op.cit, p137.

CHAPTER 10

The Seventeenth Century:
The Expanding Economy

IN a rural community most households aimed at some degree of self-sufficiency by growing a variety of crops and keeping some livestock. Many had small fields and with their garths big enough for barns and byres, it was possible to keep a cow and a calf, a few sheep and poultry while growing small crops of hay and oats in the fields. Gervase Markham, in his book, *The English Housewife*, published in 1615, assumed that the housewife would run a dairy, and so he gave her advice on the choosing of a cow (big boned, thin neck, large udder with four strong teats, and a crumpled horn) as well as on making butter.[136] He also expected the woman of the house to brew ale, produce malt, bake bread and harvest the flax and hemp. She must also be able to prepare these crops and the wool for spinning, and to dye the yarn.

These processes were all very hard work and time consuming, involving much water carrying, the digging of pits and the moving of heavy loads of wet materials, and, as the seventeenth century progressed, there is some evidence of specialisation. The malting, like the milling of cereals, was done by just one or two people in the village, the brewing by the inn keepers and the weaving was left to a weaver. Only the wealthy with large houses and a number of servants had the room for all the vats, mash tubs, kneading troughs, leads and casks needed, and both the flour and the ale could only be kept for a few weeks before they went off. Self-sufficiency might be the aim, but in practice this was difficult, and most small settlements developed workers skilled in certain trades.

This chapter will deal with a variety of occupations in Brough, beginning with the dominant one which was farming. The information is taken mainly from the wills and inventories of the period.[137] Inventories, detailing the moveable goods but not the real estate of the deceased, were generally taken within a few hours of death, by at least two sworn jurors. The custom continued in Westmorland until around 1740. Brough examples are far fewer in number and less varied than those for other places in the Upper Eden, like Kirkby Stephen and Temple Sowerby.

Note 136: Markham, G., ed. Best, M. R., *The English Housewife*, 1615, McGill-Queens University Press, (1986)
Note 137: CRO [C], D.&C. Wills and Inventories.

Farming

It is clear that the most prosperous farmers lived on Stainmore, which still included the South Stainmore vaccaries as part of the Brough manor. The 1640 Lay Subsidy Roll, listed seven taxable estates in the area of Brough and Stainmore: Kirkby Stephen had one.[138] In the early seventeenth century, a common pattern of farming emerges, among the larger holdings on Stainmore, as at Heggerscales, and at Rookby, at Borronthwaite and Ald Park. Hay and corn, mainly bigge, (barley) and oats, were grown and between six and a dozen kine were kept, with ten or more young beef cattle for fattening. The sheep flocks were around 40 in number. The exception is that of Michael Ewbank who, in 1620, had a flock of 100, some inherited from his father who had just died. Swine, poultry, and bees were also kept. There were surplus stocks of butter, cheese, beef and bacon. Stocks of yarn suggest local fields of flax and hemp. Ewbank was the only one with his own bull.[139] He had three riding mares. Other farmers had less valuable horses and these would probably be working ones. Oxen are rare in these inventories.

Christopher Blenkinsop of Helbeck and Robert Spencer of Market Brough, both freeholders, had a similar pattern of livestock, as had Robert Wardell of Sowerby Park. Cattle herds remained generally more valuable than sheep flocks throughout the century. Thomas Nicholson on Stainmore had cattle worth £68 while his flock of 48 sheep, was worth less than a quarter of that sum, in 1662. In 1692, William Ewbank of Sowerby Park had cattle worth £16 and a sheep flock worth less than a tenth of that. On the other hand, in 1664, William Richardson, the vicar, whose main interests were academic, (his library was worth £32 10s.), had 45 sheep but only four cows. This may be the result of his tithe collection: certainly in Temple Sowerby at this period the tithes were paid in kind.

At the other end of the scale were people like Henry Williamson and Thomas Waller. Williamson's clothing and household goods together only amounted to 13s. 4d. He had four kine and a small flock of sheep worth 55 shillings. He died in 1611 owing sixteen people a total of £10. Thomas Waller at High Ewbank, with children still at home, farmed at subsistence level with only a small surplus from his flock of seventeen sheep with lambs in 1609. He may have supplemented his income by being a carrier as a mare and a load saddle were among his possessions. In contrast, another

---

Note 138: CRO[K], WD/cat. 2016 [2/9/R]. This was a tax rated on freeholders with more than 5s.4d worth of movable goods:- on Stainmore, Nicholson, Davis, and Willson, at Brough Sowerby, Munkhouse, at Brough, Wardell and Shaw, and at Helbeck, Blenkinsop.
Note 139: Oxen are rarely mentioned, although there are some in the inventory of John Aiskill, 1678.

Thomas Waller, who died in 1603, lived at Thorney Scale, a less exposed site towards the lowlands, had a comfortably furnished house and reserves of butter, cheese and flesh.

Possibly the smaller farm represented a down-sizing with age. Michael Ubank (sic) the elder who died in 1617, lived at Borrans House, near to Borronthwaite, the family home. He had no debts and managed a small flock of sheep, and with his six kine, he had a surplus of butter and cheese. Another example of an older farmer may be Henry Robinson of Brough Sowerby who left just three ewes in 1680. Nearby lived another Henry Robinson who, when he died a year later, left a thriving mixed farm of wheat, bigge, oats and hay, kine, young beasts, ten sheep and three mares. He may have been the innkeeper in the village as his household goods included glass bottles, flagons and nineteen pewter dishes. When Thomas Monkhouse died in 1723, his inventory makes clear that some of his goods were still at Fieldhead, (Brough Sowerby) in his son's care. He had merely moved across the river to Starrah.

In the late seventeenth century, there is a hint of change in farming practices on Stainmore. The court records register the resentment, which had flared into physical assault. The complaints were against enclosure of the common and of obstructing the cart ways. The earliest case, soon after the Restoration, may well have been a continuation of the local rivalries of the Civil War and its aftermath. In 1661, John Laidman of Thorney Scale and three others entered the close of Geoffrey Shaw of East Rigg on Stainmore and "broke down and damaged his grass," entered his sawpit and damaged that too. Within the next two years there were three other examples reported at the Quarter Sessions, of obstructing rights of way, damaging hedges and closes at Thorney Scale and Shaw, himself was up in court for assault on William Brunskill. Eighty years on, another member of the Brunskill family was accused of damaging closes at Thorney Scale.[140]

Farming as a secondary occupation

In Brough a number of householders had other occupations outside farming but still leased a few fields to grow corn and hay, and kept a few animals for domestic use: blacksmiths like John Aisgill and Lancelot Hodgson, butchers like Robert Kidd 1739, (who also had eighteen sheep) and tanners like Thomas Rudd. Later, in 1731, the post master Thomas Lamb had two kine and two swine, apart from the seven horses he needed for his job. There was pasture for those with commoners' rights on Stainmore and Coltsford Common between the Brough villages. On Stainmore, hay was

---

Note 140: CRO(K), Appleby Indictment book.

the main crop, but to the south of Brough, next to the vicar's glebe there were two infields on which a greater variety of crops could be grown, such as peas, oats, bigge, hemp, flax and wheat.

Few agricultural products could be used in their raw state and so a number of processing industries grew up, in which the householder and the specialist could play different parts, and thus add to the value of the goods. Malting, milling and brewing are three examples. Householders, and as will be shown later, the poor, often did the preparatory work, but the heavy work requiring large equipment, hot water and space, was done by the specialist.

The mills on the Swindale Beck and the barley kiln were simple buildings which could be erected by the village masons and carpenters, but the maintenance of them required skill. Low Mill, the communal mill since "time immemorial," is marked today by a millstone in a garden wall, on the present township boundary between Church and Market Brough. Little is known about its construction at this period but it was sited below the large fall of the beck and its water wheel was probably fed by a leat.

The barley kiln, which could also be used as the village oven, was normally some distance from the mill because of the fire hazard. This was generally a stone building with a smoke vent in the roof. Inside would be a platform or floor for drying. The fire at ground level was best if made from straw, bracken or gorse; wood produced too much smoke. To quote Markham, "a soft fire makes sweet malt."[141] By this period, the making of ale was becoming concentrated on the inns. The earliest licenses to survive for Brough maltsters were for 1691 when William Dickenson, Robert Jackson and John Bur[...] are named.

At the same period there were mills at Helbeck, and in Brough Sowerby and possibly one at High Mill.[142] The Addison family had Low Mill in 1674, and a long line of Todds took over later. Unfortunately the millers left no easily identifiable inventories. The only one possibly so far found is that for Thomas Youdaille in 1613, who left milled corn and meal and old winnowing sheets. The most significant thing about his estate was the large number of small sums, often just pence, owed to him, by people like Widow Young's boy, or Cuthbert Cumpston, Widow Appleby, and Widow Wharton. He seems to have been selling something for everyday needs.

The milled cereals were varied. Wheat flour was a luxury in this area and, because the wheat was a soft variety, it could only be kept for a short time. Most bread flours were a mixture of oats and rye, and oatmeal itself

---

Note 141: Markham, G., *English Housewife*, op.cit., 1615. fac. ed. M. Best, McGill, Queens, (1994).

Note 142: 1739 Thomas Waller, carpenter, at the New Mill, Brough.

The Grapes, a lintel on Bridge Street, Brough. Drawing by kind permission of David Yeadell.

had a large variety of uses. The finest meal was for pottage and gruel, for oatcakes and mixed with blood and liver, for *haggas* (sic). The coarser oat-grits were suitable for black puddings. Oats were also used for feeding live-stock and poultry.

Bread and ale making were complementary with the ale barm producing the rising agent for the bread. In wealthy households there would be space to produce both, either in the same room or in adjacent buildings, but for most people this was not possible and by the seventeenth century, brewing was often done by local maltsters and inn keepers. Beer, with the addition of hops, kept better than ale but it could not be transported far. Thomas Lamb, the postmaster and innkeeper, in 1731 had £10 worth of goods in his brew house, but this high value probably included his own brew of beer and ale. The normal value of brewing vessels was around 15 shillings, (for example John Shaw, in 1685), and Lamb's stock of drinks inside his inn included spirits and wine, but no beer.

There are hints of other commercial enterprises in dealing with farm pro-duce. Butter factors are mentioned in the eighteenth century parish regis-ters, and earlier, in 1680, Matthew Shaw left bowls, cheese vats and churns, and a collection of debts which he owed locally, to people with whom he was perhaps trading. He had only two cows himself, so he was probably collecting milk from neighbouring farmers, and producing butter and cheese for the market.

Crafts: textiles and tanning

The main crafts based on farm products were tanning and textiles, but again, the inventories reveal little about the craftsmen and women; even spinning wheels are rarely mentioned, although Michael Shaw in 1689 had two: a hemp wheel and another wheel with stocks of yarn, while Thomas Bousfield of Brough Sowerby in 1662, had a spinning wheel and hemp. So far no mention has been found of weaving looms. These may have been claimed by other members of the family before the inventory was made, or they may have been rented. However, by this period, it does look as though weaving was no longer a household task. Gervase Markham, despite his great lists of what a housewife should do, recommended the use of a professional weaver.

Nor is there a reference to knitting, although some of the woollen caps and stockings for which Kirkby Stephen market was renowned, may have been provided by Brough people.[143] There are references to linen cloth and line, (flax yarn). Thomas Rudd had some in 1609, but whether that was made by his family or had been bought in ready to make up, is not clear and Lancelot Hodgson had both linen and woollen cloth in 1726. William Ewbank of Sowerby Park, at the end of the seventeenth century left five hanks of harden yarn, along with some cards. Thomas Nicholson had linen, and woollen cloth valued at £3 in 1662, Thomas Waller at Thorney Scale had six yards of cloth, and Christopher Blenkinsop had six stones of line. But were these all for the use of their households? After the shearing had been done, some households had several stones of wool; Harry Robinson had eight stones, Thomas Waller of Ewbank, had two stones, and his name sake, in 1603, left six yards of woollen cloth.[144]

Both flax and hemp required a lot of preparation before they could be spun. It was heavy work to prepare the retting ponds and ditches, and to lift the materials in and out. It took a long time and much muscular effort to get the crop dried, swingled (beaten), and combed. Even disposing of the water needed care to prevent the poisoning of fish in rivers.

Preparing wool from the fleece was almost as time consuming, but it could be done inside the house, once the shearing had been done. At the end of the seventeenth century, the magistrates served notices on the able-bodied poor that in order to qualify for parish relief, they must work. In Brough, they were issued with wool. In March 1683 Jane Robinson was to have twelve pieces of wool for her maintenance, in May 1685 John Todd, was to have twelve pieces, "until his children can help him." But that same year, at Michaelmas, he and his son were given sixteen pieces of wool and at the same sessions, Isobel Johnson of Stainmore got twelves pieces.[145]

These people were expected to sort, clean and toze (Markham defines

---

Note 143: Fleming, D. ed. Sir G. F. Duckett, CWAA (Record), Kendal, (1882). *Description of Cumberland and Westmorland, AD.1671.*

Note 144: A stone of wool = six fleeces. Pringle, A. in Bailey, J. & Culley, G., *General View of Agriculture in Northumberland, Cumberland and Westmorland*, (1794, reprinted 1972), p329.

Note 145: CRO[K] WQ/O/3, Magistrates Order Book beg. 1675. Williams, E. N., *Documentary history of England*, Penguin, p32. quotes the Elizabethan Poor Law of 1598, "each parish must provide a convenient stock of flax, hemp, wool..."

this as separating the strands) the wool ready for the spinners, who would probably prefer to do the next stages themselves, for the oiling and carding were crucial to the quality of yarn. Spinning was still a woman's job, and most homes must have had a wheel. It is disappointing that so few appear in the Brough inventories. There is one mention of a weaver and that is on a set of deeds, in 1749 when Thomas Waller a weaver, sold some land on the Main Street to his brother, Michael, a cordwainer.

One craft which does appear is tanning. Thomas Rudd, a tanner in 1609, left his tools to his son, and a special white hide to one of his brothers, so his trade was possibly a family business. He left tubs for tanning, and "leyther and barke" valued at 36s. 4d. He appears to have been successful, for although his home was plainly furnished he had decent clothing, as he left his best breeches to one brother, and a doublet to another. Later in the century, in 1685, another tanner was named, as John Shaw of Market Brough, and he was working on a larger scale. He left leather and bark, worth over £6, cisterns, tools and tan vats. He had a galloway, (a pack-horse) worth five shillings. He was also running a small holding with a dozen sheep and a couple of cows. But his household reflects a growing prosperity for the trade. Whereas Rudd had had only a firehouse with forms and built-in beds, Shaw had an extra room which was a parlour, furnished with a long settle, chairs and a table as well as a dish case (a dresser), and table cloths. He had sophisticated cooking facilities, and his own brewing equipment, together with linen and harden cloth worth £2 5s.

One unusual inventory is for Robert Wardale, who was described in the registers as the late Mayor of Appleby when he died in 1613. Unlike some of his contemporaries who were described as "unfurnished," (that is pos-sessing no weapons) he seems to have remained active in the Musters for he left 20 shillings worth of war furniture, (bows, arrows and pikes). Yet he was very much a Brough man, owning lands in Brough Sowerby and in Sowerby Park, and having married a member of the Waller family, he had seven children baptised at Brough. He had extensive supplies of wool, leather and skins, as well as salt, valued at over £26. He may have been a tanner or a fell monger. The main market, for the Bottom of Westmorland, with appointed searchers to test the quality of leather was in Appleby and he therefore may have become a freeman so that he could have trading rights.[146]

There must have been joiners and wheel wrights, and masons but again there is little evidence. In the inventory of Thomas Waistell 1601, on Stainmore, there is a reference to carpenter's tools, and in a court case of

---

Note 146: CRO(K), WSMB, Minute Book, Vol 1-2, The Blenkinsops and possibly the Wallers were also freemen.

Stone door lintel in Main Street, Market Brough, believed to be the work of stone mason George Dinwoodie. Drawing with many thanks to David Yeadell.

the 1660s, there is mention of Geoffrey Shaw's saw pit at Thorney Scale. Thomas Waller in 1734, described as a carpenter at New Mill, had saws and axes among other carpentery tools and a little galloway, worth £2. George Todd, a mason, of Park Houses, Sowerby Park, left no distinctive tools in 1721: all he had was a cart.

There must also have been a number of cordwainers and shoemakers but little evidence survives apart from those named in deeds and in the Quarter Sessions like John Bousfield, and Robert Pullen, both of Brough Sowerby.[147] Even Thomas Archer named as a cordwainer who died in 1727, had no tools or stock, yet he was probably still trading as he was owed £46 by his customers.

The Market

Brough, according to its fourteenth century charter, had market trading rights, but in 1671, when Fleming described it as "a little town now - decayed," he continues with further details: "A market every Thursday and a four day fair around St Matthew's day, which fair is remarkable for the selling of cattle but the market is little or nothing."[148] There is further evidence to confirm this and it seems that the market had dwindled in the face of competition from that of Kirkby Stephen. In a petition to the Earl of Thanet, in the last decade of the seventeenth century, Brough villagers pleaded for a renewal of their charter. The earl replied that as there were:

Note 147: CRO(K), WQ/SR 1733, 1787.
Note 148: Fleming, D., op.cit.

"two fairs at Brough yearly - and also the great fair at Brough Hill where they pay a good toll to me - by altering these fairs might lessen the tolls at Kirkby Stephen, for which reason I have not thought it convenient to renew the charter for Brough market."[149]

As his reply indicates the seasonal trade at the fairs remained prosperous and significant but the local weekly trading had been almost lost.[150] Although the market charter was later renewed, the market trade never recovered. No records of the trade at the fair remain, although it must have attracted drovers from a wide area. At some stage in the late seventeenth century, the site of the fair was changed from Intake Side to the site now known as Brough Hill in the parish of Warcop. A nineteenth century directory attributes this move to a period of plague when Brough wished to have strangers away from the village. Canon J. Simpson, also writing in the nineteenth century, says that the field had been too wet to hold the vast numbers of animals. Neither account gives any sources and no other documents have so far been traced. In the burial records there was William Munkhas, a driver of beasts in 1658, and William Johnson, a young man from Culgarth in Scotland, 1774.[151] Lancashire cattle drovers were recorded

Brough Hill Fair, courtesy of Mr John Walton.

Note 149: Scott, D., CWAA 1917-18. Recent discoveries in the Muniment room at Appleby and Skipton castles p16-18, (undated but in the last decade of the 17th century), in TCWAA, 1918.

Note 150: J. Simpson, *Things Old and New,* p77.

Note 151: He had driven cattle down to the fair when he was taken ill and had to apply to the Quarter Sessions for help. He was too weak to travel except by horse and cart.

by the mid eighteenth century.[152] There were pedlars and other traders such as William Lorimer, linen draper who died on his way from London to Scotland in 1780. There was even an early gypsy record, of George Jackson, an *Eziption*, who in 1588 had, "his twinnes Mycheall and Maryon," baptised.

The only records which do survive are for Appleby fair, and these are a few vouchers for horse sales in the 1620s and 1630s. They give some indication of the area that the traders came from. There were some from Halifax in Yorkshire, Northampton and Derby, from Ireland and from Lincolnshire. Two vouchers were made out to Brough people.[153]

> "1631 Solde in Appleby in County Westmorland, by William Ripley of Rippon in the county of York, batchelor, one Geldinge dapple gray shodd of all foues and of the age of sixe yeares nor thereabouts to John Waistell of Brough of the county of Westmorland, yeoman, for the price of thirtie two shillings."

> "1630 Sold - in the open market by Bridgett Jaques and Humphrey Jaques of Redmire, Countie of York, one little lame [—] horse, couller Bay, shodd of the two fore foote, to Thomas Fairer of Brough in the counties of Westmorland - price £9 6s." [sic]

For Brough, not only are there no trading records, but there are also very few mentions in the court cases. Only occasionally was assault at the fair taken to court, as in 1662 when Edward Moore and his wife attacked another couple, Leonard Lea and his wife, who then counter claimed.[154] A more serious case which was taken on to the Assizes, occurred in 1663, when Richard Moore, late of Kirkby Stephen and possibly related to the protagonists of the earlier case, was accused, in Brough of making four pieces of money from copper and other metals.[155]

Communications and transport services

The Great Highway, from Bowes to Brougham should have encouraged trade in Brough, but, until it was turnpiked in 1743, there were problems. Sir Daniel Fleming's comments in the 1670s include such colourful phrases as: "Nothing but wild desert, - the worst hard road in England, - the

---

Note 152: The fair had to be closed because of disease, a letter from Richard Burn 1749, 'not withstanding that Brough Hill Fair was stopped, many people endeavoured to bring cattle. There was no time for a sessions order, lest the people of Lancashire should do likewise, therefore the passage in was secured.' WD/QS Oct 1749.
Note 153: CRO[K] WSMB/A, vol 1, Minute book.
Note 154: Similarly there is a case in 1730 of two pedlars coming to blows.
Note 155: PRO ASS 1 44, 13.

stormy weather - and coaches [face the] hazard of overturning and break-ing."[156] It took six hours by coach to travel the thirteen miles in good con-ditions. It was worse for those on foot. The burial records list a "stranger by circumstances name unknown found drowned - in a dyke on Stainmore, an elderly woman," in 1778, and local people could also be vulnerable; Elizabeth, daughter of Henry Rudd was lost "in a greete storm," in December 1600.

And there were human hazards too. In 1683 there was a case at the Quarter Sessions which involved a number of Stainmore residents who had set upon George Gosling when he was travelling along the main highway, robbing and assaulting him. He was awarded £123 1s. So many people were involved that a general levy was ordered to pay the damages.[157]

Service industries

Because Brough was on a main road, it developed services for travellers, of which inns and blacksmiths featured most prominently in the inventories. There were smithies in both Market and Church Brough, in Brough Sowerby and in Helbeck. John Aisgill in 1674 left his working tools, horse-shoes and nails worth £2 8s. He had borrowed on bond from five local men, presumably to finance his business. Lancelot Hodgson in 1726 left bellows, and 652 horseshoes. He was working on a considerable scale; his stock included over eight stones of iron, some steel, some new iron and 40 pounds of old iron. He was still active as a smith, his stock of iron was large and he had yet to pay for it.[158] A third smith, William Outhwaite, who died in 1729, had a shop. He too had old iron, new iron and five stones of some other variety of iron. He sold household goods like pots and pans, frying pans, a girdle, candlesticks and he had fifteen pairs of wool shears in stock.

Inns

The other service which Brough could offer for travellers was accommoda-tion. In 1686 a survey listed 34 guest beds in Brough as compared with 52 in Kirkby Stephen.[159] A variety of accommodation was provided ranging from the Tramps' house, by the Swindale, (which was no more than a small shelter in the eighteenth century), to the enclosures with water and pasture for the drovers' cattle, as well as the inns for the better-off travellers.

Note 156: N&B, quote p577.
Note 157: Curwen, op.cit., 1683 Oct. for assault and robbery on Stainmore a levy of 2s.10d each to raise £123.1s for George Gosling for damage he sustained, assault and robbery by certain malefactors.
Note 158: His only debt apart from one to the iron merchant, is one to his doctor.
Note 159: PRO WO 30/48 Abstract of a Particular account on Inns and Alehouses etc. quot-ed by Marshal, J. D., *Cumbrian Market Towns, Northern History*, Leeds, 1983.

The George Hotel, Jessie Bousfield in her mother's arms, 1901, courtesy of Ann Birkbeck.

After the Union of the Crowns of England and Scotland under James I, large numbers of beasts were driven through the area, and many resting and watering places were required along the droving lanes during the season. Some of the present day inn names date from this trade: the Black Bull, the Brown Cow, the Scotsman, the Blue Bell, and the Highland Laddie.

The early inns and ale houses are a matter of conjecture. Brewster sessions were introduced in 1729 but few details survive. Inn keepers do not feature in the parish registers until the second half of the eighteenth century, and few of them were full-time even then; most had small farms or other occupations so that inventories give no clear indication either. It must be remembered that the coach trade, mentioned by Fleming, was for private coaches only. Regular stage coach services did not begin until the late eighteenth century, and most transport was done by packhorses, carts or on wagons.[160]

One of the first regular services to be set up was that of the post. Cuthbert Kay in 1611 was described as postmaster, but there are no further details of him. More can be deduced from a later register for in 1665, John Aisgill was listed as the postmaster. There were at least two men of the same name in Brough who died in the same year 1678, but the evidence points to the one who was a substantial farmer as being an innkeeper, and

---

Note 160: Williams, L. A., *Road transport in Cumbria in the 19th century*, Allen & Unwin, (1974), p108.

therefore the probable post master. He had oxen and two horses, five kine and 43 sheep, which was more than normal for an ordinary householder. Other clues are that he had a substantial purse (petty cash) and clothing worth £15, while his home had several chambers and such comfortable furnishings as cushions, brass ware and pewter.

Thomas Lamb was the post master in 1731, and he was no ordinary villager.[161] He had a valuable purse and clothing, seven horses, elaborate cooking equipment, pots and mugs, a brass pestle and mortar, and punch ladle, but also beer, rum, brandy, sack and wine worth £29, and (to clinch the matter) post mail, book, buffets (stools), and squabs in a separate room. He ran

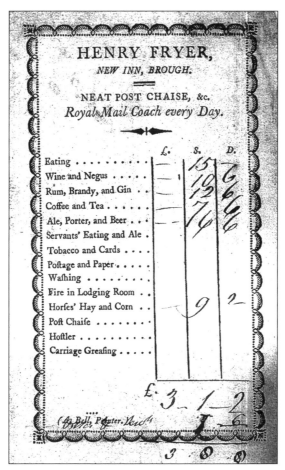

Bill for staying at Henry Fryer's New Inn, Brough, courtesy of Cumbria Record Office, Kendal, (Heelis deposit).

Note 161: This position seems to have been kept in the family for some years as a Thomas Lamb Esq. of the post office, is mentioned in 1789.

a sizeable establishment. Apart from the kitchen he had two parlours and at least six chambers upstairs, with what was described as "space for extra beds at head of cellar." His working premises included cellars, a milk house, a brew house, stables with lofts, servants' rooms, byres, and barns. He certainly had the assets of a fashionable innkeeper; a coffee mill, silver spoons, a silver punch ladle, and a little furnace in the kitchen with brass and pewter ware.

The Kidd family, who normally feature in the registers as butchers, were also innkeepers, as the deeds of their property make plain. At the beginning of the eighteenth century, the Kidd brothers and their mother owned the site of the Golden Fleece which was, at that time, on the northern side of the main road through Brough. The earliest surviving deeds date from 1701 when Samuel Kidd and his brother Robert, both butchers, bought the freehold of a dwelling house, barns, stables, with a loft, garden and garth along with the rights of turbary (peat cutting) and common grazing.[162-3] By 1739 Robert Kidd had a sizeable house, with lofts above the kitchen, a parlour (but one filled with beds), outhouses and a shop. The Kidd family continued to own the land throughout the century, letting out the business to various people like Robert Thwaites who died in 1779 and Thomas Lamb who in 1794 paid eight shillings a year rent.

Mines

Another facet of the area is that of the local geology. In Kirkby Stephen at this time there were lime kilns in the manor rental, but none has been identified at Brough possibly because some were temporary structures, erected for a particular job. There were quarries for building stone and millstones on North Stainmore, and there are a number of references to coal. The lease of New Hall in 1604 mentions, rather vaguely, *"a cole myne in Stainmore or South Stainmore, or both,"* and a *milne* stone source at Dow Cragg.

There are other hints: in 1644 Thomas Harreson, a *colyer* was buried. In earlier times this word could be used for a charcoal burner, but coal mines on Stainmore have been noted since the Medieval period. In 1674, John Aiskell had stores of peat and coals at his house in Brough. In 1682, a petition by the tenants of South Stainmore requested that "all who benefit from carrying coals do pay 2d toll for every horse, for the repair of the way to the coalpits."[164] It would appear that the pits around New Hall and along the

---

Note 162: There was a Chantry fee still to be paid of a penny halfpenny on this plot, and this continued until 1796.

Note 163: Part of the land at Maines field and Tinbridge may have been part of the property as Samuel bought these from his brother in 1709.

Note 164: CRO[K], WQ/O/3 Magistrates' Order book, QS 1660, also Curwen, op.cit.

route to Tan Hill were the ones which were being exploited, and the horses listed in the inventories may have been pack horses. The early pits were small and bell-shaped in cross section, which required little equipment.

Tourist attraction?

There was plenty of passing trade but that was hardly a money spinner, particularly as the parish often had to bury strangers who had died suddenly. An attraction was needed to encourage visitors to stay. In the fashionable world of the post-Restoration period, the continental idea of leisure and health had combined to create the Spa, as at Bath and Epsom. Thomas Machell, in his notes written around 1680 after a visit to Brough, describes what he calls Brough Spa, a well on the "north side of the bridge as you go to Church town." His sketch shows a stone built well house on top of which sits an imposing carved sandstone edifice. Here one could take the waters and be cured of all manner of sickness.[165] This enterprise does not seem to have got very far, but the top can still be seen today. It is part of the Clock Tower.

The top of the clock tower which was part of the well house. Drawing by kind permission of David Yeadell.

Professional services

As the Spa did not flourish, Brough remained basically a farming village with a small service industry for the carrying trade. Among the larger, more prosperous farmers on Stainmore, some of the sons had professional training. The Ewbank and Rumney families produced doctors who practised in the area.

Little is known about them except for Dr Michael Ewbank, who had one spectacular success which became a folk legend.[166] This episode was recounted by the Rev. Thomas Machell, who was writing about five years after the event. On 3 January 1688, Cuthbert Cumpston, who was 54 years of age, and a blacksmith at Brough Sowerby visited Dr Ubank (Ewbank) of Market Brough. He had a swelling in his throat, like a boil. The doctor found a piece of iron lodged there, and when he had made an incision he

Note 165: CRO(C), D&C, Machell, vol 3, p103.
Note 166: CRO(C) D&C Machell, vol 3, p93/103-109.

discovered it to be a breech from a gun. He put a peg through a hole in it, to prevent it slipping backwards. He then made further incisions into the oesophagus so that Cumpston could eat and drink. Two months later he managed to remove the blockage in the presence of Richard Waistell, and his daughter, Richard Burton and his wife, Michael Hodgson and Robert Nicholson. These witnesses all viewed the obstruction in the throat, and then watched its removal.

The piece was later shown to several other responsible people. Cumpston recovered enough to explain. He had been shooting a hare, (there was blood and garbage on the piece, as the witnesses noted). He said that he was thrown backwards when "his light struck out and the gun breech was lost he knew not where." Amazingly he seems to have lived, despite the risk of infection and loss of blood. It was, for the period, a remarkable operation by a doctor.

Financial Services

The end of the seventeenth century saw costly improvements not only in farming methods, like enclosure, but in living standards as houses were rebuilt with an extra storey added, and furnished more comfortably. How were these projects financed? Firstly, there seems to have been much indebtedness. Only the older and thrifty landed families were free from debt. Many of the inventories studied show great lists of debts, often more in value than the inventoried goods.

In the days before banks, there was a need to borrow from local sources. Traders relied on long term credit. When Lancelot Hodgson died, he still owed his suppliers of iron, Thomas Lamb owed his wine supplier, while farmers who bought beasts from neighbours often paid at the next Michaelmas, after the harvest or at the next fair. Rents, church dues and the poor rates were left for long periods, often until a will was being made, when the vicar could remind the testator of forgotten dues. Craftsmen and shopkeepers often did not expect to be paid immediately. The cordwainer, Thomas Archer, who owned virtually nothing, had £46 owing to him.

Thomas Youdaille in 1613, who had little more than his worn-out clothes and a small axe, had seventeen people in debt to him. Samuel Kidd the butcher in 1740, was owed £16. Thomas Bousefield in 1662, a spinner, was owed £73 while Michael Shaw was owed for yarn. Thomas Lamb, the post master had allowed his customers credit of £215 possibly for the hire of his horses as well as food and drink. Long term credit was a hidden form of lending, which many traders had to use, but there were more formal ways too.

Widows, spinsters, and retired farmers with spare cash, used it by putting it out to loan and presumably charging interest. There is no indication of the interest charged in the Brough area, but in Temple Sowerby, Ann Stable, who, in the 1720s, had taken over the business from her brother, charged 3*s*. 6*d*. in the pound but it is not certain whether this was for a year or longer.

Agnes Smith, a spinster who was in her late twenties when she died in 1665, is an example of a small scale lender. She lived on North Stainmore, with her widowed mother and several of her seven sisters. Her possessions, which included two cows, amounted to £10 but she had let out an additional £7 in loans: to her mother, to her brother-in-law and to other local people. Agnes Monkhouse, a spinster, about 30-years-old, lived at Fieldhead, Brough Sowerby. She had few personal belongings but, by 1686, she had let out nearly £250, in mortgages, in bonds and in bills. A member of the same family, Thomas Monkhouse, in retirement at Starrah, had lent £480, again in mortgages and bonds, while in Winton, Richard Monkhouse, yet another member of the family, in 1723 had over £1,000 in specialities, (bonds similar to mortgages) owing to him, and a further £73 in promissory notes.

Widows like Isabel Morland, and Isabel Barnett, lent money as required to family and friends, often without formal notes. Margaret Ewbank of Dowgill in 1675, left goods worth only £1 6*s*. 2*d.,* but she had lent out £12, and in 1692, William Ewbank of Sowerby Park was owed over £42, of which only four pounds was a trade debt. The rest was laid out in bonds. His total goods amounted to £70.

William Robinson, the vicar had lent to five people, whose names were not local, and John Gargot, a bachelor who died in 1729, had lent the considerable sum of £39 to a Colby man, and in all he was owed £66. Robert Wardell, the ex-mayor who had lent small sums to several women, forgave their debts in his will of 1613. In 1721 George Todd, a mason living at Sowerby Park, had lent over £30 from his total inventoried worth of £53.

However, there were some men who had no possessions apart from their money. Henry Buckle in 1662, was owed over £150 by a number of people, who had often taken out their loans in pairs. In 1679, John Hutchinson, who seems to have had no remaining family, no farm (a sheep iron is the only farming relic mentioned),[167] had lent out six bonds totalling in all £215, again generally to pairs of people, to the Bousfields, to the Wilkins, and to the Whartons, and the largest one, for over £107 was lent to Thomas Herdman and William Ayres.[168] Maybe Hutchinson was a middle man

---

Note 167: He left eleven yards of linen, carefully priced at 11d a yard.

Note 168: His accounts may include interest as none of the bonds are in round figures. The three lowest bonds are all for £10.12s (6% and 7.5% for larger loans).

controlling or supplying outworkers with raw materials for making up into cloth or yarn.

Thomas Nicholson in 1662, who was running a prosperous livestock farm on Stainmore, and producing linen, harden, (coarse cloth) and woollen cloth, also made his money from rents. He had let out his land at Seavy Riggs and this along with his other rents brought him in over £100. He was owed money by 23 people: some may have been trade debts, but he was certainly into money lending, for Thomas Jackson owed him for one five year bond of £20.

Local investment and initiative allowed some progress to be made in both farming and trade but it was difficult for Brough to recover from its state as "a small village fenced with a little fortress" as described by Thomas Denton around 1687.[169] It was not until the second half of the eighteenth century that new projects in the area were able to attract finance from both local and outside sources. However, before these are discussed, it is necessary to look at the social problems which the contemporary records expose and then at the changes within the agricultural sector, which remained the main source of employment in the district.

Note 169: Winchester, A. J. L., and Wane, M., eds. Thomas Denton, *A Perambulation of Cumberland in 1687-8,* Surtees Society, vol 207. The quotation continues: *a small village (in two parts,) - a street town, or high road over Stainmore and the Churchtown, where the castle stands.*

CHAPTER 11

Brough in the eighteenth century:
Widening the Horizons

TWO travellers, Daniel Fleming and Thomas Denton who journeyed through Westmorland in the late seventeenth century, remarked on the insignificance of the two sections of Brough, known then as Church Town and the Street town. Neither commented on Brough Sowerby nor on Stainmore, both of which, according, to evidence from the inventories, had some prosperous households. For these travellers, it was enough to see the uninhabited castle and the declining market, to pass judgement. But was this the whole story?

While a study of the parish and quarter session records seems to bear out the impressions of poverty, other later records give a more positive view of the scene, for once the Bowes to Brough road had been turnpiked in 1743, not only did the service sector increase in Brough but both local and outside investors were attracted to the exploitation of the minerals on Stainmore, and to experiment with water powered factories. The location, to contemporaries, was little different from Cromford in Derbyshire, or Alston in Cumberland, both areas which developed successfully in the early days of the Industrial Revolution. The main economic base of the area however, remained agriculture and the Board of Agriculture inspection in the 1790s showed up the degree of poverty and backwardness.

Administration

At the onset of the eighteenth century, Brough, like the other Clifford estates in the area, was in the hands of the Earls of Thanet, to whom it had passed through marriage. Appleby Castle was the administrative centre for these estates and the main officials, apart from the bailiff, lived there and not in Brough. In 1695 the castle keep was gutted, and a few years later, the furniture and fittings of the rest of the castle were sold.[170] The church, which Lady Anne had restored around 1660, continued to function. It had even functioned during the Commonwealth period despite the fact that its vicar, William Richardson, was called before the commissioners appointed to examine 'the scandalous, insufficient and ignorant - ministers' in 1655.

Note 170: Charlton, J., *Brough Castle*, op.cit., p20. N&B: Simpson, W. D., op.cit. p247. Also 1763 repair of Brough mill.

However, he was not ejected.[171]   Queen's College Oxford, still had the advowson, and by 1703 Thomas Barnett, the clerk, i.e. the vicar, received not only the small tithes but also the great tithes, worth £25, which previously had been given to Queen's. He also had the 'Parson's Garth', or glebe.[172] This was a valuable living.

Todd's manuscript[*] gives an insight into the population of the parish before census returns. In 1720 he notes the number of families: "within its limits the villages of Burgh (Market Burgh) of 52. Church Burgh (where ye church stands) 36. Sowerby 36. Hillbeck 12. South-Stainmoor 40, North Stainmoor 33, and Argil-row 20 Families."

The parish was the basis for much of the local administration, both ecclesiastical and secular. The church wardens were responsible for the church buildings and the congregation, but, in each parish, or in some areas in each township, there was a group known as the Vestry, which was a secular institution. All men who paid the poor rate were entitled to attend its meeting and to vote to elect the poor law guardians, the constables, and the highway overseers. In many respects this was an important form of local government, as it augmented the work of the magistrates, in maintaining the roads and bridges, and in dealing with poverty. Many of these Vestry records have been lost.

The church wardens' accounts, however, survive for part of the eighteenth century, showing that certain events were important in its calendar, namely celebrating 5th November, from 1716 onwards (after the scare of the Jacobite invasion of the previous year) and in 1745, the "rejoicings of the Duke of Cumberland's victory" cost 7s. 6d. It appears that the church bell sounded the curfew at eight o'clock each evening, as long as it was kept well oiled. At the end of the eighteenth century, the choir stalls were finished and the singers were accompanied by at least one instrumentalist, a bassoon player. The church wardens were responsible for keeping down the vermin in the area, and paid out the large sum of seventeen shillings in 1716 for fox and badger heads, (in Kirkby Stephen, at the same time the going rate was 6d. a head), see Table 7.

The accounts for the constables, the poor law guardians and others only survive from the end of the eighteenth century. This is still an era before the comprehensive collection of statistics had begun, but at least the Brough parish registers are intact, and by the middle of the eighteenth century, the clerk began to put in a few extra details. It is from these that some of the poverty in the area is revealed.

Note 171: Curwen, J., op.cit.

Note 172: CRO(K), WDX/3.

* Hugh Todd was Vicar of Penrith, CRO(C), reference thanks to Dawn Robertson.

TABLE 7: Extracts from the Church Wardens' Accounts

[In 1713 Rush-bearing is mentioned]		
1716	To ringer on 5 November	5s.
	For vermens heads [fox and brock heads]	17s.
1717	To ringers on gunpowder, treason [night]	8s.
	[also in 1738, 1748, 1756, up to 1827]	
1719	To clerk for washing and liming the church,	
	ringing eight of the clock, finding oyle [oil] to bells	£1
1729	To Thomas Cook for sweeping the church and whipping	
	out the dogs and other work	17s.
1734	For conveyancing the land bought with the publick	
	stock and expenses	£1
1745	Rejoicings at the Duke of Cumberland's victory	7s. 6d.
	[Bonnie Prince Charlie was on the run]	
1748	New pewter instead of old flagon	?
	20 stone of hair [for plastering the walls?]	
1791	To a bassoon	£2
1796	Ale when singers pew was done	5s.
	Two seats in coach to Carlisle	£1 6s. 8d.
	Two seats in coach from Carlisle	£1 6s. 8d.
	[possibly for a diocesan meeting]	
1827 First mention of organist		
[Note - Eighteenth century spellings used.]		CRO(K), WPR/23A&B

Poverty

Opening any page of the burial register at random, one notices the number of those listed as poor.[173] The decade from 1738-48, shows that between a quarter and a third of those buried were described as such, and in both 1741 and 1745 the percentage reached nearly a half. November and January were the worst months. Again, the details for another year chosen at random, that of 1766, gives a further indication of the problems of the period. Out of the 24 deaths only four were householders. Another six were widows and boarders, unable to support their own household, either because they were just starting out in jobs, or because they were too old to work. Eight burials, that is one third of this annual death total, were of children still living with their parents. Finally there were six poor people, and all with local surnames.

These figures illustrate the hazards of childhood illnesses, and the ease

---

Note 173: Taking the year as starting on 1st January.

with which poverty could overcome a family following the death or sickness of the bread winner, and the effect of hard winters and poor harvests on the nutrition standards of those at risk. In this particular year, there were no records of strangers buried, but it is not unusual to find, as in 1768, "a stranger, name unknown," and in 1778, "a tramper unknown found drowned or suffocated in a dyke on Stainmore, an elderly woman."

Parish authorities were quick to disclaim responsibility wherever possible, and Brough suffered more than many places from people moving along the Great Highway. Strangers who needed help were the responsibility of the parish in which they had been born, sometimes this was difficult to reach. In 1754, Thomas Cooper, born in Cornwall, aged 54, was discharged from the army, having served for almost 40 years. He had a wife and three children to support. The magistrates allowed him to pass through from Stainmore to Sedbergh, but he was ordered not to claim settlement until he got to Cornwall.

Legitimate traders were often overtaken by events. When William Johnson, a 30-year-old Scottish driver of cattle to Brough Hill Fair, was taken ill in 1774, he could not travel except in a cart, and Brough Overseers appealed to the Quarter Sessions for help. All overseers, not just those at Brough, were very quick to pass on anyone born elsewhere. In 1730, they petitioned that Bridget Bowman, described as single and very pregnant, be removed from Brough yet her legal settlement, was very close, on Stainmore.[174] In 1740, a deserted wife, Ann Moor and her son, were rapidly sent on their way from Appleby, to Mallerstang where the husband had been born, the son of the clerk there. Ann Wharton of Romaldkirk was sent home as was Thomas Swaile of Aspatria and, in the other direction, James Raw, rope maker of Brough was returned from the Carlisle district in 1741.[175] In 1770 two Brough men were paid 4s 6d for taking their horses to Appleby, "for taking Mary Foster away."[176]

Some of the stories which emerge from the Quarter Sessions records throw light on why there were so many strangers moving through Brough. For example, John Carrus worked in a trade which was notorious for the fluctuations in the work available. He was a 43-year-old weaver from Carlisle, and in 1765, he required a pass to get home. Seven weeks earlier, in the hope of earning some money, he had gone to the harvests in

---

Note 174: Eventually Anthony Ward of Appleby was charged 4d a week towards the upkeep of the bastard. Ward reappeared in several assault cases up to 1745.

Note 175: Burial 1773 at Brough, Abraham Watson a poor traveller, said to be of Keswick, a weaver by trade. Details of removal orders etc. CRO(C)/Q/11, Quarter Sessions Cumberland, CRO(K) WQ/ SR, Quarter Sessions, Westmorland.

Note 176: CRO(K), WPC/33 Account book.

Lincolnshire where he had caught the ague leaving him too ill and weak to move far.

Another example is of Jane Scott, a pedlar and a vagrant who, in 1767, was 80-years-old. She was one of many traders trying to make a living in the rural north. She said she had been born in Annan, in Scotland and "upwards of fifty years ago" she had married Andrew Scott, also from Scotland. He had carried a pack, and 40 years previously she had travelled with him. He had died at Yarm in Northumberland, she thought, between 30 and 40 years before. Since then she had worked the harvests in the north and begged.

A third case is that of Richard Wilson, a shoemaker from Northumberland, who was found in Brough in 1734. He was, he said, suffering from the falling sickness and he explained that on the recommendation of a Newcastle alderman, he was on his way to Dr Harrison of Westmorland, who, he was assured, would cure him.[177] He got as far as Brough and while drunk, he took some linen clothes lying on a hedge at the back of the garth behind Robert Kidd's house, (probably the Golden Fleece). When Kidd, a butcher, went to the house of a neighbour he found Wilson there along with the linen he had stolen, namely a man's shirt, three womens' shifts and two childrens' shifts.

Although the records of the overseers of the poor do not survive until the late eighteenth century, requests for relief often reached the Quarter Sessions. In 1741, George Waller of Brough claimed that both he and his wife were lame, they had three children and he could not work. He was granted one shilling a week. In 1767, Ann Waller, now a widow, with six children was ordered to the poor house, but, later that year, it was acknowledged that she was very lame and infirm with four small children and she was given five shillings a week.[178] At the same time, George Tinkler of Brough and his wife, both described as very old and infirm had their petition rejected. Whenever possible the costs would be passed on to the family. In 1767, Mary Cumpston a widow with three infants, was chargeable on the rates as her father in law, Cuthbert Cumpston, had refused to help, until the court ordered him to pay 3s a week.

In 1770, an attempt to regularise the relief of the poor was made in Brough. A Vestry (meeting) was set up to "consult on the poor house."[179] It was decided to buy a house. In 1772 the minutes discuss the rebuilding of the house and it was agreed that it was to be re-thatched. In October 1772, £9 was paid for a property, with a house, garden and garth in Church

---

Note 177: Dr Harrison lived in Morland. He died in 1747.
Note 178: Her elder children had perhaps been apprenticed out.
Note 179: CRO(K) WPC/33.

Brough, which lay between "those of Henry Allison and John Harrison."[180]

There is a list of the poor and impotent people of the township of Brough for 1774:

> Moses Cock, [Cockson] dyer, wife and three children
> John Wharton, wife and six children
> Jane Loadman
> Agnes Hops
> Elizabeth Hamilton
> Ann Hougill
> Isobel Harrison and child
> Catherine Waller
> Mary Sisson
> Mary Thwaites
> Widow Cockerton [Cockson]

Three years later another list shows many of the same names, and suggests that the overseers found it more helpful to give outdoor relief rather than use the poor house. By 1780 they were letting out the poor house for 6s.8d a year, but whether this was let as a business or as a work-house, is not clear.

Some of the long-term poor, who were cared for in their own homes, were too old to work. Ann Nanson in 1777, Mary Atkinson in 1778, (aged about 90) and Mary Thwaites in 1788, for example, were all described as ancient when they died. Others were widows like Margaret Cockson and Widow Howgill. Some were crippled or ill and needed neighbours to bring their dole. Ann Waller (Walters?) had relief administered by Robert Kiplin while George Petty, a single man of Intakeside, looked after someone called Wiseman, who was probably Tabitha Wiseman who died in the Poor House in 1779, a few months after George himself had died. Tabitha had been receiving help from at least 1775, when she had £2 12s. 6d. for twenty weeks and her clothes mended for 6d. Most claimants received two shillings for four weeks.

Some, however, like John Wharton, a labourer, received ten shillings for four weeks. He was on both the 1774 and the 1777 lists, with a wife and six children to support. Having married in 1755 after the birth of their first daughter, they had at least eight children, including a set of twins. Jane, the wife died in 1777, and John, by then described as ancient, died in 1781. Another family in trouble were the Cockfields. Moses, the head of this household, a dyer, had had a tempestuous youth. He had been up before the

---

Note 180: CRO(K) WPC/33, Account book (J. Middleton). It is not clear if this was a second poor house.

Quarter Sessions several times when younger, in 1743 and 1745, when he had been bound over to keep the peace. He was in trouble in 1771 for non-payment of his poor rates, and by 1774 he was on the poor list.

Some relief seems to have been given for temporary ill health. Thomas Hopkinson had sixteen shillings for four weeks in 1777, but claimed no more. He died at the age of 75 in 1792. George Horn, similarly, died eleven years after he had last claimed relief.

Specific examples of help come to light. In 1771, a Vestry was called for putting out Catherine Coulthore's son, Moses, who was about thirteen-years-old, as an apprentice. He was also provided with clothes worth 16*s.* 6*d.* Catherine's husband, William, described as a poor man, had been buried in February 1768.

A number of personal tragedies are covered by the statement in 1770 that Elizabeth Bousfield was paid three shillings every two weeks, to keep Elizabeth Thornber's child. Elizabeth Bousfield may have been the recently widowed wife of Thomas, the blacksmith, who "was killed by the fall of a crag upon him in Borrowdale, in a coal pit." Elizabeth Thornber, a single mother, whose daughter Alice had been baptised in 1767, was buried in March 1769.

Unavoidable expenses included such items as the cost of Mary Baxter's funeral which was 17*s.* 6*d.*, in 1775, while that of Isable Harrison in 1783, cost 18*s.* 6*d.*, and her son, then about fifteen-years-old, also needed *showes*, (shoes) and clothes, at an additional 2*s.* 6*d.*[181] Clothes often had to be supplied to the needy. Ann Waller was given a shift, an apron and handkerchief, a bedgown and "mending by Nelly" costing a total of eight shillings. Frances Graham was given two shifts, a gown and a petticoat, worth just under a pound. These were provided by George Middleton and James Devis, both local shopkeepers. Nearly 30 years later the payment for petticoat, handkerchief, clogs and mending to Nancy Gregson was 11*s.* 3*d.* Sometimes a bed and bedding were required at a cost of £2 17*s.* 4*d.* When children had to buried by the parish the coffin cost three shillings in 1780 and 4*s.* 8*d.* in 1824.

In the 1780s the poor rate collected was about £31 of which Market Brough contributed two thirds. Stainmore was a separate area. A striking innovation, presumably in the hope of saving money, is recorded in 1824: "to Robert Ranson and family in expenses to America £25 16*s.* 7*d.*" Does this tie in with an earlier record in 1805 when Eleanor Johnson of Ramson, was buried? She was described as wife of Henry, "now in America." This could be a fruitful topic for further research, as already it is known that

---

Note 181: CRO(K) WPC/33

several families from places like Ousby migrated as a group to North America around this time.

Other records from the Quarter Sessions include the crimes of the area. Most were small scale. John Perkin of Brough Sowerby was in court for taking timber belonging to Philip Musgrave at Great Musgrave, in 1755. John Dickenson, also of Brough Sowerby, a yeoman, was accused of stealing one glass bottle and a quart of rum worth two shillings. In 1754 John Strickland stole a silver spoon worth ten pence, for which he was to be whipped privately in Appleby gaol, and in Brough John Monroe, described as a barber and wig maker, was accused of stealing a gold ring, worth eleven pence from a widow, Frances Allison, and on a second occasion, of stealing a looking glass, of the same value. He was committed to gaol but although there were six local people named to appear in the bill of indictment, he was found not guilty.[182] A major theft took place on Stainmore in 1752 when John Thompson of Asby was robbed. He lost £126 in gold and silver. There are no more details.

Otherwise the Quarter Sessions dealt with the condition of the roads and bridges, which were often in a terrible state. There was a general complaint following the Jacobite invasion, when, "several people - of late being much oppressed - by providing horses, carts and men to drive - for the carrying baggage for the soldiers, passing into Scotland and the Northern parts seek three pence a mile from the county for their trouble."

These records show a generally law abiding community, to whom the main road could be seen as a mixed blessing: a source of expenditure and disturbance as well as a valuable trade route. The next section will deal with the state of agriculture, which was crucial to the economy of Brough.

Note 182: CRO(K) WQ/SR/1738, 1743, 1748, 1752.

CHAPTER 12

Farming:
The Board of Agriculture's Survey

POVERTY was endemic in this area of marginal farming and as the infant mortality rates dropped during the eighteenth century, the families outgrew the resources of their small holdings. The traditional farming system could not be easily adapted to population growth, and the improved agricultural techniques elsewhere in England had hardly reached Westmorland. In fact many places were unsuitable, being the "high, hilly, solitary country" of Fleming's earlier description.[183]

It is necessary to look at the contemporary view of land-use to see where the problems lay. In the second half of the eighteenth century two descriptions of rural life were published. One was Arthur Young's *Tour of the Northern Counties* in 1768, which contained very few details about the Brough region, for he concentrated more on the Swaledale and Penrith areas. The second was the Board of Agriculture survey of Westmorland, made in 1793, by Andrew Pringle. Unfortunately he could only spare three weeks to cover the whole county, and although he found everyone very helpful, he did admit that his survey was a little brief. Both writers were primarily concerned with the state of agriculture, and this, in Westmorland, did not impress them.[184]

Pringle's first view was that most land was held by yeomen who had estates worth £10 to £50 per year. These small farms were held by customary tenure, with the landlord responsible for the repair of buildings, and retaining control of the timber on the land.[185] There were few *'mere'* cottages, he wrote, as "even the labourer and the mechanic" had small farmhouses with some land. The yeomen lived poorly and worked hard, often needing another occupation to supplement their income, while the women and children were knitters or spinners. Pringle found that over the previous 40 years, many had sold their land and become labourers. This meant a loss

Note 183: Fleming: "the air in winter is a little sharp yet very healthful."
Note 184: Pringle, A., in Bailey, J. & Culley, G., *General View of Agriculture in Northumberland, Cumberland and Westmorland.* (1794, reprinted 1972). The Westmorland section is by A. Pringle and will be referred to as such in the footnotes.
Note 185: In 1720, the Earl of Thanet had authorised his tenant Whelpdale, to take timber to build a house at Blue Grass from the land leased by Shaw and Nicholson. As they refused to allow this, the Earl prosecuted them. George Earle was prosecuted by the Earl for cutting and selling timber off his customary tenement on Stainmore. He was fined three times the value.

of common pasture rights, and therefore of cheap fuel, wool, and milk. Meanwhile he found that, "it is painful - to behold the beautiful servant maids of this county toiling in the severe labours of the field. They drive harrows, - the ploughs, - (and) the dungcarts."[187]

A typical labourer could earn nine shillings a week in summer and a shilling less in winter. These may be compared with those given by Arthur Young's figures for 1768 in the table below. Pringle gives some idea, in very round terms, of the weekly living costs: rent one shilling, fuel one

---

TABLE 8: Prices and Wages, late eighteenth century, Penrith.

Arthur Young, *Tour through Northern England*, 1768.[186]

Wages: Daily
>   In harvest 1*s*. 6*d*. with beer
>   Haytime 1*s*. 3*d*. with beer
>   In winter 10*d*. with beer
>   Reaping corn 3*s*.-5*s*. an acre
>   Mowing grass 1*s*.-2*s*. 6*d*.
>   Ditching 8*d*. a rood
>   Threshing barley 1*d*. halfpenny
>   Threshing oats 2*d*. halfpenny

Provisions: 1768
>   Bread , oats and barley one penny a pound
>   Cheese 2*d*.
>   Butter 6*d*. for 18oz
>   Beef 2½*d*., Mutton 2*d*. halfpenny, Veal ditto, Pork 3*d*.
>   Milk 1*d*. three pints
>   Candles 7*d*. a pound, Soap 7*d*. a pound.
>   Labourers house rent 20*s*., firing 30*s*.

Non-agricultural Wages:
>   Mason and carpenter: 1*s*. 8*d*. a day
>   Thatcher 1*s*. 6*d*. a day
>   Headman's wages £12-£14 p.a.
>   Boy £3
>   Dairy Maid £6
>   Other maids £3-£4
>   **Women** per day in harvest 10*d*. and beer
>   In Haytime 8*d*. and beer
>   In winter 6*d*. and beer

Note 186: Hutchinson, op.cit. Pringle, A., op.cit., p302 ff
Note 187: Pringle, A., op.cit., p302 ff

shilling, and oatmeal one shilling. His figures are much higher than those of Young and yet other sources suggest that the cost of living had not risen much over that period.[188] He maintained that this left the labourer in a position to eat as well as the farmers of 40 years previously, with three meals a day. Breakfast was potage, bread and cheese, dinner was meat and potatoes and supper either potatoes or bread and cheese. The bread was clap bread or oat cake, made up once a month on a girdle, with sixteen quarts of oats making 16lbs of meal.

Farms in the Bottom of Westmorland, (that is the Upper Eden valley) contained much coarse pasture land, and were rented at 20s.-24s. an acre. The main structure on these farms was the barn, which included the cowhouse, the stables and enough storage space for the crops and the hay. The average Westmorland farm of 100 acres, (and presumably a lowland one), Pringle asserted, would have fifteen acres under barley or oats, 35 acres of hay, and 50 acres of pasture. On this could be raised ten dairy cows which produced 20 firkins of butter.[189] This could give a profit of £60 on the capital outlay of £260.

The terms of the lease often included the rotation of crops required. The normal one, of twelve years around Brough, was to keep a field in grass for seven years, then to plough it and sow oats. The following year barley was sown and this was followed by oats, before a return to grass. Turnips and potatoes were sown on some land after a summer fallow, to feed the livestock. Flax, and hemp, previously found in most small garths were no longer grown, while new crops like clover were not popular. However, in much of the area, hay was the most important crop, partly because nearly every farmer had livestock but also because there were many areas where cereals could not be grown. Much of the better land was subdivided into tiny half acre closes, but the commons were still left as wastes, in a deplorable state, allowing the intermingling of diseased animals and with little control over the stints, (or numbers allowed).

Livestock farming

The most notable trade of livestock was that of cattle, for 10,000 Scottish cattle were sold each year at Brough Hill Fair at the end of September. The *'History'* by Nicolson and Burns, published about the same time, describes the fair as, "remarkable for the sale of horses and cattle." Many beasts were destined for southern markets although many were bought by local farmers. The influence of the fair can be seen when, in 1749, it had to be closed due to disease, and the problems were to stop not only the Scottish drovers, but

Note 188: Pringle, op.cit., p306.
Note 189: A firkin held 56lbs.

also the vast numbers of cattle expected from Lancashire.[190]

Pringle noted that the attention formerly paid to black cattle "had diminished of recent years." Even so, he found numerous herds on the commons.[191] Most of the cattle kept in Westmorland, were longhorns with the "desirable property of laying the fat upon their backs and other valuable parts." He had been told that the local expectation was that a profit of twenty shillings within a year, could be made from a Scottish beast, (no mention of breed or age) but in reality, when the cost of wintering on low ground, and the loss by fatigue and disease was taken into account, the profit margin was much lower. Young cattle, bought either at Brough Fair in the autumn or from the drovers of Galloway and Dumfries in the spring, were kept on inferior land in summer with straw and hay in winter, and were fattened for market at three years, or sold to the graziers of Yorkshire and Lancashire from £5 to £8 a piece.

Pringle's report states that dairy farming, however, was more common than stock fattening. A *milch* cow was expensive to buy; it cost £10 and therefore most were raised on the farm, a practice which, he felt, had led to a notable degeneration of stock. He estimated that it cost £5 a year to keep a cow which could generate annually £8 worth of produce, mainly in the form of butter for the London market.

Sheep were most numerous on the commons. These were the native breed with some crossed with Scottish rams. They were described as horned, dark faced, thick pelted with coarse stringy wool. No attempt had been made to improve them. The wethers over a year old were kept all year on the hills but the others were brought down to be wintered in lowland areas, where a tenth would die before Christmas. The canny farmers would pay two shillings per head for their over-wintering, but only on those which survived until April. They were mainly bred for their wool although there was some export of mutton to Lancaster and Liverpool.

When the old ewes with lambs were sold off to lowland farmers for fattening, at the autumn sales, Scottish hogs (young sheep) were bought at about 8s. 6d. a head. These were generally kept for two years on the commons, and then sold for 11s. To this value may be added the price for their fleeces, (another three shillings), making a total of 14s. a head. Again this left hardly any profit when the costs of salving, clipping and other expenses were taken into account. Then there was always the worry of disease. In 1792 one third of all the sheep in Westmorland had died.[192]

It was reported that a small experiment aimed at improving the breeding

---

Note 190: CRO(K), WD/QR, 1749.
Note 191: Pringle, A., op.cit. p321.
Note 192: Pringle, A., op.cit. p355. No explanation given.

Cattle for sale at Brough Hill Fair, Westmorland, photograph courtesy of John Walton.

had taken place in Westmorland, in 1789, but there is no indication of which landowner was involved. Twenty Lincolnshire ewes, which had been tupped by Mr Bakewell's breed in 1789, were brought in. They survived the winter and lambed in 1790. The aim was to cross breed them with the native sheep. The first cross bred lambs were described as the best sheep in the county, but over a five year period, problems appeared which had not been sorted out when the report was written.

Other livestock for the market in Westmorland included a small number of swine, and, by the 1790s, these were professionally cured. One other product deserves mention and that is the raising of geese, mainly on the commons. The birds were sold on to drovers, for markets in northern towns.

There is some indication that efforts were being made to improve agriculture in the area by the beginning of the nineteenth century. When Thomas Whelpdale took a lease in 1802 for Blue Grass on Stainmore, a farm of 62 acres, the Earl of Thanet laid down the crop rotation to be practised, which included grass, followed by a two year fallow then two years of grain and finally cropped with either beans, peas or clover. He also laid down the amount of lime and dung to be used. The lease was for seven years so that long term measures could be practised. It is noticeable that there were a number of his tenants in the Brough area who were gradually enlarging their farms. Edward Halliday at New Hall and High Ewbank between 1767 and 1801 accumulated 420 acres, for which he paid £240 a year rent. Thomas Hodgson between 1775 and 1801 built up a compact

A drawing of the native breed of sheep in Westmorland when A. Pringle surveyed the area's agriculture in the 1790s.

estate around and including Brough Castle. John Wilson and John Bailey had also enlarged their holdings on long leases for up to nine years.

The need to enclose and improve the commons was Pringle's main recommendation, but this was not an easy task on the fells, especially where the common rights for cottagers were at risk. There had been piecemeal enclosure from the medieval period. Helbeck common had been at least partly enclosed by the eighteenth century for a court case in 1731 was brought against Richard Allison of Brough. He was accused of grazing two horses, which ate 11*d.* worth of grass, in a private close on Helbeck Common. It was the late nineteenth century before most of the Brough commons were enclosed. It was a massive undertaking to sort out the legal problems of the commons and in the pre-railway era, a second factor had to be considered, which had major implications for the area. This was the disruption which would affect the traditional drovers' routes.

Pringle's assessment was influenced by his knowledge of agriculture in other parts of northern Britain. His survey left a valuable record of the main aspects of Westmorland life as seen by an outsider, at the end of the eighteenth century. A more intimate view is found for the same period in a small notebook of a Brough Sowerby farmer: Jonathan Alderson, the subject of the next section.

A yeoman farmer of Brough Sowerby: Jonathan Alderson[193]

The most common occupation of a male householder in the parish registers of the late eighteenth century is given as that of yeoman, a term usually taken to mean a farmer with his own land. In the Brough area it was used more generally to mean a countryman of respectable standing.[194]

In the Kendal Record Office, there is an account book of Jonathan Alderson of Brook Farm, Brough Sowerby, who, when he died in 1801, at the age of 76, was described as a yeoman. The note book gives a glimpse of his activities. The booklet was irregularly used from 1751 to around 1789, to keep family records, weather details and trading accounts. It is well worn, the pages are crumpled, and a number have been cut out. There is no order and often no date. Every spare inch has been in-filled, and some notes start at the front and some at the back of the book. It therefore raises more questions than it answers but it remains a valuable resource.

Alderson lived in Brough Sowerby all his life. There he and Ann, his wife, brought up the family of ten children, born between 1749 and 1770. He was a dutiful member of the community. He had his children baptised and paid his church dues. He served as overseer for the poor on at least two occasions and as constable for one year. He was literate and numerate, and he sent his children, including the girls, to school. Amongst his accounts are scattered sentences like: "Alays (Alice) entered school in October 1772" and "George and Mary started at Sowerby School" in 1781. (George later went on to Winton school). Alderson was a regular subscriber to the newspapers; in 1775 he paid 12*s*. 11*d*. for newspapers for one year and ten weeks.

For five years he gives brief summaries of the weather starting on 16th November 1771 with a comment "the greatest flood we have ever known." The following two years had fine summers and hay-time but wet harvests. In 1774 there was very stormy weather, with a wet, dark summer and a long hay harvest, and in 1775 there was a very wet winter and a very *'drouty'* summer (sic).

His account book begins with the dates his four cows were bulled in 1751, and this information is listed for most years somewhere in the book. Yowes (ewes) were included in the accounts, as well as swine, but it is not clear if they are his, or if he was trading, as the ink has faded badly in that corner of the book. Again there are references to cereals but there is no certainty that they are his. In 1768, he had done some work at the vicarage. His bill shows that he could cope with all aspects of arable farming: sowing,

---

Note 193: CRO(K) WDX 341/1. The notebook has been deposited by Mr Alan Bell of Nateby, and it is used with his kind permission. I am extremely grateful for the chance to use this information.
Note 194: See *Oxford English Dictionary.*

hedging, muck spreading, winnowing. This bill was never paid.

J. Alderson: 1768 Work done at Vicarage (original spelling)	
12 days blowing	£3 12*s.*
loading maner (manures)	£1 2*s.*
sowing oats and harrowing	6*s.*
sowing barley and harrowing	5*s.*
throing out maner	2*s.*
1 day hedging	1*s.*
2 day hedging	2*s.*
mending a gate	4*d.*
Total	£3 1*s.* 8*d.*

His accounts are chaotic, except when he was recording parish business. As overseer for the poor in 1758, he listed what he paid out to Palmer Nicholson, to Dobson, to Debra Colthard, Thomas Swailes and the Cumpston family, (some have already been mentioned in the Quarter Sessions appeals described earlier). He had to pay 1*s.* 6*d.* for clogs for one of the Cumpstons, he bought line cloth for £2 7*s.* 6*d.* (for clothing) and paid 10*s.* 6*d.* for housing Mary Cumpston. His expenses as constable are equally carefully listed: 1*s.* for his swearing-in, 2*s.* to appoint an overseer, 3*s.* for attending the window sessions (for the tax), plus 2*s.* for collecting the window and land tax. (Brough Sowerby's land and window tax, he recorded as 6*s.* 10½*d.*) Paper cost him 3*d.*

There is no record of which year he was constable, but it may have been in 1769, when he records that he paid in the boon coals at Appleby Castle. It is clear that he owned a cart and that some of his work was carrying heavy goods, for in the same year, on at least three occasions he took slat(e)s to Bowes from Brough, one load of five tons, another of 7½ tons and then another of 1½ tons. Slate was the term used for the local sandstone flags of Stainmore, which could be cut thinly along the bedding planes and used for roofing. The accounts show fifteen unspecified loads from Appleby to Brough, three horse cartfuls to (*Baringham?*), some grey slates to Mr Harrison and two cords of wood to Appleby Castle , and three to (*Langton?*) He was then able to pay off one guinea from a bill he owed Edward Fothergill: a neat illustration of long term credit financing a small business.

In 1772, 173 loads of lime were carried and in 1775 he spent five days in April and nine days in June at Helbeck, carting lime, at 6*s.* a bushel. Meanwhile he was still carrying timber and slates to Appleby, and coals, costing 2*s.* per load, presumably to local farms. In 1780 his loads seem to have changed to butter in bulk, milled cereals and brandy. He noted eight years later, that the carriage to Sunderland were 3*d.* each, for three lots of

Brough Sowerby photograph by kind permission of Alan Bell, Nateby.

butter, 6*d.* for a bundle (unidentified), and 3*d.* for a parcel.

There are a number of other, undated, lists of spices, currants, raisins, nuts, tobacco and clay pipes as well as cloth, thread, flock and flannel. On another occasion he listed *fig* blue and *puder* blue, starch, and twelve firkins of soap. Some have prices, some have not. Were these his own shopping lists, or was he buying them for a customer or shopkeeper? Did he supply a shop, a dye works or an inn? Why, when he received parcels did he pay? In 1758, for example, he 'bought off William Cooke a parcel for 17*s.* 6*d.*' He bought two more that year and one from Mr Bell (possibly a Brough shopkeeper), the following year. It seems likely that the bundles and parcels which he bought were part of the carrying trade, in that he paid for them and then collected the customer's money on delivery. Unfortunately, although a number of his customers appear in the parish registers, their work is either not mentioned or is under the general term of husbandman.

It is possible, therefore, that these accounts show the early stages in the development of the carrying trade, which was evolving along the new turn-pikes. Alderson had no regular runs, and no regular places. The carrying was done as required and could be fitted into a farming routine, so providing a sec-ondary source of income at a time when farming was less secure than before. He seems to have been reasonably prosperous, as he had his daughters, as well as his sons, educated, and his newspaper bills suggest regular reading. He certainly had the initiative to take every opportunity to widen his trade.

Brough Sowerby blacksmith at work. Photograph by kind permission of Alan Bell, Nateby.

By a remarkable coincidence, another set of contemporary accounts of a local business have survived: these have been published in *An Eighteenth-century Shopkeeper: Abraham Dent of Kirkby Stephen* by T. S. Willan. Abraham Dent was a substantial shop keeper in Kirkby Stephen with connections with the London trade. Farmers in Brough and Stainmore are recorded as selling him small quantities of wheat. These included John Ellison of Barras Hall, John Sawkell and James Petty of Stainmore, James Bird of Helbeck and Thomas Cannon of Brough, while William Shaw of Stainmore was selling malt for his brewery. Other people were buying a variety of goods. James Raine, a glover, bought alum. Jonathan Ewbank was buying copies of Horace, Virgil, Ovid and other Latin texts, while Thomas Hodgson, the vicar of Brough, bought "one parish book bound." William Walton, who bought groceries and cloth in 1762 worth £1 18*s.* 8½*d.*, used extended credit to pay off 10*s.* 6*d.* in 1764 and the rest in February 1765. The most important feature, in light of the area's mining history, is that George Harker, John Coat and Co., bought powder for 'Awgill' from Abraham Dent. In 1762 they had 20lb, then 38lb and by 1765 their bills show that they were buying powder on a regular basis. Dent, like Alderson, was trading at a time when there were marked improvements to the transport system in the area. The next chapter will discuss the development of the turnpike roads.

CHAPTER 13

New Developments: The turnpikes

ALTHOUGH Brough was an insignificant village in the early 1700s, it was not isolated. It was certainly difficult to reach in the rainy periods but because its highway connected the Newcastle area, a fast developing industrial region, with the west coast, and because the London traders preferred the Stainmore route to that over Shap, there was a fair amount of through traffic. Even in Fleming's time the post came through twice a week. However, the upkeep of the road was an almost impossible task as it was based solely on the six days of parish labour due from all the rate payers.

The growth of commerce, of manufacturing and of mining in northern England along with the political necessity of being able to move the armed forces after the 1715 rebellion, made better roads essential. Legally, the parishes were responsible for the roads, but usually failed to keep them up to standard, as the Quarter Sessions records demonstrate. A new system of road management had been introduced early in the Restoration period. This was the Turnpike Trust, where a group of entrepreneurs financed the improvement of a road, with professional oversight, and paid builders. Tolls were charged to off-set the costs. Each trust was established under an Act of Parliament, initially for a period of 21 years.

In 1743, the Act establishing the Bowes to Brough Turnpike Trust was set up.[195] The preamble stated that, "the several roads leading from Bowes to Brough - are so very bad and ruinous, especially in the winter season, that travellers cannot pass without great danger." The Act named 129 Westmorland, Yorkshire, and other worthies as trustees, and investors, "for surveying, ordering, amending and keeping the said roads." It laid down the tolls to be charged, allowed the trustees to obtain road building material, and required magistrates to oversee the work of the Trust. The trustees included Sir Philip Musgrave, Sir James Lowther and Sir George Dalston. From outside the area, came Sir Conyers Darcy, and Chomondely Turner, Esq. The Northumberland coal interests were represented by Henry Vane, Esq. A number came from the Barnard Castle area, such as Richard Coates and William Robinson of Rokeby Park, Philip Brunskill of Bowes, and Joshua Dixon of Raby.

Note 195: Local Turnpike Acts: 26 Geo. II Cap LXVII. Brough-Bowes, 28 Geo II Cap. XVI, Brough-Eampnt Bridge, 1 Geo III Cap XLIII, Kirkby Stephen-Tebay.

Practically every clergyman in the Appleby deanery was among the investors, along with the mayors of Kendal and Appleby and the Archdeacon of Carlisle. Local men, from Stainmore, Brough and Kirkby Stephen, like Jonathan Ewbank, John Rudd, Thomas Lamb, Joshua Nicholson, Richard Waller and Thomas Harrison were all included.[196] This was seen as a long term investment. At least one family handed its shares on to its junior branches. In 1859, Sir Richard Tufton was paid £26 4s. 3d. one year's interest on £600 at four and a half per cent.[197]

This was the first such venture in the area, and the road westwards from Brough to Eamont Bridge was not turnpiked until 1753 and that southwards to Kirkby and beyond, until 1760. An important development was the application in 1769, for extending the Bowes to Brough road, from the Turnpike at Maiden Castle through Kaber to join the Turnpike from Brough to Kirkby Stephen, and also another branch from the Stainmore turnpike to "the coal works at Taylor Rig, and Tan Hill and King's Pitts in the county of York, and also from the foot of Barrow's Brow until it joins the Coal Road - and also from Tan Hill to - the Market Town of Reeth." This established a network of roads on South Stainmore enabling the coal traffic from such places as Hard Hills as well as Tan Hill, to increase. Other mines were opened along the Middleton road, (built by the London Lead Company) north of the original turnpike and in 1820, this too became a turnpike. The tolls from the carriage of coal may well have been the most important source of revenue by the 1830s.

In Nicolson and Burn's *History* published in 1777, there is an enthusiastic comment on the Stainmore road, "it is nearly as good as the best road in the kingdom. Whereas it took up to six hours to cover the thirteen miles,"[198] (it was, in fact, over sixteen miles long), "it now took with ease an hour and a half, and since the turnpike was made, there is no need for a halt so the Spittle inn has become useless."[199]

No early records of the work on the road have as yet, been found, but later ones give some details. The width of the main road was seventeen feet, with gullies at either side; the secondary road to the coal diggings was narrower, at three yards width. It was made of six inch deep broken stones from local quarries, like the one at the Grained Tree, (Maiden Castle), at the Punch Bowl, at Oxenthwaite, and at Barras Brow, and Tan Pitt, to give a few examples. Local owners rented their quarries to the Trust; William Simpson

---

Note 196: CRO(K) WST 2(1-9), WD/HH 193.
Note 197: Less property tax at 15s.9d.
Note 198: The surveyors measured it as just over sixteen miles and the Kaber extension as eight miles.
Note 199: N&B. op.cit., p578.

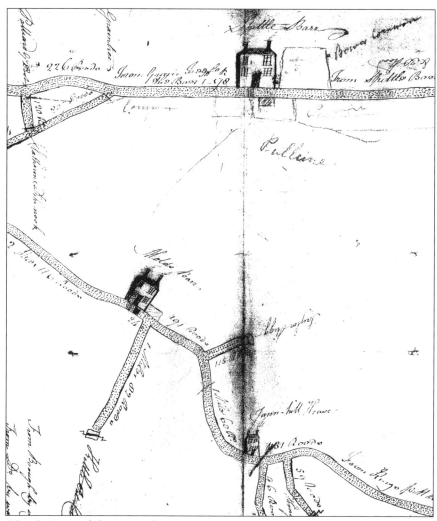

Map 8: Part of the Turnpike plan to improve the Brough, Bowes and Tanhill roads, from the Heelis papers with kind permission.

charged 2*s*. 6*d*. a year for his at Birkbeck Pastures. In 1857, 50 yards of stone was bought from the East Ward Union, (Kirkby Stephen workhouse) at 1*s*. 9*d*. a yard. There was severe wear and tear on the road surfaces. In 1836 a pot-hole near Pit House (Mousegill) measured seven roods in length and two feet four inches in depth.[200]

The construction of these roads and their maintenance required more than one man and a shovel, and an important development in the area was the formation of small companies. In 1829 Joseph Johnson, William Baine

Note 200: CRO(K) WD/HH 200.

and Co. were paid £8 6s. for levelling up 24 roods of road at Maiden Castle, In 1824, Thomas Hobson and Co. were paid £20 4s. for repairing the road near the Slip Inn, and James Parkin and Co. for breaking stones at Oxenthwaite £1 2s. 6d. Six different companies, for example, were paid for work in the last quarter of 1831. This did not exclude individuals from being employed as casual labour, especially in times of crisis. In January 1829, two men were paid six shillings for one and a half days snow clearance. In February, five men were paid two shillings each for snow clearance from Maiden Castle to Kaber Cross. Similar payments continued sporadically in March and April of that year too.

Another development was the employment of a surveyor in charge of the work. Michael Ewbank had an annual salary of £15 15s. in 1832, and in 1836 Joseph Whelpdale held a similar position. The Trust's legal affairs were under the supervision of the Heelis family who occasionally had to deal with complaints from the General Post Office. In November 1827, a letter from its Leeds office stated that:

> "Sir, Since I saw you on the 27th Ult at Appleby relative to the Brough and Stainmore Road I have walked over it on purpose to examine it and must say it is in general in a very bad state and as such have represented it to the General Post Office and will thank you to make it Known to the Trust that unless it is put into a good state of repair it will be indicted the next Quarter Sessions.
>
> "On the 30th Ult we had the misfortune to break a Splinter Bar in going through the Gate of Spittle solely in consequence of there being no lamp up which caused delay of eleven minutes. I am decidedly of opinion that the Gate is not of the width that the Act requires and it is quite impossible for us to attempt to keep time at this Season without requesting every thing to be done that the General Act provides for. There are no Guide Posts put up yet."

The clerk of the trust, Mr John Heelis, replied, on 21 November, 1827:

> "Sir, I - have to inform you that at the last meeting on the 31st October the Trustees made an order that Posts should be put up on the road under the direction of Mr Hopes, one of the Trustees (the treasurer) and I understand that the Surveyor immediately proceeded in the business and they will be put up so soon as they can be procured.
>
> "I have communicated your complaint about the repair of the road to the Surveyor and also to several of the Trustees and he of course will repair where he thinks necessary but it is the first complaint that the Trustees have received of the road being out of repair."[201]

Note 201: CRO(K) WD/HH 200.

Toll Charges , by Act of Parliament 1742.[202]

For every:	Drawn by:	Toll:
Coach, chariot, landau, Berlin Chaise	6 horses, mares, geldings	2*s.* 6*d.*
ditto	4 horses, etc.	2*s.*
ditto	2-3 horses, etc.	1*s.*
ditto	1 horse, etc.	6*d.*
Wagon, wain, cart, carriage	4 horses or oxen	1*s.* 6*d.*
ditto	1 horse 2 horses, 3 horses	4*d.* 8*d.*/1*s.*
Horse, mule, ass, laden or unladen	Not drawing	2*d.*
Every drove of oxen, cattle		10*d.* per score or in proportion
Every drove of calves, hogs, sheep or lambs		5*d.* a score or in proportion

Two toll gates, one at Spittal and the other at Colliery Gate, were the responsibility of the Brough-Bowes Trust and these were farmed out to consortiums.[203] For example in 1829, three men from just over the Yorkshire border, (two coal owners and a publican) bid £345 for three years rights to the tolls on the colliery road. After this the lease changed hands each year, often to local men. In 1848, the auction was held at the Swan Inn, based on the previous year's prices of £322 7*s.* 11*d.* at Spittle Gate and £174 5*s.* 5*d.* at Colliery Gate. However, within five years there was a considerable fall in the value of the tolls. Although the railways had not reached the Eden Valley, they had affected some of the through-trade across Stainmore and the tiny local coalfields could not compete with the major ones of the north east.[204]

The other turnpikes had their own surveyors and toll gates, but the procedures were all very similar. The toll gate to the west of the village towards Brough Hill, for example, belonged to the Eamont Bridge-Brough

---

Note 202: CRO(K) WD/Hoth. Box 34/21.
Note 203: CRO(K) WD/HH 198/193, Toll gate leases.
Note 204: Shepherd, M. E., *From Hellgill to Bridge End, Aspects of economic and social change in the Upper Eden Valley, 1840-95.* Herts. University Press (2003), p185-7, Tolls. These local turnpikes trusts were dissolved in the 1870s, p 128.

Trust. The one on the Middleton road was at Milking Style Gate. Evidence from an undated, but late eighteenth century, document gives lower tolls for Brough Bar, (on the Brough-Eamont road), with the droving traffic being charged only half the tolls recommended in 1742.[205]

The income from the local turnpikes shows their relative importance. In 1821, based on an average over the previous three years, the Brough to Bowes tolls, which included those of the Coal Road, amounted to £652, but this was only about 60 per cent of the value of the Brough-Eamont Bridge section. The Middleton road had, at that time, only had one year's return of tolls, at £98.

By 1843, income had dropped by a quarter along the whole length from Bowes to Eamont Bridge, (including the coal road). The Middleton Road tolls had increased to £230 and continued to rise to £300 in 1850, accounting for about a quarter of the tolls for the four roads.

The effect of the turnpikes: Coaches and Carriers
For nearly a century, these roads were of great importance in opening up the Upper Eden area and as such they boosted the economy of Brough. Only with the building of the railway across Stainmore did the situation change. Once these roads were built, coaches and wagons brought people and goods through the area. Soon regular coach and carrier services were set up and by 1829 these services were advertised in the directories. The Royal Mail, from London to Glasgow left The George, in Brough daily, northbound at 2am, southbound at 11.30pm, while two services left from The White Swan. One was the Express, from London to Carlisle, which went three times a week, and the other was the Lord Exmouth, connecting Newcastle and Lancaster which also went three times a week.[206] There were therefore, regular connections to London, to the north east as far as Newcastle and to the north west, either north to Carlisle and Scotland, or south to Lancaster with connections to Liverpool.

Carriers provided a cheaper and slower service, for both people and goods. Considerable distances were covered. In 1790, Messrs Handleys of Carlisle advertised their weekly service of stage wagons which took ten days from Carlisle to London via York. From York, coming northwards, they called at Richmond, Barnard Castle, Brough, Appleby, Penrith and Carlisle.[207]

Note 205: CRO(K) WD/HH.
Note 206: It had been the first direct service between Kendal and Newcastle in 1818. The first mail coach from Kendal to Carlisle was in 1796, and the first over Stainmore in 1809, on the London-Edinburgh route. Williams, L. A. *Road Transport in Cumbria in the nineteenth century*, (1975), p110.
Note 207: Williams, op.cit., p104, quoting D. Scott.

CASTLE INN, WOOD-STREET.

Kendall, Lancafter, Whitehaven, Penrith, Carlifle, Edinburgh, Glafgow and Paifley

Flying STAGE WAGGONS,

Twice a Week, fets out and comes in as follows, viz.

Comes in to the above Inn every Monday and Thurfday, fets out every Tuefday and Friday;

Arrives at *Wigan,*		Returns from *Wigan,*	
Chorley, } Monday and Thurfday		Chorley, } Tuefday and Friday	
Prefton, }		Prefton, }	
Lancafter, Tuefday and Friday		Lancafter, Monday and Thurfday	
Kendall, Wednefday and Saturday.		Kendall, Wednefday and Saturday.	

Carry Goods and Paffengers with the greateft Care and Expedition, by the way of *Litchfield, Stone, Newcaftle-under-Line, Sandback, Brereton Green, Holms Chapel, Warrington, Winnick, Newton, Afhton,* and the following Places:

Ayr	Cartmell	Egremond	Ireby	Maybole	Strathaven
Annan	Chorley	Falkirk	Irvine	Machlin	Shap
Allonby	Chewbent	Flookborough	Jedburg	Milnthorpe	Stranrawer
Allftone	Calderbridge	Garftang	Kirby Lonfdale	Newton	Troutbeck
Amblefide	Clithero	Gervan	Kirby-Stephen	Newtonftewart	Ulverftone
Appleby	Colne	Glenluce	Kefwick	Old Cumnock	Unrigg
Beetham	Cockermouth	Greenock	Kelfo	Orton	Warrington
Blackburn	Dent	Haltwiftle	Kilmarnock	Ormfkirk	Wigan
Bolton le moors	Deffington	Haverfham	Kirkcudbright	Prefton	Walton
Brampton	Dalton	Hawkfhead	Kirkham	Poulton	Whaley
Broughton	Dalfton	Holme	Leigh	Port-patrick	Wray
Bootle	Drigg	Hornby	Lockmabin	Ravenglafs	Warcop
Booth	Dunbarton	Hefketh New	Longtown	Ravenftondale	Wigton
Brough	Dumblain	Market	Lockerby	Sedburg	Wigtown
Burton	Dumfries	Ingleton	Lowther Hall	Standifh	Workington
Burnley	Ecclefechan	Ireton	Mary Port	Sterling	Wharton
Carnforth	Ecclefton				

Performed by the Public's obedient Servants, { J. SHELLY, E. BRADSHAW, J. BRADSHAW, J. WRIGHT,

Advertising poster for the new stage coach service, with kind permission of CRO(C) and the Lonsdale estate.

Six carriers, all local men with one possible exception, advertised their services from Brough in the 1829 directory. One went from Kendal via Appleby and Brough to Newcastle, and another weekly one through Kendal via Kirkby Stephen. There was a twice weekly service to Penrith, one each market day to Kirkby, and a twice weekly one to Stockton. Finally one which stopped at the Shoulder of Mutton, twice weekly, on its journey between Penrith and Stockton, offered to "forward goods to all parts." There was also *ad hoc* carrying, often by farmers with space in their wagons who would do odd local deliveries.

The effect of the turnpikes: Accommodation

The timetables show that the inns were an integral part of the transport network. The odd hours of arrival and departure, and the long journeys meant that travellers and horses, needed refreshment, the wagons needed repairs and the horses had to be changed. The 1794 directory lists ten innkeepers in Brough, and one in Brough Sowerby. In 1829, there were nine in Brough, including the Packhorse, and the Bridge in Church Brough, the Black Bull in Brough Sowerby, and eight inns on Stainmore. The Punch Bowl, the New Inn, Cooper House and the Blue Bell served the main road, but there were two at the Slip Inn, and another at Mousegill which served the Coal Road and another, the Rippon Arms, for Dumma and the North Stainmore mines. There were also unlisted alehouses, whose occupiers sometimes appear in the parish registers. Where, for example, was the King's Head Alehouse, which Mason Howe, who served on the Poor Law Vestry, occupied for at least eleven years up to 1782?

The history of one particular inn in the centre of Brough illustrates the confidence which local people had in the early nineteenth century transport developments. An earlier chapter has already shown that the Kidd family, two butchers and their mother, had bought the freehold of a large set of buildings on the main road next to the Swindale Beck in 1701. They had developed this as an inn alongside their other, butchery business. It must have had a good reputation as the innkeepers were addressed as yeomen or gentlemen. From 1794 Thomas Lamb held it for six years, and George Bland for ten. It was then called the Golden Fleece and by 1819 Bland held it along with six cottages, and a large collection of outbuildings, stables, cowhouses, two orchards and two gardens. During the first two decades of the nineteenth century the Kidds seem to have sold at least part of their holding, to a farmer at Parks, on the outskirts of Brough for his son, William Dodds, working as a turner and brush worker in London, sold his part in 1807.

The deeds do not reveal what happened next except that in 1818, it was bought by Stephen Cleasby and his sons, all merchants of London, who also held Palliard, and two neighbouring farms on Stainmore. In 1820, they leased out to Joseph Watson, what was described in the deeds as a newly built dwelling house, "now on the site of the former Golden Fleece inn - which is now called the Castle Hotel." It was a seven year lease, at a rent for the first three years at £90 a year and for the last four at £100 a year.[208] The 1841 and 1851 censuses show the Kilvington family in charge of the hotel, and running it as a post house, with five servants. This was, then, a luxury establishment.

This brief description of a commercial venture is important in a number of ways. First the Kidds, as the long term owners had prospered especially

---

Note 208: CRO(K), WD/RG 1701-1927 (Vaux Brewery).

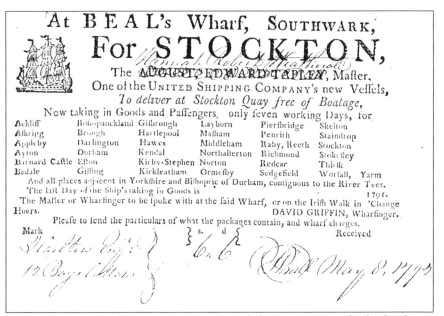

Advertising poster for water transport and the carrying trade, by kind permission of CRO(C) and the Lonsdale estates.

after the 1740s and the last one had reached the status of being known as Mr Robert Kidd. Secondly, with the success of the Brough turnpikes, investors with local connections, although living elsewhere, had the confidence to plan large scale projects. It is notable too, that not only had the commercial classes, like the Cleasbys, moved to London, but so had others like Dodd, a skilled craftsman, taking advantage perhaps, of the coach or carrier networks.

By 1851, the Mannex directory shows a changing situation. There were still the same number of inns but the transport pattern was shifting. The only regular coach service was the Royal Mail from the Swan Inn to Penrith. There were four regular carrier services, but with more frequent services. There were three weekly to Barnard Castle from Appleby, and Kirkby Stephen, (Hilton and Bell), two to Newcastle, from Appleby and Kirkby Stephen, (Robinson and Young), four weekly between Kendal, Penrith via Brough to Barnard Castle (Rudd) and one for each market day to Kirkby Stephen, Appleby and Barnard Castle, (Sowerby and Dent). By 1885, there were no coach services advertised and only Bell the grocer, ran a carrying service to Kirkby Stephen on a Monday and to Appleby on a Saturday. Heavy freight in the north east and the north western coalfields could, by then, use the new rail systems and avoid the road between Bowes and Brough.

The viability of Brough as a service centre on the turnpike is worth considering. An examination of the deeds for the Swan Inn from 1765 to 1829 can be used to throw some light on the situation. During this period, this was an important inn served by the Carlisle to London stage coach in 1790, and by a number of others by 1829. The parish records and directories show that this inn was occupied by long term tenants, first the Augnier family and later the Grindreds, suggesting that it was successful as a small family business. The deeds, in Kendal Record Office, however, illustrate the problems.

The inn is named in the will of Elizabeth Rudd, a widow, who left the freehold of it to her sister Ann Robinson, in 1765. It lay between the messuage of John Thornburr and that of John Lambert. Two years later the property was sold by the heirs of Mrs Robinson to Jonathan Ewbank of Borronthwaite. At the time of the sale, James Augnier, a farmer and innkeeper, was the occupier, and in 1769 he bought the freehold for £150.

In 1769, it was described as:

A messuage, a dwelling house with a brew house, a barn, two stables, one cart house and a garden lying on the backside thereof adjacent to Mr Thomas Lamb on the east and the house of James Augnier on the west.

(Later deeds mention an orchard, and the brewhouse was still there in 1829).

Three years later Augnier bought a field half an acre in size, called the Croft, from Robert Hardy, of Brough. Like the inn, this field was part of the Helbeck manor and held from the Carleton family. In 1777, finance was needed and Augnier took out a mortgage of £250 at four and a half per cent with James Elliot of Middleton, County Durham. Elliot's heir, John Walton Elliot, called in the mortgage five years later as none of the principal had been paid off. In 1784, Augnier took out another larger mortgage, for £450 at five percent from Catherine Hardy of Kendal. When he died in the following year, his property was left to his family, which included his daughter Elizabeth, who was married to John Marshall, an innkeeper of Greta Bridge. When the heirs of Catherine Hardy pressed for repayment, Marshall bought out the family interest and became the new owner, still with the £450 mortgage to pay off. But he too was unfortunate, and in 1798, when he was described as an innkeeper, dealer and chapman, he was declared bankrupt.

The economic situation was difficult at this time and there were no bidders when the receivers put the property up for sale. It eventually sold in a Barnard Castle auction in 1799. Not until 1812 was it in the hands of another Brough person: Christopher Grindred bought it first with a mortgage from John Lough of Kirkby Stephen, and then in 1815 this was transferred to one from George Thompson. By 1821 the mortgage was held by Thomas Mason and William Dawson although the Grindreds still ran the business, even after the death of Christopher in 1825.

The problems of finance at this period are only too apparent from this description. Although there was an increase in the number of investors from outside the parish as a result of the expansion of travel, private mortgages were generally short term, and often from elderly people whose heirs needed to release the money. In Brough there was too much competition from the large number of inns, and the profit margins cannot have been high enough to cope with the rising prices of the period. The ambition to own the business was soon lost in the realities and in the case of both the families mentioned, they became occupiers rather than owners.

CHAPTER 14

New Openings: Mines and Mills

TWO aspects of the economic activity associated with the Turnpike Age will be considered. These are the exploitation of minerals in the parish and on Stainmore and the water powered mills built along local streams.

Mines

Early nineteenth century directories emphasised the mineral wealth of Stainmore. This consisted mainly of coal and lead. The coal, found generally in small broken seams, was of the same period as that of the Durham field, but in much smaller quantities, and much more difficult to extract. It was the poorer quality of Carboniferous coal, suitable only for household use, except in one or two places where steam coal was found. The coal to the north, around Borrowdale, North Stainmore, was of lower quality. The lead veins, running through the Great Scar Limestone, were productive, but again, there was no great quantity. The limestones and gritstones of the uplands provided building material, ganister for furnaces and lime for the kilns, but these were expensive to transport, and as they were found in vast quantities elsewhere in the Pennines, there was no market for them apart from locally.

Earlier chapters have made brief mention of coal mining activities, dating back into the Medieval period. By the mid-1640s this had become, apparently very lucrative as Lady Anne Clifford, writing from London asked Sir John Lowther, (who seems to have been acting on her behalf), to be especially vigilant about coal mining on Stainmore.[209] When Lady Anne was in possession of her Westmorland estates, her account book shows that she had eight score and two loads of coal from her own pits on Stainmore, at 12d per load, "for firing my house at this Appleby Castle." This was in August 1673. In the same year, on 7 October she had 122 loads delivered, and on 24 October another 150 loads.[210]

Outside these accounts, evidence remains patchy except in archaeological remains, and there are no descriptions of the mining areas or of the miners. By the end of the eighteenth century, the parish registers give small hints of mining activities. When, in 1775, George Pearson was killed by accident in the coal work, he was working on Helbeck Fell. Other deaths,

Note 209: CRO(C), D Lons L/1/28.
Note 210: *Accounts of Lady Ann Clifford*, as quoted by Sir Martin Holdgate, op.cit., p158.

such as Simon Bullard a young man, in 1786 who was killed in a coal pit, and William Hodgson, a collier, in 1774, who perished in the snow, "coming from the coals" are not located. Then, although not a miner, John Blake, a "Scotch driver of cattle," suffered "an untimely death" on his way from the coal pit turnpike house on Stainmore.

Another source, the Quarter Sessions, illustrates an unexpected reference to coal, in a court case which had nothing to do with mining.[211] In 1730, Thomas Stable of Brough Sowerby had horses grazing in the fields of John Peacock. One horse had its throat cut and the blame fell on Elizabeth Summers, the widow who actually owned the field. Peacock had sub-let the grazing to Stable, at a rent of one shilling and three cartloads of coal yearly. The implication is that Stable had access to a good supply of local coal; the nearest was probably at Mousegill, (Barras), a half an hour's walk from Brough Sowerby. In nearby Winton, the Manor Rental Book at the beginning of the eighteenth century, records 35 loads of Boon Coals, "to be taken up at the pit."[212] This might have been from the same area or from the Redgate mine first mentioned in the Medieval period.

Jeffery's map, surveyed in the 1760s, and the large scale OS maps surveyed a century later, have some old pits marked where the present day landscape shows evidence of man-made disturbance. There are bell pits, adits and waste tips around Borrowdale and Dummah Crag, Hard Hills, Mouthlock to Crag Green, and to Tan Hill, to name but a few. There were some on Middle Fell and around Tarn House to the north of Helbeck. On the whole, the poorer quality coal found north of the main road, was in thin and broken seams. To the south the coal comparable in age with that in Durham, was unfortunately, not found in any quantity. Around Argill Beck, steam coal was still mined in 1946.

However, not all the old workings to be seen today are from coal mines, some are from lead mines, as at Augill and at Swindale Head, while others are quarry waste and lime diggings. In addition, there is documentary evidence of mining in the Westmorland census of 1787, (luckily the Stainmore copy survives), in directories, and in the censuses from 1841 onwards. The indications are that the mining industry was important locally, providing alternative employment for the rural population, and supplying a purely local market. It was never big enough to attract much outside labour, and it collapsed once the nearby north eastern coalfield started to move its coal by rail.

In the second half of the eighteenth century, there appears to have been a concerted effort to develop the minerals. The Earls of Thanet, successors

Note 211: CRO(K), WD/QR 1730.
Note 212: CRO(K) WD/Cat/9177, Manor Book of Survey, 23 Dec. 1702.

to the Clifford family, held most of the local mineral rights but the Carletons of Helbeck also had coal on their land. This was mainly used for their own enterprises, as will be shown later in this chapter. The Thanet leases for the exploitation of coal show a methodical approach to the development in the eighteenth and nineteenth centuries. A typical advertisement for an eighteenth century lease is:-

> "To be let by Proposal for a term of twenty one years and entered upon the first day of January next All the Coal Mines Collieries and Seams of Coal within the Lordship and Forest of Stainmore in the Manor of Brough and County of Westmorland as well those opened and discovered as those unopened and undiscovered and as well those in or under the Commons and waste Grounds as in and under any of the inclosed Grounds within the same Lordship and Forest." (sic)[213]

Later the conditions required the tenant to pay rent each half year, to employ twelve men daily in the workings, ensure the workings were supported to avoid collapse, and make good afterwards. He was not to encroach on any other diggings, nor to enter any price-raising arrangement without the Earl's agreement. All diggings were to be filled in after exploitation to prevent sheep or cattle from falling in. If the tenant failed to observe these and other conditions the agreement could be terminated at three months notice. The requirement to employ twelve men (this was in 1823) is interesting as it may have reflected the number of miners living locally.

In an earlier lease, in 1763, the Reverend Gilpin Gorst, (son of the steward of Appleby Castle) took a lease for coal in Stainmore, Mallerstang and Knock for twenty one years at a rent of twenty shillings per annum.[214] The wording suggests that mining was an established industry locally, for the workings were to be "according to the usuall Course and method of working Collieries..." (sic). Among the assets included were "...the House and Shop at Nether pitt," (sic) near Mouthlock. By this time, coal mining was well established in Lancashire, County Durham, Northumberland and on the Cumberland coast, especially at Whitehaven. Techniques and practices were well known, and Gorst was either to follow what was done in those places, or such practices as were already established in Westmorland.

Attached to this lease was another agreement limiting Gorst to £100 profit per year, any excess to go to the Earl of Thanet. It also stated that the Reverend Gorst could have the living of either Kirkby Thore parish or of Long Marton when either became vacant. (He got both eventually). He

---

Note 213: CRO(K), WD Hoth, Box 34.
Note 214: CRO(K), WD Hoth, Box 25.

Coal miners at Borrowdale Pit, North Stainmore. Photograph by kind permission of John Walton.

was occasionally associated with another man, Lancelot Harrison, who also had a number of interests in both Yorkshire and Westmorland.

Before the twenty one years were up, the colliery rights on Stainmore were leased in August, 1777, to Lancelot Harrison, gentleman, of County Durham.[215] His rent, for the Nether Pit House site, was much higher; £30 per year for six years, and thereafter £40 per year. His selling price for the coal was limited to four pence per load of six pecks, "got from the south side of the Kirkby Stephen turnpike... and coal from the north side at seven pence per load," suggesting that there was a difference in quality. One matter still unresolved is the size and weight of a load of coal. Pringle, the Board of Agriculture inspector, only gives dimensions of carts and not capacity.[216] In 1780, another Westmorland record suggests that locally used carts could carry 40 stones, (five hundredweight), although some could carry up to 48 stones.[217]

Outside investors became interested and the leases were renewed every few years as different Swaledale men joined the group, and in 1823, one from Liverpool. By 1824, the rental was £420 yearly. This was the

Note 215: CRO(K) WD Hoth Box 25; Lead & Collieries, 1763-1845.
Note 216: Pringle, op.cit. p307 states that a Westmorland farm cart was commonly 52 inches long, 36 broad and fourteen and a half deep, containing less than sixteen cubic feet, which may give an indication, assuming Brough colliers used similar carts.
Note 217: A peck was a measure of capacity, the fourth part of a bushel or two gallons but could also be an indeterminate amount.

highpoint in the venture. Twenty years later, it was £340 yearly, and taken by two men with local connections, William Cleasby and Henry Hopes of Stainmore, along with Simon Harker from Richmond. Thus, over 80 years the rents for coal mining had gone up from £1 per year to over £400, and then had fallen slightly.

Those who leased the mines made their own arrangements with the miners and few records have survived. The Yosgill documents show that Carleton was working both mines and the mill. In 1788 he paid James Beckwith £15 15s. for sinking a new shaft. Another payment of £10 to an unnamed worker was for "the driving at the Howle pit - 25 fathoms, and to mending the shaft." John Rudd was paid 5s. for carriage of wood, perhaps pit props. In 1789 Isaac Topping sent 64 loads to Hillbeck from William Bland's workings at Winber (sic), and that same year there were deliveries from Loadman's colliery (seven loads), from Blue Grass (one load), from an unnamed source, 24 loads and one from Hungriggs worth £24. The prices varied from a farthing to over two shillings a load, but as there is no indication of load size, there can be no comparison.[218]

In the 1787 census, miners made up one tenth of the male inhabitants of Stainmore. Fourteen of the householders were full time miners, others were part-time farmers or sons of miners. The ones that can be traced lived near to Dummah, Windmore End, Hither Pit and High Ewbank. Two, John Oyston and John Moor, were described as poor, and the latter, who was also described as old, died in a blizzard in 1794. There were also two household heads who were coal carriers.[219] At the time of the 1829 directory, Stainmore was still noted for its collieries. There was Robert Buckle, a colliery owner, and at Mousegill Row (which seems to have included all Stainmore from south of the turnpike to Tan Hill), there was a consortium of five miners working at Low Pits and Light Trees colliery, under the supervision of John Gibson. By 1851, no colliers were listed in the directory and the remaining

Note 218: CRO(C), D/Lons/L, 10/3-10, Box 1052, D/Lons/L 12/3-10. D/Lons/L12/310/4, Coal: Some records in the Yosgill documents link some miners with workings. In July, 1789, Isaac Topping sent 64 loads to Hillbeck, costing 10s.8d, at two pence per load, from William Bland's workings at Winber (probably Windmore). Topping was very literate and had a good hand. In September that year William Beckwith, William Varley (possibly *Varty*), Jon Birkbeck, John Brunskill and Robert Simpson sent seven loads at a total cost of 15s.10d from Loadman's colliery. More coal was sent, by John Scott. James Beckwith sent coal from Bluegrass Colliery in October. An undated fragment (possibly from 1790), shows John Thompson delivering 24 loads of coal to Yosgill at 10d per load, 18 at 7d, and two at ½d per load. In April, 1790, three loads, costing 2s.6d, were delivered by someone called Elwood, three by Bent at 7d, three by Matthew Gill for 2s.6d, and six by Thomas Catteral for 5s. In 1789 Catterall had brought coal from Hungriggs for £24. Loadman's colliery may have been on Stainmore. Bluegrass was on the old road from Brough to Bowes.
Note 219: Westmorland Census, 1787.

inhabitants of Mousegill were either farmers or inn keepers.

This highlights the problems of relying on directories as the census for the same year tells a different story, as it lists a number of miners living on Stainmore and in Brough, who would be within walking distance of local mines or some had weekly lodgings near the mine.[220] In the 1851 census, there were 20 heads of households in Brough, who were coal miners, plus 26 other members of the households, (aged between eleven years and 65 years of age), and eight unspecified types of miner. The latter were in Helbeck and could have been working in either lead or coal. Over the previous 60 years, more than 90 individuals in Brough parish had been named as miners in various documents. For some it had been a secondary occupation, alongside farming, but for others as for example, the Beckwith family, it may have been a long term employment for they had developed the expertise to drive shafts into the hillsides as well as to mine coal and they had developed a coal carrying business (see Appendix VIII).

In the latter part of the nineteenth century, the mines were owned by the Walton family, who had interests in both lead and coal mines over a large area of northern England, stretching from Alston to Stanhope, as well as businesses in Middlesborough and Darlington. They may have had land in Helbeck from at least the 1820s, and in the 1841 census, Jacob Walton had a farm on Stainmore. He originally came from Alston. The family were connected with the Augill smelter which will be discussed in the next section. The family also owned the Borrowdale coal mine on Stainmore which operated into the twentieth century.

There is a description of conditions at the mine in March 1912, because, with the exception of Borrowdale, all the country's miners were on strike, and it was the only pit in England working. Newspaper reporters arrived and together, their accounts give a contemporary impression of the workings. It was a "diminutive affair," "a quaint little pit head, - nearly 2,000 feet up on the Stainmore Fells." (In fact it lies around 1,550 feet). The reports stated that it employed only about a dozen men, "who are non-union and unmoved by the general stoppage, - (they) are now the only miners at work." The working conditions were difficult, but this was a drift mine, near the surface, with, seemingly, no problems of gas. The seams were eighteen inches thick and the workings cramped at two feet six inches high, with a low roof.

On the day when one reporter visited, there were eight miners at the face, each using only one two inch high candle. The heavy waste material and the coal were moved along rails in horse-drawn tubs, led by two men. The excavated material now forms the uneven ground around the entrance,

Note 220: CRO(K) WD Hoth. Box 25.

which can still be seen. Between four and six tons of coal were mined each day, which was enough to supply the households of Brough and Stainmore.

The mine had suffered only one serious and unexpected flooding during the period of the Walton's ownership and this had been in 1870. While inspecting the workings, the owner, Mr Thomas Walton, and a miner, Michael Steel, had been trapped by a sudden flood. A seventeen-year-old boy ahead of them managed to wade out although the water was up to his chin. He was sent home to change and on his way back to the mine, he discovered the cause of the flood. A stream had changed its course and was flowing into the mine through old workings. The miners were able to dam this, and when the water subsided, the other two were rescued, perched in a partly excavated face, having been there for 36 hours. The lad, William Deighton, later became the mine manager and died in 1924. According to his obituary, he was up at 4am everyday and walked the three miles or so to the mine. In the course of his 50 years of work, the writer estimated that he must have walked over 50,000 miles.[221]

Lead Mining

In the 1851 census, there were six lead miners listed, but no-one engaged in smelting. Ten years earlier, the 1841 census, although difficult to read because of the fading ink, had recorded at least six times that number. Did this represent the beginning or the ending of an industry?

The Earls of Thanet and their predecessors had long exploited lead on their estates, and this continued well into the nineteenth century, when such little lead ore as might remain was undercut by cheaper imports. Brough, unlike the Yorkshire Dales and Alston, was not a major lead-working area, but seems to have been reasonably productive. The remains of a smelter can be seen at Augill, on Stainmore. Relatively little evidence for the period has been found so far. The 1829 directory mentioned the lead vein at Augill, and as a foot note, stated that at Swindale Head a vein of lead ore had just been discovered that, "is said to be the richest at present worked in Northern England."[222] In 1829, it gave employment for a group of five miners, (Gill, Robinson, Rogerson, Hutton, and Capstick). Later the North Stainmore Mining company is mentioned with an agent Philip Robinson and a mining clerk, John Horsley, in Brough and, the 1851 directory continues, "There is a prolific lead mine and smelt mill, erected in 1843, in a secluded and romantic vale. Robinson is the managing partner for this

---

Note 221: The Walton family scrap-book of newspaper cuttings. Also details from John Walton for which I am very grateful.
Note 222: Parson and White, *History, Directory and gazetteer of Cumberland and Westmorland*, Leeds (1829) fac. (1976), p535.

concern, the machinery being exceedingly complete."

Lead had been mentioned briefly in earlier documents, although in a negative sense in the Steward's accounts of the fifteenth century where a mine was said to have been unworked. The 1780s seem to have been the time for a renewal of interest, for then a number of indentures were issued by the Thanet estate. Gilpin Gorst and Lancelot Harrison (who were also concerned with coal on Stainmore) were to be allowed to search for lead on an area 6,000 yards long by 300 yards broad, on Stephen Cleasby's land where, it was stated, a smelt mill already existed.[223] Again in 1780, Gorst, Harrison and a third adventurer, Collingwood, took a lease on all "groves, mines, rakes..." on East Stainmore. By this time, Gorst had been involved with mining for at least seventeen years.

Also in 1780, six gentlemen, (four of whom: Francis Richardson, Henry Alderson, George Emerson and Anthony Harker, lived in Brough) took the lease at Swindale Beck, at Peaks Moss, to search for ore in an area 1,000 yards long and 600 yards wide. The rent was to be one seventh part of the treated ore. This group may have been the finders of the rich vein mentioned in the 1829 directory.

The development of other lead mining regions in Teesdale and Alston encouraged investors near Brough and a number of new leases were issued, to Richardson again, for example, for working the land around Palliard and to John Bland for 1,200 yards around Augill.[224] Most activity seems to have been around North Stainmore. However, there is a later reference, in 1826, to a lead vein in Ewbank Park extending from the Park wall for 1,200 yards, which a consortium of five local men under James Moor leased.[225]

Today the Augill smelt mill is a scheduled monument.[226] The mill may be on the site of an older one but the present building is the one mentioned in the 1851 directory as being constructed in 1843, by the North Stainmore Mining Company to process the lead found up the valley. Located on the east bank of the Augill Beck, it was converted, about 1859/60 to roast iron nodules found in the local mines. By 1894 it had ceased to operate.

The smelt mill was built of stone, with its east side built into the hillside and powered by a water wheel, fed from a leat east of the Augill Beck and by a reservoir from above. The ore was mixed with fuel, (peat and coal), on open hearths and the water wheel powered the bellows to fire the

---

Note 223: CRO(C) D/Lons L12/3/10/10). This may have been Augill , but there was a smelt mill quarry near Slapestones marked on a later OS map.
Note 224: CRO(K) WD Hoth Box 25.
Note 225: CRO(K),WD/Hoth Box 30. James Moor and Thomas Jefferson, both of Kirkby Stephen, Parker Crosby of Barnard Castle and Christopher Holliday and Christopher Kearton, both of Stainmore. The workings can be seen near to New Hall.
Note 226: Schedule of Ancient monuments: AA 13762/1, No. 32897 on 9.3.2001.

hearths. There were also slag hearths for a second smelting. The Augill smelter has been preserved because although lead smelters of its type are not rare, this one is unusual because of its conversion to iron smelting which required a higher temperature. But even more important is the fact that the flue and chimney, which were led out to a higher site, broke through a Roman signal station above the Stainmore Gap.

Stainmore also provided other raw materials: ganister from near Tan Hill, road and wall building material, wherever necessary and lime. Lime kilns were very common and are marked in many places; one of the largest groups is near Borrowdale. Few lime burners are listed because often the kilns were erected, by farmers and builders for specific jobs and then abandoned.

The Helbeck lime kilns are an exception. They appear to have been part of John Carleton's enterprise.[227] There was plenty of good quality limestone around Helbeck and the coal for the kilns could also be found locally. One cart of coal was needed to two carts of limestone. Lime was required by builders as well as farmers. The weekly accounts for part of 1784, show that the lime was being bought by a variety of people in the neighbourhood, from Crag House on Stainmore to Musgrave, Bankend and Walk Mill (Haver Gill) on the west. Musgrave, Warcop and Sandford were frequently mentioned along with Brough and Brough Sowerby.

This particular set of accounts start on 1st May, when 209½ bushels were sold. Weekly sales of around 175 bushels continued until June when there was a marked increase reaching 434 bushels for the week of 21 June. By the second week in July the total had dropped to 139 bushels. This pattern suggests that much of the lime was used for the fields, but Pringle, the Board of Agriculture observer, wrote a few years later, that the application of lime had not become general in Westmorland. He reckoned that to improve the grass 75 to 480 Winchester bushels per acre (that is a minimum of 25 Westmorland bushels) were needed. Very few customers of the Helbeck Kiln were buying more than 20 bushels at a time, and although some were doing this two or three times during the season, this was nowhere near enough for Pringle's recommendation. He reckoned that the cost at the kiln was between three and four pence a bushel.

Most people were buying four or five bushels, and this included women like Mary Toppin and Sarah Davison. Mr Hudson a Brough attorney and the miller at Helbeck, each had one peck. It looks as if the kiln was supplying the local householders as lime was much used for lime washing buildings. Jonathan Alderson of Sowerby (chapter 12) took delivery of 24 bushels in June and may have been selling them on, and there may have

Note 227: CRO(C) D Lons/L/12/3/12/7.

been other carriers buying at the kiln, like Thomas Atkinson of Hogarth.

The local mines and quarries were small and dispersed, but until the middle of the nineteenth century, they served the local market, while giving alternative employment in an area of marginal farming, which was facing competition from other areas in England. The production of lime and building material continued throughout the century. However, the area could not match the quality, the quantity, or the price of Durham coal, or of imported lead, once transport costs had been lowered by the building of the railway network throughout north eastern England. The next section will examine another attempt to introduce new industry into the area: a water-powered cotton mill.

Yosgill Mill: an experiment in cotton spinning

In the eighteenth century cotton spinning and weaving became a "get rich quick" industry in, mostly, northern England, Wales and Scotland, where fast-flowing streams provided power. The technology of the established woollen and linen industries had been adapted to cotton and partly mechanised, and, by 1760, cotton was a very big industry. The Eden Valley did not want to miss this development, and, downstream, a flourishing and long-lasting cotton industry developed at and around Carlisle, as in Lancashire and elsewhere.

A short-lived cotton spinning and weaving works was established at Yosgill, slightly west and north of Market Brough, owned by John Metcalfe Carleton of Hillbeck (or Helbeck) Hall, who had a curious reputation.[228] The records found for Yosgill date from 1784 to 1792, and give only an incomplete picture. Its life was brief, as was a comparable enterprise at Kirkby Stephen, just north of the church, set up about 1790 by Manchester businessmen.[229] In Brough also Mr John Wilson had established a dye-house, an indigo mill and corn mill. A directory reference of 1790, said: "Here is a considerable dye-house, situated about two hundred yards below the bridge, belonging to Mr John Wilson... he has also erected a huge corn mill and an indigo mill on the same river."[230] Little is known about John Wilson except that by the late eighteenth century, he had inherited a number of houses along the main street in Market Brough, from his father in law, Thomas Hodgson, the late vicar. Wilson with his family along with that of his brother-in-law emigrated to Ohio, USA, in 1796, shortly after the

---

Note 228: Carleton was apparently a spendthrift who went bankrupt in 1792. Sharpe, J., *John Metcalfe Carleton, Georgian Rake of the Eden Valley* (undated).
Note 229: CRO (K) WCC OL, 743.
Note 230: *The Universal British Directory*, 1790.
Note 231: CRO(K) WDX 341/4.

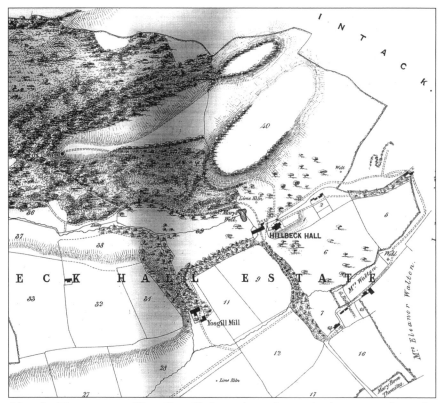

Map 9: The cotton mill at Yosgill from the sale particulars map, from the Heelis collection CRO(K).

failure of Yosgill.[231]

There had been dyeing of some kind earlier in the eighteenth century, as Moses Cockfield was named as such in one of his Quarter Sessions appearances in 1743, and the parish registers list two others: Anthony Tate and Edward Lamb, in 1743 and 1760 respectively. The dyehouse and indigo mill continued after Wilson had left and were still working in 1841. There are some vague references to another, later, attempt to establish a cotton industry in Brough but, so far, nothing definite is known. Trades mentioned in the parish register include weavers and dyers, who may well have been self-employed.

Processes, machinery, equipment and the product

Yosgill cotton mill was on the hillside, by a stream flowing from the fells. It drew its water power, probably via a dedicated mill race, from a dam further up the hill. It presumably resembled local water-powered corn mills, with a mill wheel transmitting the drive to various floors. The raw cotton, mostly from St Domingo and Brazil, was imported into Liverpool, with brokers there or at Manchester buying for Yosgill. Coasting vessels transported it to Lancaster, or possibly Milnthorpe, with road carriers bringing it, through either Sedbergh or Kendal, to Brough. All this would be slow and costly, putting the company at a disadvantage to the Lancashire spinners who got their raw material from Liverpool quickly, and the important rival cotton industry sites around Carlisle and in Scotland with their own ports.

Initially Yosgill was a spinning mill, and it dealt with the first stages of preparing cotton yarn. Briefly, the raw cotton mass was first opened in carding machines, then converted into rovings and then, by drawing and spinning, made into the yarn, known as 'twist'. This was sold on to merchants in Glasgow and in Lancashire. The quality initially seems to have been low, possibly intended for coarse knitted ware or cheap cloth, perhaps fustian. The Glasgow merchant frequently commented that the yarn was difficult to sell because of its poor quality.[232]

The mill had several floors, with separate processes on each level. On the ground floor the heavy bales of raw cotton were 'opened' and fed into carding machines (or 'cards'). These were basically multiple large diameter rollers, fitted with large spikes set in leather ('card clothing'), which rotated at high speed and tore the bundles of cotton apart, thus freeing the individual fibres. After this crude opening 'ropes' of the fibres were taken off (or 'doffed') as 'rovings' on to roving machines which started the process of applying a 'twist', which strengthened the roving, to enable it to pass through the later processes. This work was done by men, women and boys.

On the next floor above, further roving would be done, giving more twist (for strength) and drawing out the roving into something more recognisable as thread or yarn, and lengthening the roving considerably. 'Doffers', probably young children, would take the roving off one machine and pass it to the next roving machine, for further processing. When roving was complete the material would be further twisted and spun, and the yarn drawn out until the process was complete, with the spinning being done on large multiple machines.

Some anonymous modern drawings of the site suggest the internal building dimensions as 60 feet in length, and 72 feet externally, but about 26 feet in width internally, and externally about 30 feet.[233] Each of the four floors

Note 232: CRO(C), D/LONS L12/3/10/9, Box 1052. As late as July 1791 the merchant, Christie Smith & Co, of Glasgow, complained about the poor quality, saying he had to reduce the price in order to sell it.

Note 233: CRO(C), D/LONS/L/Carleton of Hillbeck/10/13. The authorship of these excellent drawings is unknown. They are dated 1967, modified in 1988, and were found in the Lonsdale file.

was about nine feet high. There was a fireplace in each room. The water wheel was at the west end, and a staircase at the east end gave access to all floors. Given other data available the draughtsman calculated there were six cards and seven roving or 'tomming' engines, on the ground floor.[234] The first floor contained six roving engines and the two upper floors had spinning machines with over 1,100 spindles.

The mill water wheel probably transmitted power by vertical wooden shafts to each level, through crude bevel gearing, then to horizontal shafts with belt drives to individual machines. An undated drawing shows a proposed water wheel of 26 feet diameter, driving, via a rocker arm or 'Bob', to a drive shaft, eight feet in diameter, and then to a nine inch bore pump, probably for the water supply.[235] A detailed specification which may be for the same wheel and equipment, or for a modified design, gave a total cost for the project of £127 8*s*. 10*d*.[236] Around 1788, proposals for an enlarged mill included:

> "In each room to have Seven Drums and Each Drum to Carry one Hundred and twelve Spindles, (therefore) in One Room will be Seven Hundred and Eighty four Spindles... (and) including those in the Smithy, the whole will amount to 2,016 spindles."[237]

Women, assisted by children, usually did the roving, drawing and spinning, and the multiple spinning machines meant that one woman could produce a great deal of yarn. Carding and opening was very heavy labour, needing men, as well as women and children.

The machinery specification above includes a reference to the smithy, raising the question of mill maintenance and the type of engineering facilities available in Brough. There were several local blacksmiths, but their expertise would be mainly in farriery and agricultural equipment. Who would make cast and wrought iron or brass components which had to be extremely accurate? The textile machines of the period, although they were made mostly of timber, included metal components requiring precision work. At least two blacksmiths are named in the accounts; William

---

Note 234: 'Tomming'; the meaning of this word is unknown. Possibly it meant a device for stripping cotton from the cards.

Note 235: CRO(C), D/LONS/L/Carleton of Hillbeck/10/13, Box 1052. The drawing appears to be original.

Note 236: Ibid.

Note 237: It continues, 'Allowing one Pair of Cards one Roving Engine And one Drawing Engine to 336 Spindles in 2 Rooms where 14 Drums are going and 1568 Spindles Will take four Fine Cards and 5 tomming. Ditto.' It concludes that 'By a fair Calculation of Allowing 448 Spindles in the Smithy which at present will on the whole Amount to 2016 which will keep 6 Fine Cards And 7 tomming. Ditto Constantly with 6 Roving Engines and 4 Drawing Ditto.

Metcalfe, and Thomas Catteral(l). The latter is a puzzle. In 1790 he was described as the factory blacksmith, and in another as the spinner. Certainly, one Thomas Catteral, was doing maintenance work for the factory, as well as bringing in coal and other jobs.

In Lancashire, where there was a high concentration of textile factories, specialised engineering firms and machine tool makers developed to serve the industry, and large mills there employed their own mechanics. Brough was too remote to benefit easily from these services, but the drawings for the Yosgill water wheel suggest that there was someone, perhaps from Barnard Castle where there were several mills, with local knowledge who was a skilled draughtsman, and mathematician.

Weaving had started at the mill around 1790, although some may have been done earlier under contract. The Brough parish registers referred to Roger Lee, as a "factory weaver, Yose Gill" in 1795 and 1796, and to Charles Jackson, a weaver at the "Thread Mill" in 1801 even though the factory was then closed. Weaving had still not been effectively mechanised and handlooms adapted from wool weaving were used, with weavers tending to work in houses rather than in factory sheds. There is a contract, dated 1794, involving Jonathon Tod and Richard Devis for "house carpentry and joinery" at Yosgill Factory which may have been for the building of weavers' houses.[238] This, however, was after Carleton's bankruptcy, and remains a mystery, not that Carleton allowed bankruptcy to stop his ventures.

There are no clear cut descriptions of the products but an account book has references to, "Calicoes sent to Mr Thomas Burrow, Lancashire," and to "weft cotton and warp cotton," implying weaving. In 1791 one reference[239] mentioned, "93 peices (sic) Calico at 6*s*. 9*d*." totalling £3 7*s*. 9*d*.[240] William Raine, a contractor, in Barnard Castle, submitted accounts, probably in 1791, and 1792, mentioning loom parts (slays), pickers[241] and "loom altering."

The length of a piece of cloth was about 28 yards. Most looms still usually wove a cloth 27 inches wide, although larger looms were in existence. The mill seems to have been weaving calico, a low grade material, but requiring finer threads than the original coarse ones which the Glasgow agent had found so hard to sell in the early days of the mill.

It is difficult to make precise statements about the output, as the accounts are sporadic. What can one make of such figures as those for the sale of

Note 238: CRO(C), D/LONS L12/3/10/16, Box 1052.
Note 239: CRO(C), D LONS L12/3/10/11, Box 1052.
Note 240: (possibly April, 1793) following Carleton's bankruptcy.
Note 241: CRO(C), D/LONS/L, 12/3/10/11, Box 1052.

yarn in 1787, in Glasgow, one of 500 pounds weight and another of 2,540 pounds? The first load cost £1 10s. and the second £8 1s. 4d. to transport. In 1791 the Glasgow merchant disposed of 1020 pounds of twist, reducing the price for 90 pounds of exceptionally low quality yarn to 1s. 4d. per pound weight.[242]

In July 1790, the accounts show that 100 pieces of calico (2,827 yards in all) were sent to London, and, in May 1792, 144 pieces of calico were sold for £48 12s. 0d. (six shillings and nine pence per piece), with William Raine, of Barnard Castle, acting as the selling agent.[243]

There were references in Raines' accounts to dyeing, implying a widening of production to include wet finishing. This may have been done at the mill, but more likely at the dye works, just downstream from the High Mill. The Parish register mentions dyers, but little is known of their work.

Employment, Wages and Conditions
The mill may have employed few people directly, preferring to contract with individual men to carry out certain processes, with these men employing their families or other people to do some of the work. There were some workers with local surnames, like the Allisons, and Crumptons (sic), while others came from Lancashire and Scotland. In April 1790 for example, two boys and two girls in one family, from Scotland, arrived, the girls to work in drawing, and roving, and the two boys in carding. But these outsiders could be highly mobile. In December 1789, a number of adult workers and their children left to work in Caton (near Lancaster) where they could earn more money, and where there was more job security, or where the wages were paid more regularly.[244]

In March 1790, Thomas Catteral, the factory blacksmith (already mentioned) demanded half his wages weekly in cash "or he will go." Catteral's position was unclear. In the April, when described as the head spinner, he was ill, so that the spinning process was falling behind and he blamed his illness on the spinning. He and his wife did leave, but left their children behind. They went to Mosley in Lancashire, but returned some weeks later. In May 1790 Catteral and all his family left, it appears finally.

The size of the workforce varied. In September and October 1784,[245] for example, seventeen, mostly adults, were paid in one week, thirteen the next, and nineteen in the third. By 1789, there were probably 30 children at the mill, listed under adults' names, so they may have been family members or

Note 242: CRO(C), D/LONS L12/3/10/9, Box 1052.
Note 243: CRO(C), D LONS/L/Carleton/10/1A, (large memorandum book).
Note 244: CRO(C), D/LONS/L/9/29.
Note 245: CRO(C), D/LONS/L/12, Box 1052.

possibly even orphans or paupers. Their ages ranged from six to seventeen. It seems that, by 1790, the mill was doing well and employing larger numbers than previously. Details of the children and known workers are given in Appendix VII. Some pay sheets for 1791 and 1792 suggest there were between 60 and 75 workers, including children. There were also several casual workers doing odd jobs. Not all would be full time workers; some only put in 2½ days per week. To local people, the mill had yet to prove itself as a full time regular employer. To be on the safe side, they continued with the more traditional work, in farm or road work: rather than learn new skills they preferred to stick to casual labour at the mill.

Training was certainly needed for newcomers, as shown in a memorandum from May, 1792:[246]

> "An Agreement made by and between John Carleton Esquire and Roger Ley, May 1st 1792 Roger to Instruct William Sayers in the Trade of a Weaver of Calicoes and he the above Roger Ley to have 2/6 per (piece?) allowed by John Carleton Esquire for every (one) done by the said William Sayers in a workmanlike manner and delivered by the said Roger Ley to John Carleton."

This was not an apprenticeship indenture, and probably referred only to training an adult worker. As in the Lancashire mills, training was by learning on the job; "sitting alongside Nellie."

The 1784 data suggest that, in the opening and spinning processes, the pay rates for the spinning masters were two shillings a day, but, it was traditional for them to pay their child helpers out of their own earnings, which they may have done here. While other men received up to one shilling and four pence per day, ordinary spinners were paid between 3½d. and 6½d. per day. The lowest paid man was Thomas Gill, receiving 2½ per day. Women and children were paid far less, some only two pence per day, and again may not have worked full time. The rates in weaving were similar. Roger Lee (or Ley) received 1s. 9d. per day, while "Charles" (possibly Charles Jackson) was paid two shillings per day. The wage bill for the week ending 22 January 1791, for 69 people, amounted to £9 13s. 5½d. The highest payment, sixteen shillings, was to John Graham for six days. Thomas Allison, received ten shillings for six days. That week most people worked at least 4½ days, and some six days, and possibly a night shift that week.

The working week was six days, but this would vary with trade and, sometimes, the water supply. Carleton seems not to have paid his water bills on time, and the water owner threatened to cut it off, and then there were occasional water shortages due to either freezing or drought. Payment

---

Note 246: CRO(C), D/LONS/L12, Box 1052.

of wages became erratic. In January, 1790, the manager wrote to Carleton advising him that the workers had not been paid for six weeks and were proposing "to take their children away" as they could not procure bread. One possible reason for their going may have been short working during a prolonged dry period in the spring, with reduced water for power. Certainly in April the manager reported to Carleton that there was a water shortage, allowing only half-time working. There was also a shortage of rovers (women).

Work was erratic, with, it seems, limited full time working. From 18 December 1788, into February 1789, the mill was closed for a number of consecutive weekdays; even when open, half of the days were on short time.[247] It may have been a hard winter, or it may have been due to problems with supplies of raw cotton.

The working time for a day would be limited by light, but a full working day could be twelve hours or longer. The mill constantly had to buy candles, to keep production going in the limited daylight of mid-winter. One fragment of paper (undated but possibly after 1790) carries a calculation that one candle (at twelve to the pound weight) could burn for four hours.[248] Fourteen burning constantly could burn for twelve hours, and for night work, three candles would be adequate for reeling and twisting. The costs of a night shift, usually twelve hours long, needed to be closely monitored, but when the trade required an increased output, women, as well as men, would work these shifts.

Coal Usage

Coal was obtained locally, possibly for space heating in the mill or in Helbeck Hall. Some was sold to the workers, for in August 1789, Thomas Catteral(l) was charged 2s. 6d. for three loads of coal, as were others. There was no reference to steam power. On 1st July 1788, Isaac Topping[249] invoiced for 64 loads of coal from 'Blands at Winber[250] Colliery,' at two pence per load, total ten shillings and eight pence. In October 1789 James Beckwith[251] supplied 50 loads of coal from Bluegrass Colliery at seven pence per load.

Nothing has been found referring to humidification in the spinning sections, but it was often used to strengthen the yarn for spinning.

Note 247: CRO(C), D/LONS/L/Carleton of Hillbeck/10/10.

Note 248: CRO(C), D/LONS/L12/3/19/14, Box 1025.

Note 249: CRO(C), D/LONS/L12/3/10/16. See reference to Isaac Topping and James Beckwith in the section on mining.

Note 250: More commonly 'Windmore'.

Note 251: CRO(C), D/LONS/L 12/3-12.

Humidification was achieved by maintaining a high temperature to heat vats of water. If this was done it would warm the mill, possibly excessively, and may have harmed the workers' health. Nothing has been found to suggest other illnesses linked to cotton dust, such as byssinosis (a lung condition), but the processes were probably too slow at this stage. Cotton mill workers tended to be susceptible to respiratory illnesses, partly because of humidification, not then controlled by legislation. There are references in the archives to workers being ill, but nothing indicates possible causes. Some uncertain references seem to suggest the 'Doctor' was brought in to treat workers, but these are questionable, as the 'Doctor' may have been a job for some workers. 'Doctor' was also the term for a particular machine part, often a blade designed to sweep over a machine to clean it.

It seems that the mill owned at least four cottages which it let out at 7d a week to its workers. There are references to the sale of boots and shoes. This was a necessary provision for a workforce unable to get to shops because of the long working hours, but no reference has been found to the truck shops found in the Lancashire and other mills which supplied food at inflated prices, by docking the wages of the workers.

Later problems

Carleton's enterprise was an over confident attempt to join the new wave of industrialists of the late eighteenth century. Based on new inventions in the spinning processes, many mills were set up in Lancashire and Derbyshire, but they also faced financial problems. Yosgill was chosen as a site because it was on Carleton's estate. The only thing in its favour was the water power, which was cheap to run but expensive to maintain. Even with a mill leat and a dam, there would always be problems controlling the water supply in drought or frost.

Transport costs for the raw material and the finished product were high, because there were no nearby markets or ports. The labour supply had to be trained or brought from elsewhere, and the factory system, whereby regular shifts and controlled hours were worked, was an alien concept for a rural population. Carleton does not seem to have had the knowledge for directing such an enterprise, and he needed to find highly trained supervisors and managers at a time when the whole cotton industry was in its infancy and facing continual change. He probably did not invest enough to keep his plant up to date and with his own apparent financial incompetence, the Yosgill enterprise foundered.

Around 1790 Carleton appears to have had difficulty in paying bills. Various suppliers were demanding overdue money. In January, these included a spindle supplier at Greta Bridge, near Barnard Castle, the contractors Barnfather & Hodge, Thomas Bowes for the Brough poor rate, and a chandler at Barnard Castle who emphasised that he was demanding, not asking, for his money. The situation got worse: in February John Armstrong was owed £1 11*s*., and Mr Strickland, a Kendal supplier was owed an unspecified amount. In the March a Kirkbride supplier demanded £8 18*s*. and in May, a local carrier, George Robinson put in his claim. Worse still, in March 1791, the water supplier stated that, unless paid, he would cut off the water supply. More cheerfully, the quality of yarn had apparently improved and sales at Glasgow were better.[252] Despite all these claims, Carleton does not seem to have understood the problems. He liked spending money in London and at Helbeck Hall, and was keen on employing gardeners, as well as ensuring his horses were well looked after and housed. More was written about a new foal and its accommodation and the death of a favourite horse than about the workers.

But to set this failure in context, it is important to remember that at the time (1770-90) the cotton industry of Northern England and in Scotland, was still developing, and much of it depended on hand power, water power, and some (literally) horse power. Steam power took a long time to have any significant impact and water power remained dominant for many decades, even in spinning; power-driven looms were not really viable until well into the next century. In other words, Yosgill mill was typical of most of those in its industry throughout the north of England. Vastly bigger steam-powered mills were developing in Lancashire and elsewhere, but the enterprise at Brough is likely to have been nearer the norm, both in its size and in its transience.

The mill apparently ceased to operate in 1792 and that seems to have been the end of the organised cotton industry in Brough. The nearly contemporary attempt at Kirkby Stephen was even less successful.[253] It started about 1790, and lasted barely three years, despite several later attempts to resuscitate it. Various operators involved went bankrupt and eventually its buildings were bought, about 1812, for use as the Kirkby Stephen Union workhouse.

Corn and other Mills

Since the records began there had always been a corn mill in Brough, using a water wheel. The earliest was in Church Brough, but as the community grew, others developed, in Helbeck, in Market Brough, in Brough Sowerby and one on Stainmore. All these were water powered.

The mills were needed to grind cereals to produce not only flour but oatmeal, malt and animal food. An important point, made by M. Davies-

Note 252: CRO(C), D/LONS/L/9/29.
Note 253: CRO(K), WCC/OL 743.

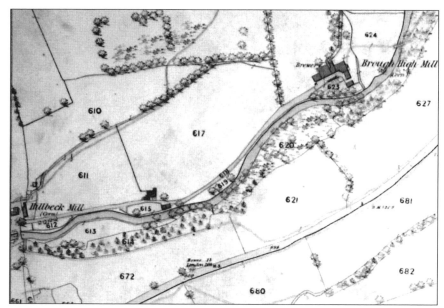

Map 10: Two mills to the north of Market Brough - High Mill and Helbeck Mill from the OS map, December 1860, by kind permission of Mr Chris Dent.

Shiel in his study of Cumbrian mills, is that meal and flour, ground from local cereals did not keep for more than a fortnight.[254] It was therefore necessary for millers to produce small quantities frequently and it was better to have a number of small mills, one for each village, rather than one large one for an area. The early mills were simple wooden or stone buildings with thatched roofs beside a stream, with a pit for the wheel. Swindale Beck was the main power source for the Brough mills. High Mill, on the north side of Brough, with Helbeck Mill downstream and Low Mill in Church Brough all made use of the same erratic but generally fast flowing stream as it fell from the Pennines to the Eden valley, with its uneven bed providing falls which could be made into weirs. Leats were built to regulate the water to both High and Low Mill, and the first edition OS map shows a pond below the latter.

The mill stones were from locally obtained millstone grit. In the nineteenth century, a mill with one wheel normally worked three pairs of stones, but by the end of the century, the import of large quantities of hard wheat from Canada and other parts of the world, altered the situation. The grit millstones could not cope and those of tougher rock had to be imported. In addition, it was becoming cheaper to mill at the ports or at the railheads serving the main centres of consumption, like the industrial towns. As the

Note 254: M. Davies-Shiel, *Watermills of Cumbria,* Dalesman, (1978).

scale of milling increased, more power was needed and the local mills could not compete in the wheat trade, although in Brough, milling continued throughout the nineteenth century producing animal fodder, oatmeal, and barley for malting.

Another point made by Davies-Shiel is that, in the damp and humid climate of Westmorland, drying kilns were a necessity, and to prevent the spread of fire, they were often set apart from the mill. However, as they were still used as communal ovens, they were located within the village. The present place name, Kilngate, may give a clue to the location of one in Church Brough. The early references to a kiln, beginning in 1425, have already been mentioned but little was known of the layout. By the eighteenth century more details of a typical kiln can be found. By then, a kiln was usually a two storey building of stone, with the fire below the floor made from separated tiles or stones, on which was laid a horsehair blanket for the grain drying. A hole in the roof, or a chimney, took the smoke away.

Low Mill, according to Davies-Shiel, was a typical example of a bank mill, built into a slope, alongside a falling water course, and easily accessible to the village. Many of these buildings in Cumbria date from the late seventeenth century. Lady Anne's diary records that she rebuilt Low Mill, at Brough, in 1661, and later evidence shows that it was again rebuilt in the 1790s.[255] Usually there was a kiln, then the water-wheel and a store for the stones. Next was the stable, (so that rising damp did not penetrate the living quarters), and finally the miller's cottage. The main head race began at the weir at Bridge Street, dropping enough to turn the small over-shot wheel, which was placed downstream, in Church Brough. The tail-race emptied into the Augill Beck, in Church Brough, near the old site of the Bridge Inn. There was a smaller leat below the mill and the area downstream was a 'wash' to contain the flood water.

The High Mill was a much bigger project.[256] An entry in the 1794 directory, states that it was built by John Wilson at the same time as he built the Helbeck mill complex. The early OS maps surveyed in the late 1850s show no link with the Middleton road. All trade was along the narrow lane which followed the Swindale into Brough at the main bridge or across the pack horse bridge by the Black Bull. In 1813 it was occupied by William Todd, but then let to Thomas Hodgson and his son Jeffery, who had been millers at Acorn Bank for 21 years. The site contained a water corn mill, a drying kiln, malt rooms, a house, stables and the pigsties. According to the deeds, the mill contained mill-stones, the engine,[257]

Note 255: Clifford, D. J. H. ed., *Diaries of Lady Anne Clifford*, Sutton, (2003).
Note 256: CRO(K), WDX 341/3.
Note 257: A term used to describe the working parts of the mill.

Brough High mill - photograph courtesy of Mr Chris Dent.

along with gears and cloths.[258] A few years later, it was occupied by Sawyer and Fawcett. Throughout the century there were two separate enterprises on the site: one was a brewery, the other a corn mill. In 1888, when it was auctioned as part of the Black Bull's holdings, sales particulars describe both enterprises very much as they had been in 1813, yet five years later, when it was again up for auction, the brewery was said to be disused.[259]

Helbeck Mill, however, is the most interesting. Built as an indigo mill and workshop complex in the 1790s alongside a water mill, it was occupied throughout the nineteenth century. John Pattinson, gentleman, who advertised in the 1829 directory as a dyer and fuller, lived there in retirement in 1851. He had paid £140 for a two acre field nearby in the 1830s, possibly for tentering (drying finished cloth), which suggests that cloth finishing had continued in Brough after the closing of Yosgill Mill.[260] This was in the days before synthetic indigo had been developed, and the Brough works seem to have been small, possibly a family business. Raw materials could have been dyers-knapweed and woad. Some may have been produced in

Note 258: The occupiers had to maintain the drains and waterways.
Note 259: CRO(K),WD/HH, bundle B.
Note 260: CRO(K), WDB/35. The 1860 OS survey notebook which gave details of every field surveyed indicates that Yosgill Mill was still in use but as a corn mill. WDX 341/3 Pattinson's field at Robert Head.

One of several leats in Brough to supply water for mills. Photograph by kind permission of Dr. Stephen Walker.

England but by this time much was imported and unfortunately, for this area, there are no records of imports from India or other foreign producers. The dyers needed a plentiful supply of water and urine, for the vats and drying space for the cloth or yarn. At one time, water seems to have been taken from the mill-leat of the adjacent corn mill, to feed the indigo works below, for dyers needed a good supply of clean water. The water was then fed back into the beck, no doubt highly coloured. There may at one time have been a fulling mill too, as Pattinson advertised that he was both a fuller and a dyer. Also on the Helbeck site, in an adjacent building and using the same leat, was a corn mill which in 1829, was run by Rudd and Robinson, and in 1851 by Dodd and son. The 1881 census lists both a saw mill and a corn mill on the site.

The directories illustrate the decline of milling. In 1829 there were corn mills at Helbeck, with two millers, at Brough Sowerby, and at Mousegill on Stainmore, but the main ones were Low Mill in Brough, and the High Mill, both worked by consortiums. Throughout the nineteenth century, all except Mousegill were working, with High Mill both a corn mill and until 1893, a brewery, while Helbeck Mill was also a sawmill. In 1905, only Low Mill advertised in the directory, but the 1910 rates valuation survey recorded both it and High Mill as corn mills, and Brewery Lane, which linked Helbeck and High Mills, was occupied by tallow works, and a slaughter house.[261] This may have been on the site of High Mill, which had been a working farm throughout the nineteenth century, with Fawcett's tallow works there in the 1851 census. Thirty years later, Fawcett's tallow works were listed at Row Bank, at the southern end of Market Brough.

Brough Sowerby Mill lay on the track eastwards out of the village, near to Bloan Farm. For most of the nineteenth century the Brogden family, were the millers who lived and farmed at Whitriggs. Mr Thomas Raine, a descendant of the family and the present owner of the mill site, does not remember the mill in use, although in his grandfather's day it had been used to mill cattle feed. The water which originally came in a leat from the Powbrand Syke and drained into the Belah, had long been turned off. The wooden water wheel, in need of repair, was removed, probably in the 1960s and re-instated at Brampton Mill, near Appleby. A sketch and details of the crown-wheel and gearing, which were originally below the stone floor of the mill, are to be found in Davis-Shiel's book already mentioned.[262] All has since been demolished.

Like other places, Brough was no longer isolated and immune from outside influences, therefore the growth of large scale milling elsewhere in Britain, had a major impact on the fortunes of Brough millers, and brewers,

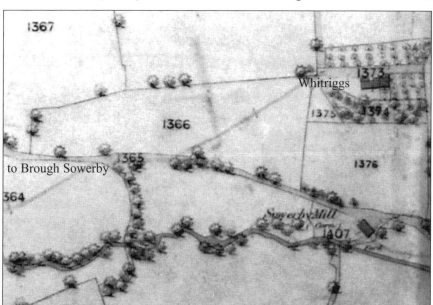

Map 11: Brough Sowerby corn mill on the 1860 Ordnance Survey map by kind permission of Chris Dent.

Note 261: CRO(K) WT/DV/2/11, 1910 survey for rates.
Note 262: Davis-Shiel, M. op.cit, p 79.

as well as on the miners and cotton workers mentioned previously. The last quarter of the eighteenth century was one of transition and it is possible to judge the situation in part of the parish by examining the 1787 census.

In October 1787, a census was taken at the direction of the local Justices of the Peace covering the whole of Westmorland. This was to record all members of each household together with their relationships with the head of household, and their occupations.

Many of the returns are missing and there are none for Brough or Brough Sowerby, but there is a list for nearby Stainmore and Kaber.[263] The Stainmore census was compiled by William Whelpdale, the local constable, who was a farmer and innkeeper, living at Bluegrass. His family had been on Stainmore for most of the century, and one of the family had been involved with the Turnpike Trust. The census was carried out over a few months, and compiled by the constable. This was not a record of the situation on one particular night as later censuses were, but a general gathering of information by the constable.

Whelpdale's comments show considerable knowledge of the inhabitants. In the Sayer family one daughter was a knitter, but the entry for Henry, a son, was "play." Elizabeth Oysten was "past any business" and her husband "poor" while John Armstrong was "out of health and on the township." Margery Waistell, a servant in the household of Mary Ewbank, and Mary Dent, in another nearby household, had their work listed as "drudgery."

The census, well ahead for its time, named everyone and gave the relationship to the household head. It shows that farmers were able to benefit from new employment opportunities, which could provide alternative income, should the harvests fail or other natural catastrophes strike. These opportunities were based on the wider exploitation of the local mineral deposits, which had been made possible by the improvements in road communications.

This census also reveals the part played by women and children. Some listed their work as housekeeping, seamstry, and spinning, (although all five weavers living locally were men). However, knitting was recorded in 60 per cent of all households. Whether they were lone householders like the widow, Agnes Jackson, or living in a large farming family like the five daughters of George Atkinson knitting of stockings. It appears that it was a common occupation for women and children in the area.

No returns for the 1787 census have survived for the town of Brough but there is quite a detailed entry for it in the *Universal British Directory* three

---

Note 263: *Vital Statistics, the Westmorland Census of 1787*, Curwen Archive Trust, 1992, Berwick and 1790 Directory.

years later in 1790. Although some of the information needs to be treated with caution, this entry does illustrate a contemporary view of Brough as a thriving centre, catering for the needs of travellers, with regular coach services, inns and shops. Half a century after the turnpiking of the main road, new enterprises, like the cotton mill and the dyeworks had been set up, and with two banks represented, the prospects of expanding the economy looked hopeful. The thrice yearly fairs were well attended, but there was said to have been no market for many years. This is not the view of a nineteenth century directory writer, (as shown in a later chapter), but the 1790 entry includes the small details which suggest that its writer had close contact with the community. It is worth quoting the first paragraphs: (original spelling).

Brough is a small inland town, 6 miles from Appleby and 252 from London. It is also called Brough-under-Stanemore, i.e. a borough on a stoney mountain. Its being situated on the great road from London to Glasgow, and the Southern parts of Scotland and North of Ireland, (crossing at Port Patrick) occasions the town to be much frequented by travellers. It has two very good inns, viz. the Swan, kept by Mr James Aunger, and the New Inn, kept by Mr Henry Fryer; to the latter of which inns arrives every morning, about nine o'clock, the Glasgow mail-coach from the south, and another arrives every day, at the same inn, from the north, about two o'clock in the afternoon.

The Earl of Lonsdale has lately let an elegant house, called Creckendrop hall, (formally a gentleman's seat) to a Mr Ives who hath fitted it up as an inn, about half way between Brough and Penrick. There are two other good inns in this town for wagons and country travellers, viz. the Fleece, kept by Mrs Thwaits, and the Black Bull, kept by Mrs Cook....

Two bankers' agents, for the respective banks of Durham and the joint bank of Whitby and Malton in Yorkshire, reside here; Mr Thomas Hodgson for the Durham, and Mr Michael Horne for the Whitby; who transact business in the same manner as their principals....

The Carlisle stage coach from London arrives at the Swan Inn from the South, every Tuesday, Thursday and Saturday, about six in the morning, and returns every Monday, Wednesday and Friday, about one o'clock in the afternoon.

There are two stage coaches from London to Brough, daily; one from the Saracen's Head, Snow-hill, at half past seven and eight o'clock in the morning: and the other from the Bull and Mouth, Aldersgate at seven in the morning, and one and seven in the afternoon. Waggons go from the White Horse, Cripplegate, and Castle, Wood-street.

Then follows a list of principal inhabitants beginning with Gentlemen etc. This was headed by Carleton, John Esq., Justice of the Peace, and included substantial businessmen or their widows, like John Kidd, and Mrs Lamb, both had been innkeepers, and George Middleton, a retired shop keeper. Others, Thomas Hodgson and the Ewbank widows were landowners. The F which stands beside some names indicates a freeholder with the right to a Parliamentary vote. The rest of the list is devoted to traders.

The following are the principal inhabitants:

Table 9: 1790 directory (compare Appendix IX)

GENTLEMEN, etc.	TRADERS, etc
Carleton John, Esq, (F) Justice of the Peace	Aselbie, John, Butcher
Ewbank Mrs Hannah, widow	Abison, John, Carrier
Ewbank Mrs Nancy, widow	Armstrong, ..., Victualler
Emmerson Mrs Elizabeth, widow	Atkinson, Richard, Shoemaker
Hamilton Mrs, widow	Aungier, James (F), Innkeeper
Hodgson Thomas, Esq (F)	Atkinson, John, Taylor
Horn Michael, Esq (F)	Alderson, John, Miner
Hodgson, Miss	Alison, Richard, Mason
Kidd John, Esq	Bird, James, Victualler
Lamb, Mrs	Bird, James, Tea-dealer
Lowson Mrs Ann, widow	Bainbridge, John, Peruke-maker
Middleton, Miss	Baumer, John, Victualler (Badger)
Middleton, George, Esq (F)	Bushby, Thomas, Carpenter
Ryder, Mrs	Berket, Michael, Horse-dealer
Richardson, Francis, Esq.	Boar, Robert, Yeoman*
	Bell, Matthew, Miner
	Bainbridge, Timothy, Gardener
CLERGY	Bayles, John, Yeoman
Barnet, Rev. Thomas (F), Vicar	Bowe, Thomas (F), Innkeeper
Sewell, Rev. James (F), Curate, and Master of the Grammar School	Bowe, Michael (F) Dealer in Wood
	Brown, Christopher, Miner
	Cook, Mary, Innkeeper
PHYSIC	Cook, Robert, Dealer in Horses
Rumney, John, Surgeon and Apothecary	Coulson, Thomas, Miner
	Compson, George, Coachman
	Carr, John, Pedlar
LAW	Cleasby, Robert, Weaver
Nelson, Wm. Attorney and Post-master	Deighton, William, Sadler
	Deighton, John, Shoemaker

Darby, William, Mason
Darby, William, jun., Mason
Darby, John, Mason
Darby, Matthew, Shoemaker
Devis, Adam, Ras...-merchant
Dodgson, Thomas, Schoolmaster
Fryer, Henry, Innkeeper
Falder, Robert, Butcher
Gill, John, Blacksmith
Gill, John, jun., Carrier and
Butter-factor
Graham, John, Steward to the
Cotton-mill
Holton, Christopher, Stone-cutter,
etc.
Hewetson, Henry, Victualler and
Farmer
Hodgson, Isabel, Baker
Hilton, Thomas, Cheesemonger
Hodgson, Christopher, Taylor
Harrison, John, Weaver
Horn, John, Shoemaker
Johnson, Richard, Miner
Johnson, John, Shoemaker
Johnson, William, Innkeeper
Irish, William, Dealer in Horses
Kidd, Robert (F), Butcher
Lamb, William, Butcher

Lambert, John, Carpenter
Monkhouse, Miles (F), Cooper
Metcalf, John, Clogger
McNaughton, Robert, Taylor
Monckhouse, J. Spinning wheel-
maker
Newbolt, John, Butcher
Outhwaite, Barbara, Shopkeeper
Petty, John, Blacksmith
Richardson, ..., Carrier and
Butter-factor
Rickaby, John, Miller
Ransom, John, Weaver
Simpson, Thomas, Blacksmith
Simpson, John, Miner
Spencer, John (F), Farrier
Salkeld, John (F), Yeoman
Taylor, John, Excise-officer
Thwaits, Mary, Innkeeper
Todd, Jonathan, Joiner
Todd, William, Miller
Waller, Edward (F). Yeoman
Walker, Peter, Yeoman
Wilson, Thomas, Weaver
Wilson, John (F), Dyer
Yare, William, Schoolmaster
Yare, Ann, Shopkeeper
Yare, Joseph, Carrier

* By Yeoman is to be in general understood a person who occupies his own farm and lands.

These show a good spread of occupations, with smiths, horse dealers and inn keepers for the passing trade, along with carriers, a saddler and a coach-man. The building trades are well represented, and include the well established Lambert family whose business continued throughout the nineteenth century. There are professional people, a surgeon and several school masters. Tailors, shoemakers and food dealers were numerous and there were weavers and a spinning wheel maker. A paragraph on John Carleton Esq. gives details of the changes discussed earlier:

He has also erected a cotton-mill, and carries on a very extensive cotton manufactory, which employs a great number of people, and is of great benefit to the poor, whose children can earn their living at six or seven years of age. There are no other manufactures carried on at or near this place, except the knitting of white yarn stockings, which is the chief employment of most of the poorer sort of the female inhabitants. Here is a considerable dye-house, situated about 200 yards below the bridge belonging to Mr John Wilson, who carries on an extensive business in that line; he has also erected a large corn mill and an indigo mill, on the same river, over which he hath also built a neat bridge for the convenience of the residents of the upper part of the town who have business at either of the mills. Next this bridge is a spa well.

The directory was primarily a trade directory, but details of historical interest were added. When these describe contemporary events there is a rare insight into the period. For example the entry on John Carleton mentions his newly built Fox Tower:

John Carleton Esq., one of his Majesty's Justices of the Peace for this county, and lord of the manor of Hilbeck, hath a beautiful seat about a quarter of a mile north of this town, called Hilleck-hall,[sic] which, being situated on an eminence, commands an extensive prospect every way except the north and east, which is intercepted by a chain of rocky mountains, which runs behind the hall, and extends many miles north. This gentleman has also erected a romantic round building on a rock, which projects from other rocks, in a hanging wood, and which is called Fox Tower, from the number of those animals with which the wood abounds. The building is surrounded by a platform, on which he has planted seven cannons, which he fires off on birth and rejoicing-days.

The other buildings named are the church, which only merits a brief description, and the castle. The dramatic collapse of part of the keep had happened only a few months before the directory was written, and the discovery of the hoard of Roman coins was within living memory.

The parish church is a short distance from the town, in a little village called Church Brough; it is a neat building, but no way remarkable for any thing, either internal or external, except the pulpit, which is cut out of one entire stone.

Near the church, on a hill, are the ruins of an ancient castle, belonging to the Earl of Thanet; the walls of the square tower of which stood pretty perfect till the beginning of the present year 1790; which, as is supposed, the ground giving way, the bottom part of the south east corner fell down, leaving the upper part, with the turret at top, suspended, and without any other support than the cement of the wall parallel with it; it is called, according to ancient records, Caesar's Tower, and is supposed to have been built by him. An evident proof of its being built by, or in possession of, the Romans, appeared about twenty years since; for, as some labourers were digging the foundation of a house to be built near the castle, they found an urn, or earthern pot, full of Roman silver coins, about the size of our silver three-penny pieces, but thicker, many of them in high preservation; one in particular, bearing a fine impression of the head of Titus Vespatian, and on the reverse, a female figure, in a weeping posture, representing, as is supposed, the city of Jerusalem, which that Emperor destroyed.

Dr Rumney, who had contacts with the antiquarians of Newcastle, was put in charge of the finds.

The improved road system therefore, can be seen to have widened Brough's connections in both the commercial and the cultural spheres. However, the situation altered in the next century as competition from a new form of the transport grew. This was the development of the railway network, which will be discussed in the next chapter.

CHAPTER 15

The Railway Age

THE opening of the Carlisle to Newcastle railway in 1838 had a major impact on the Brough to Bowes road. It meant that east to west freight could move more quickly (at 24 mph) and more cheaply than by wagon along the Stainmore turnpike. The railways could easily carry much greater weights of bulky goods as well as many more passengers and in more comfort at any one time, than the wagons and stage coaches. One large stage-coach could only take up to eighteen passengers, (including those outside) while the common load for a draught horse and cart over hilly country was between fifteen and eighteen hundredweight, based on the estimate that a single horse-cart carried ten pigs of lead each of twelve stone.[264] In contrast, in its first year of operation, the Stockton-Darlington line carried 42,000 tons of coal.[265]

In 1846 the Lancaster to Carlisle railway was opened, and over in the north east, a close network of lines had developed from the early Stockton-Darlington one, connecting with Newcastle and other coalfield towns. The inhabitants of Barnard Castle realised the potential of the rail and petitioned for their own link to Darlington. This was opened in 1856.[266] To both east and west of the Pennines, it was possible by 1850, to reach Scotland or London and the Midlands by rail. Local carriers adapted to the innovations by offering services to the railheads. As early as 1839 a Carlisle firm was advertising a service to meet the Newcastle train at night and to take passengers down to Preston so that they could catch the early morning train to London.[267]

Why did the 'railway mania' miss Brough?
In the mid 1840s three schemes had been drawn up by companies keen to provide east to west links across Northern England. The York and Carlisle company proposed a link from Northallerton via Barnard Castle and Brough to Clifton on the Lancaster to Carlisle line. The York and Glasgow company proposed one via Thirsk, Hawes, Kirkby Stephen and Appleby to Clifton, and the Leeds and Carlisle company promoted one from Leeds

---

Note 264: Pringle, J., in Bailey and Cullen, op.cit, p273.
Note 265: Simmons, J., ed. *Rail 150 Years, The Stockton & Darlington Rai*lway, Eyre, Methuen (1975), p41.
Note 266: Simmons, op.cit, p30.
Note 267: Williams, op.cit, p152.

1910 · Bealah Viaduct, near Brough.

The Belah Viaduct, near Brough, 1910, by kind permission of John Walton.

through Hawes and the Eden valley to Clifton.

In 1846 the three companies amalgamated to form the Northern Counties Union Railway, still with the aim of promoting an east to west line, but with at least one branch line along the Eden Valley to Appleby. However, the major problems which the surveys showed, were the difficulties of building across Stainmore, with the steep gradients and the need for expensive tunnels. Problems were also foreseen in maintaining the line and running trains throughout the winter months. Eventually it was realised that this was an over-ambitious scheme and that there would be little room for profit making. The company could not raise the necessary finance and the plans were abandoned.[268]

A common idea today is that the landowners of Brough were against the railway. However, Margaret Shepherd has found that the Earl of Thanet owned over three quarters of the land needed by the line in the Brough area, and there is no record of any objection from him. She speculates that the problems may have been caused by the customary tenure, whereby many of his tenants held "de facto ownership."[269] It would be a complicated legal matter to sort out who could give the necessary assent and who would get the compensation for the loss of land.

Certainly the successor to the Earl of Thanet, Sir Richard Tufton, did not oppose the railway across his land for in 1852, he commissioned a survey

---

Note 268: Walton, P., *Stainmore and Eden Valley Railways,* Oxford Press, (1992).
Note 269: Shepherd, M., op.cit, p199.

to explore the possibility of a line from Appleby to Clifton. Public meetings were held at both Appleby in 1854 and at Brough in 1856 to discuss the promotion of railways and their prospective routes across Stainmore, but there was one great problem: the schemes were too expensive for such small communities to finance.

It was events outside the local region which finally determined the railway routes. The rapid growth of heavy industry in the North East Coalfield in the mid-century needed railways to move bulky materials across the country. To provide this, a subsidiary of the Stockton-Darlington company proposed a line across Stainmore. The aim was to transport Durham coke to the Furness and Cumberland iron ore districts and to return with loads of haematite. The company planned to link the railways of South Durham with the main north-south line on the western side of the country at Tebay. The new railway, to be called the South Durham and Lancashire Union line, was to be built across Stainmore but well south of Brough.[270] The economic advantages of this link attracted the necessary finance; 146 local landowners and farmers bought shares.[271] The Act for the South Durham line was passed in 1857. A year later, after much disagreement, the subsidiary route, that of the Eden Valley Railway was agreed. It was to link the South Durham line at Kirkby Stephen with Warcop, Appleby, and Clifton.

The construction was as difficult, dangerous and expensive as the former Northern Counties Union engineers had foreseen. Thomas Bouch, the engineer in charge, had to oversee the construction of dramatic viaducts, (Belah, Merrygill, Podgill among others), which were necessary to overcome the deeply incised valleys. The cost of construction averaged over £12,000 per mile.[272] The gradients were near the limits of the capacity of the locomotives. The long pull on either side of Stainmore summit, at 1,370 feet above sea level, included two miles at 1 in 72, after a six mile climb of around 1 in 60.[273] The line was opened in 1861, and the Eden Valley line in 1862. Both were worked by the same company. The Eden Valley Line did not touch Brough, but at the request of George Bailey, the bailiff there, (who pleaded the case for eighteen shopkeepers, three millers, and sundry other local businesses), a station was built at Musgrave. The first trains carried up to 600 tons of coke westwards and 150 tons of haematite eastwards.[274]

On the South Durham line, in the first year of operation there were around fifteen freight trains a day in each direction, and two daily passenger

Note 270: Shepherd, M., op.cit, p200.
Note 271: Walton, P., op.cit, p12.
Note 272: Walton, P., op.cit.
Note 273: Simmons, J., op.cit, p30-32.
Note 274: Kirby, M. W., p162 quoted by Shepherd, M. p204.

Construction of the Smardale Viaduct on the South Durham and Lancashire Union railway.

services in each direction, with an extra one on Wednesday, from Barnard Castle to Tebay. The journey took just over an hour and a half each way. The first excursion train, from Darlington to Windermere took place just three weeks after opening. Peter Walton in his book *The Stainmore and Eden Valley Railways* notes that 21 first class tickets at 7s.6d each and 154 second class tickets at four shillings each were sold for this journey.[275-6]

There is no evidence of any great opposition to the railway by Brough people but neither was there any active promotion. This first line near Brough was in response to the demands of industry outside the area. It was a means of covering difficult ground as quickly as possible and so enabling the industries to lower their costs. Throughout England, the railway companies based their application to parliament for new routes, on the amount

Note 275: Walton, P., op.cit, p149.
Note 276: On the return journey, at Bowes the train was derailed and the driver died later.

of freight available.[277] The resources of the Brough region were simply not enough to encourage outside investment in a line. The Eden Valley line also by-passed Brough, because its route had been determined by a very powerful lobbying body representing Appleby's interests.

When a second company decided to build across the area, it too took a route well away from Brough. The Settle-Carlisle railway, which opened in 1876, was built by the Midland Railway, as part of the company's great scheme to capture some of the trade with Scotland, by linking the Midlands and the West Riding, via the Lancaster to Carlisle line, with the industrial areas of Scotland. This Lancaster line, by the late 1850s, was in the hands of one of the Midland's major rivals, the London and North Western company, and co-operation between the two seemed unlikely. In 1866 the Midland company introduced a bill in parliament for the construction of the cross country link which they needed from Settle to Carlisle. This was passed, but over the next two years, an agreement was reached with the London and North Western that the Lancaster line could be run jointly if the Settle-Carlisle act was abandoned. However, parliament refused an abandonment act and the line had to be built.

In 1869, the first sod was cut. Six and a half years later, it was finished; two years longer than planned and a million and a half pounds over budget. To quote a recent third leader in the *Guardian*, (30.12.09): "The line charges across some of the finest upland country in Britain, through fourteen tunnels and over twenty four viaducts, the highest mainline railway in the country." The nearest stations to Brough were at Appleby and on the far side of Kirkby Stephen, so the carriers and carters of Brough had extra trade. The line was running goods trains by 1875 and the passenger services were started on 1st May 1876.

Although neither of these lines came through Brough, their influence was felt. They provided alternative employment in an area already short of work. The baptismal register of the Primitive Methodists of Brough dates from 1844 and continues throughout the period of railway building. The earliest entries are those of farming families and small businesses, but in 1855, when the Jackson family baby was baptised, the father was described as a "plait-layer." There were other plate-layers soon after: in 1859 there was the Stott family of Kendal, then in the early 1860s there were the Longstaffs, the Wilsons, and Bousfields all from Tebay, and the Sandersons of Spittal. In the 1870s the names included Dents, the Dickensons and the Richardsons as well as the Allisons, the Fawcetts and Smiths.

Once the lines were opened, others (Longstaff, Stamper, Hunter), got

---

Note 277: One of the few applications built on the number of passengers available was the Liverpool to Southport line in the 1840s.

more permanent jobs, as signalmen, porters and engine drivers. Their addresses ranged from Orton and Tebay, to Knock, Milburn, Kirkby Stephen and Spittals. Without extensive family history research it is impossible to prove that all these families had connections with Brough, especially if the link was through the wife, but by this period, there were other Primitive Chapels nearer to their places of residence, in such places as Kirkby Stephen, Tebay and Kaber, yet the families travelled to Brough for the family celebrations.[278]

It can be argued that the construction work of the 1870s, which employed over 6,200 men, altered the demographic profile of Brough. The 1881 census reveals a lack of young men in the parish, while several hundred with Brough surnames are to be found in County Durham and other areas needing strong workers. The building of the line had attracted young men from all the villages around. They could earn up to ten shillings a day and there was no Sunday work. The contractor building the stretch of line from Kirkby Stephen westwards complained that his men were from farming families and they disappeared for a month around June to get the hay in. When this line was finished, many followed the gangs to other sites or to the related industries in County Durham. The Shildon Works Company in 1872, advertised for engine drivers. These could earn seven and half pence an hour driving trains on the main line, and five pence an hour as a shunter. Workshop workers earned three pence and three farthings an hour.[279]

In the short-term, Brough and Stainmore benefited. During the construction work there was a great demand for local stone and lime, and the farms found a ready market for their butter, cheese and bacon. There was thus more work for local carriers. The railways excelled at the transport of heavy, bulky goods, not just from the outside areas but also from the area which they crossed. They stimulated the opening of new quarries and lime works. When the South Durham and Lancashire Union line was closed in 1962, it was still earning over £3,000 per week, from Brough Quarry and £10,000 a month from Hartley Quarry.[280]

Another aspect of the local economy changed with the railways: the droving trade took to the rails, and local farmers could reach the markets more quickly with their stock. By special request sidings were built for cattle trucks at Barras, and the Auction Market at Kirkby Stephen was moved to the East Station. In the first year of opening, the *Penrith Observer* reported that Brough Hill Fair was "the worst known, the horse sales were a drag," and, the report continued, there was no Sunday trading. This was

Note 278: CRO(K), Register of Baptisms, Brough Primitive Methodist Chapel.
Note 279: Walton, p149.
Note 280: Walton, p193, letter from W. E. Sayer, Helbeck Lime Works.

Musgrave Station, by kind permission of Mark Keefe.

blamed on the facilities, "now offered for speedy travelling by the Darlington Railway."[281] These complaints continued in the following years, and were aired by the *Westmorland Gazette* as well as the Penrith papers.[282]

Advertisers for Brough properties were keen to mention the new opportunities offered by the railways. In 1852 in the pre-railway days, when Helbeck Hall had been offered for sale, much was made of the fact that a daily mail coach ran from Brough to Penrith so that London could be reached in ten hours. Seven years later, Brough High Mill was stated to be within a short distance of the South Durham line: a line which at the time had not even been completed. When Augill Castle, a prime gentleman's residence was offered for sale in London in 1897, the advantages of being within two and a half miles from either Musgrave or Barras stations were emphasised.[283]

These lines opened up a wide area to the inhabitants of the Eden Valley, with connections to London, Leeds, Liverpool, the Lancashire towns and the Midlands and, via Carlisle with Glasgow and Edinburgh. All the major industrial regions were within reach and offered better employment prospects than Brough. Here were job opportunities which did not involve a complete break from the family home. The next chapter will look at Brough while these changes were taking place.

Note 281: *Penrith Observer*, 1st October 1861.
Note 282: Walton, P., op.cit, p13.
Note 283: CRO(K), WD/HH/bundle 3, sales particulars.

CHAPTER 16

Brough in the Nineteenth Century

FOR many settlements in England, the nineteenth century was a period of success and change, often accompanied by a fast growth in population as a response to the job opportunities offered by the new industries of the period. This was not so in Brough. This chapter will look at the characteristics of the township

At the approach of the nineteenth century, there were some positive signs suggesting that the economy of Brough was growing and diversifying. True the cotton mill had closed after only a brief period, but that was blamed on the extravagance of the owner, and although there were fewer independent farmers, there were still jobs in the agricultural sector for labourers. There was still a dye works, and there were flour mills and a brewery.

Moreover, the mineral wealth of the surrounding area continued to look promising, with a newly discovered lead vein and the coal pits able to produce enough for the immediate needs of the area. The main cause for optimism was the traffic on the turnpikes with goods and people crossing Stainmore regularly. The inns in and around Brough were seen as good investments, with their tenures taken up as soon as they became vacant. The retail trade had increased and had been varied with new specialist workshops, such as milliners and mantua makers rather than seamstresses, three resident tailors, instead of a peripatetic one and, (a touch of luxury), a barber and peruke maker.

Brough had not changed in its administration. It was still a part of the estate owned by descendants of the Clifford family, and the church still belonged to Queen's College, Oxford. Nicolson and Burn claim that in 1777, there were 210 families living in the parish, and all were Church of England.[284]

This situation did not last long, for in the nineteenth century a number of dissenting chapels, financed by local people, were built in Brough. In 1803 John Rumney, surgeon of Market Brough sold a piece of land on the south side of the road, and east of the lane leading from Brough Bridge for "the erecting of a Chapel or preaching house," for the use of the Wesleyan Methodists, and when the legality of the sale was called into question in 1812, it was duly enrolled at the further payment of five shillings. The men

Note 284: N&B, op.cit, p565.

behind the original purchase were from Brough and the surrounding villages under the guidance of William Fenwick, preacher of Barnard Castle. The land appears to have been part of Rumney's garden, on the opposite side of the road to his house. The chapel was built on Back Lane, behind the site of the present building which dates from 1905.

This started off a chain reaction. Charles Davis built an independent chapel in 1824, and the following year, the Primitive Methodists, or as described in the deeds, the "Ranters" built a chapel in Church Brough on land bought for £6 from William Jackson and his wife, at the north end of their garth, behind his dwelling house, and the common (Coltsford Common) to the north.[285] Five years later, on Stainmore, Mouthlock Chapel was built for the same sect, on a plot of land by the road leading to New Hall. In 1850-2, a chapel and graveyard for the Particular Baptists, was built on the land of Thomas Magee, called Chapel Garth, which lay between the Back Lane and the high road to Kirkby Stephen. Joseph Yare of Brough, Joseph Jameson of Crackenthorpe, and William Burtegill, a farmer, were the instigators of this project.[286-287]

The establishment of the Primitive Methodist Chapel on North Stainmore illustrates the way in which a small section of a scattered community set about building a chapel. This work may have been spurred on by the establishment of an Anglican chapel in 1861 just behind the Punch Bowl. In 1868 the Primitive Methodists opened their own chapel nearby on the main road at North Stainmore, and the minute book of the annual meetings of the chapel trustees begins in 1869. A separate note found in the book states that before that date, a group had held services in Lane House near the Punch Bowl. The chapel was built of stone from a nearby quarry, on land owned by the lord of the manor. Robert Clemitson (sic) the minister of the Primitive Methodist Chapel in Brough helped to set up the project and chaired the first meeting at which trustees were appointed. These were John Nicholson, Thomas Metcalfe, Robert Barker, John and James Croft, Christopher and John Coates, Christopher and John Bousfield. They came mainly from the area around Hard Hills, and Borrowdale Beck, and were either farmers or miners. None of the families was wealthy, and there was no endowment to draw on.

The first resolution passed, after the trustees had been appointed, was that £80 should be borrowed at four and a half per cent interest from Mrs

---

Note 285: 1905 Directory, Primitive Methodist Chapel at Brough was rebuilt at a cost of £820 in 1877, but was struck by lightning three years later. It was rebuilt to hold a congregation of 300.

Note 286: Curwen, J., Records, see also first ed. OS six inch map.

Note 287: Today the Memorial Hall stands on the site.

Etching of Brough, looking north towards Helbeck Hall, from Poet Close.

Joseph Robinson of Hartley. It was expected that a regular income would come from collections, and the letting of seats, which were to be one shilling and sixpence a year, to be paid half yearly. As the chapel became established, the harvest festival and chapel anniversary brought in a few pounds each October, and the Sunday School was asked to pay twenty shillings a year. A successful bazaar in the early days brought in more money and by 1871 it was reported that not only had the interest on the loan been paid regularly but that part of the principal had been paid off so that it had been reduced to £45.

Thereafter an annual sum of £4 or more was paid off the principal; a remarkable achievement for a small community. Occasional repairs to the structure must have been a worry as, after the annual donation of half a crown to the orphanage had been paid, only a couple of pounds a year were kept in hand. When new lamps were needed, for example, the carol singing groups were sent out. Women do not figure in the administration at this time, but it is obvious that much of the care of the building was in their hands. In 1871 Mary Bousfield was to have "one of the best hymn books for her use" as remuneration for cleaning the chapel. The minute book shows a determined and loyal congregation, with a number of the trustees remaining in office for several decades. It also shows how other activities, such as the choir, and the Band of Hope, flourished around the chapel and its community.[288]

These non-conformist congregations are all examples of local initiative, which loosened the traditional hold of the Anglican Church. Other aspects of traditional control were also changing and with the development of mining, the terms of the leases were altered. The Thanets issued short leases to groups of people for the exploitation of specific veins or seams of minerals. Some lessees were outsiders. The influx of labourers for the mines and later for the railways brought new customs. The labourers were often lodgers, who had no manorial ties with the land, or with the lord. Meanwhile many locally born people took advantage of new opportunities for travel, using the coaches and carriers, and later the railways.

Brough, as seen in the directories

Throughout the nineteenth century, the local directories register remarkably little change in Brough. But then their job was to attract people and to show the positive side of a district. The general descriptions were often culled from older directories. Brough Hill Fair continued to be attended by "vast multitudes" although both the mining and the fair had suffered dramatically. Bulmer's directory of 1885, while copying the usual assessment of the Brough Fair Hill crowds was more critical in its assessment of the situation.[289] It commented too, that the "dreary landscape" offered few attractions to tourists, and continued: "the South Durham railway, it was fondly hoped would give an impetus to mining - but this consummation, so devoutly to be wished, has yet been but sparingly accomplished."

Market and Church Brough, were still predominantly farming villages when the 1829 directory was published.[290] There was some small scale processing of agricultural products, so there were also flour dealers, a bacon curer, a brewery (or possibly two), tallow works and a saw mill. There were still some remnants of the textile trade, as there was a dyer and fuller, and there was a weaver. The village shops provided for everyday needs, such as grocers and drapers, shoemakers and tailors. But there was also evidence of the importance of the main road for the coaching trade. There were nine inns, and four smithies, together with long distance carriers. In 1829 a

---

Note 288: Minute book of North Stainmore Primitive Methodist Chapel, kindly loaned by Joyce Scott, secretary to the trustees.

Note 289: Bulmer, T. E. *History, topography and directory of Westmorland 1885,* Manchester, (1885), p144.

Note 290: Parson and White, *History, Directory and Gazetteer of Cumberland and Westmorland,* 1829, fac., Whitehaven (1976).

The Castle Hotel from an old postcard kindly loaned by John Walton.

number of miners lived in Market Brough as did the owners of the mines.

As the century passed the directories record fewer miners: Albany Bell was described as "late manager of the Augill Mine" in 1885, and Charles Davis was the secretary of the Brough with Hilbeck Mining Company. There were no long distance carriers, and no coach services were advertised. Farmers were still the most numerous group listed and there were a number of small shops and workshops, (tailors, shoemakers and bakeries). Two Temperance cafes had been established, reflecting the new anti-drink movement, and only seven inns were advertised.

In the first half of the nineteenth century, Brough Hill Fair attracted large crowds for the sale of horses, cattle and sheep, and the livestock were driven considerable distances. A letter from the Lowther estate shows that the Scotch cattle bought at Brough Hill Fair in 1814, were to be driven across to the Whitehaven estate, "if the cattle are unruly, please to send some person to help - until they are tamer."[291]

There is a description of the fair, written in the 1870s by Canon James Simpson, which recounts events earlier in the century.[292] He mentions the throngs of Scottish breeders and English graziers. The tradition of "haltering the stags," the highlight of the fair, always brought crowds of onlookers

Note 291: CRO(C), D/Lons/3/158, Letter, Bowness, Whitehaven to Robert Lumb, Lonsdale agent at Lowther.
Note 292: Simpson, J., *Things Old and New, at and around Kirkby Stephen, 1863-1886*, rep. (2006), Upper Eden History Socity, p77.

as it was the custom for the unbroken horses (stags), brought to the market in vast numbers, to be separated and haltered only after a buyer had selected one. Strong lads delighted in showing their prowess, encouraged by "much shouting and waving of sticks." The fair was attended by Yorkshire clothiers, who started arriving the evening before and were still coming twelve hours later. They sold blankets and household goods, petticoats for the ladies and broad cloth for the men.

There was also another fair in March in the 1820s, "a good one for cattle." Again the Yorkshire clothiers had attended and before trading could begin the fair had to be walked. This meant that Matthew Horn and John Deighton, one on the fiddle and one on the clarinet, walked "the different avenues of the town three times," playing *God save the King*. Trading once started, would carry on until mid-afternoon. At six o'clock a "merry neet" began with dancing round all the inns. Most people gave the fiddlers a penny a dance, and that added up to quite a tidy sum. This spring fair no longer existed by the time Simpson was writing in 1863.

The autumn fair had also declined. It is hard to reconcile the statement in the 1885 directory that "vast multitudes" were still attending the event, with contemporary press reports quoted earlier of "the worst Brough Hill fair ever," in 1861.[293] In 1865, according to the *Westmorland Gazette* "there were now few regular attenders at the Fair."[294] The Mannex directories throughout the 1850s had stated that the weekly market was not prosperous, and the 1885 directory commented that "its market has been obsolete for some eighteen some years." The most telling phrase was that, "Its one street is as silent as a city of the dead."

The Register of Electors, 1820 and 1832

Another source of information about Brough is to be found in the Register of Electors. The volumes for 1820 and 1832, compiled in those years by William Kaye, give not only the names of the voters, and which oaths they had taken (freeholders oath, bribery oath and so on) but also for whom they voted.[295]

The register published in 1820 is important because it records the pre-Reform bill situation, when the vote was limited to male owners of 40 shilling freeholds. This meant that there was a vote with every such holding and the voter did not necessarily live in the area where he had the right

---

Note 293: 1st October 1861 the *Penrith Observer* reported card sharpers on the hill in great numbers and a fatality as Robert Taylor of Appleby drove home in his van which overturned.
Note 294: *Westmorland Gazette*, 7 October 1865, quoted by Walton, P., op.cit.
Note 295: Kendal Library, *Register of voters for the Shire of Westmorland 1820*, compiled by William Kaye, published 1820.

Brough, High End from Bridge (Westmoreland)   No. 1918.

Old postcard kindly loaned by John Walton.

to vote. In Market and Church Brough, together with Brough Sowerby and Helbeck there were 64 men with the franchise, some of whom were entitled to several votes. Of these sixteen lived outside the area, with six in London and one in Newcastle. On Stainmore there were a further 42 voters. Most held their voting right as farmers, or quarry owners, but in the Brough villages they included the clergy, the school master, a miller, a blacksmith, and a cabinet maker.

The Register of Electors of 1832 illustrates the changes caused by the Reform Act of that year. Brough was part of constituency called the Shire of Westmorland, which included Appleby; the latter no longer had its own members. There was no secret ballot and women still had no voting rights.

The act widened the qualifications for the franchise, giving voting rights it has been estimated, to 60 per cent more of the male population in England than before. The qualifications were based on property ownership or on the occupation of property held by long term leases, and these qualifications had to be registered. These included freeholders and customary tenants, (copyholders), of property worth at least £10 a year, together with £10 leaseholders on a 60 year lease, and £50 leaseholders on a 20 year lease.

In Brough, Helbeck, and Brough Sowerby 101 men had the qualifications to vote. John Bailey at Tofts, Thomas Lancaster at Tinbridge, John Fryer at Demesne Farm, and William Brogden at Whitriggs were all freeholders, while the Cleasby family qualified by the freehold title of the Castle Inn. Others got the right through the ownership of the cattle-gates on the Intack. Richard Addison of Helbeck Hall qualified with the customary property of High Brewery. Robert Buckle at Thrush Hall, and Joseph Dobinson and Robert Percival, both of Brough Sowerby were among the occupiers of a house and land worth £50.

As in earlier years, many of those who gained voting rights were farmers. Only one voter, Mr William Sargeant, was described in the 1829 directory, as a gentleman with no other occupation. Robert Buckle was an owner of mines. Others who qualified included John Arrowsmith, who ran an academy, Adam Davis, the bailiff, John Rumney, the surgeon and the vicar, the Rev. Lancelot Jefferson. Robert and William Lamb, both living in Carlisle, owned the Swan, and Thomas Collinson, living in London, owned the Black Bull. The Hindmores owned the freehold of Helbeck Mill and Charles Davis, the tallow works on Raw (Roe) Bank. Richard Spencer owned his smithy, so did Joseph Balmer.

A number of others had the freehold of their workshops. These included Thomas Lambert, a joiner's workshop and house, George and Isaac Robinson who were weavers, Thomas Lowden, a mason, John Pattinson a dyer, and James Blakelock who owned a quarry. Others entitled to vote were William Wilkinson, a tailor, Robert Deighton, a saddler, John Horn, a shoemaker, several grocers, and two carriers, John Robinson and John Young. The right to vote had clearly been widened to include property owners, craftsmen and tradesmen.

Of these voters around a third lived elsewhere. Twelve of them lived in

Looking down Brough's Main Street from the top Market Cross. Photograph by kind permission of John Walton.

London, (in Regent's Park, Lombard Street and other central addresses), and most of the others had moved to neighbouring counties. Only one, living in Liverpool, had moved to a northern industrial city. At this stage in the nineteenth century, the people who had moved elsewhere, like the Cleasbys who were London merchants, were those financially better off, or with specialised occupations.

In both 1820 and 1832, there were the same three candidates standing for the parliamentary election. These were the Right Honourable Viscount Lowther, Colonel Lowther and Henry Brougham Esquire. In both years the area voted staunchly for Brougham, who, in 1820, won every vote on Stainmore, and all except one in 1832. In the Brough villages including Helbeck and Brough Sowerby, where more people had multiple votes, Brougham again was the victor with 51 votes against eighteen for Viscount Lowther and fourteen for Colonel Lowther.

Brough as seen in the censuses

The censuses of the nineteenth century, beginning in 1801, could be expected to give a more accurate picture but these too have their problems. Comparison between censuses is fraught with difficulties as the early ones were generally organised by the clergy and based on the parish registers. These were mere totals of males and females. The 1841 census was a bold attempt by the Registrar General to collect data on every individual, but it was soon apparent that it did not go far enough.

The 1851 census therefore required more detail of birthplaces and households. It also set the pattern of holding the censuses in spring. The one in 1841 had been in June when groups of hay makers and other agricultural workers were moving around the countryside, and in Brough on census night there were eleven people living in tents, and four travellers at one lodging house, and six drovers, (two from Ireland) at another. This was the week of the horse fair, although that hardly explains the ten stonemasons staying at the Swan Inn, all from outside the county.

Another problem to be considered is that the enumeration districts did not remain the same and some areas, particularly Helbeck[296] in the Brough area were treated differently between successive census counts, and in the late nineteenth century, the new civil parish boundaries were not those of the old ecclesiastical parishes.

Most householders gave one occupation but in reality, many had second jobs. Miners kept small holdings, carriers kept inns and auctioneers were often inn keepers. Women's work was almost certainly under recorded, and the definition of their jobs depended on the enumerator. In Brough, in 1841,

Note 296: The 1841 enumerator reported that he was uncertain of the boundaries.

many were called labourers, whereas in later censuses, they were listed as charwomen, laundresses and the like.

The census records Brough as a small community with a parish total in 1801 of 1,437 inhabitants, with roughly half those numbers focused on the townships of Market and Church Brough. Over the next 30 years the figures rose so that in 1831 there were 1,882 inhabitants in the parish. This, the highest total for the nineteenth century, was followed by a decline in numbers, which was only temporarily halted in the 1851-61 decade with the influx of the construction workers on the nearby railway. In 1881 the population figures were lower than those of 1801 when the censuses began.

The 1841 census shows that 20% of the inhabitants of Brough parish had been born outside Westmorland, confirming that part of the earlier population growth had been by in-migration. On the other hand in the same census, 31 unoccupied houses were recorded in the parish. Although it was a June census, it is unlikely that the empty property represented holiday makers, or even changes of tenancy, as the next four censuses were taken in spring, and repeat this pattern. Even at the period of its greatest growth the parish had no more than 324 incomers in a decade. The 1851 census, the first with details of birthplaces, reveals just how stable the community was. For example, on Stainmore, 60% of the householders had been born within the parish of Brough, and another third came from just over the border of Yorkshire and Durham.

Pre-1841, the early censuses included rough estimates of household occupations in the parish. These show that a third of the householders were engaged in the primary sector of the economy, as farmers, miners or quarrymen. Another tenth were in the small scale manufacturing and processing industries, leaving the rest, apart from the ten per cent retired householders, engaged in the service industries. On the surface this seems to be an equable distribution across the employment sector, but it gives no indication of the profitability of the enterprises, or the degree of under-employment, when family businesses struggled to support all the family members who needed work.

The competition in the mid-century was against the formidable growth and scale of industry, mining and commerce which had developed on the British coalfields. There was no way that the meagre resources of the district could compete with the nearby coalfield and ports of Durham and Northumberland. Although, at this time, there were no railways near Brough, the effect of the close rail network elsewhere, particularly around the perimeter, both on the east side and on the west side of the Pennines, meant that heavy goods could be distributed throughout Northern England without using the road crossing Stainmore.

Farming was the main occupation with one third of the household heads dependent on farming. In the mid-century, the parish including Stainmore contained a total of 95 farms, with an average size of just over 60 acres. There were large farms like High Ewbank and New Hall for example, both over 400 acres in size, but at the other end of the scale, there were a number under ten acres, which had to be worked as a supplement to another occupation, like inn keeping or quarrying. This period was seen as an opportunity for those with money, and the larger owners, the Bainbridges, Tallentires and Baileys, took over the uneconomic farms to enlarge their own holdings.

Some small farms were sold, and family members became labourers on larger farms or they moved into other employment. Hiring fairs were held twice a year, so that the farm servants from outside the village could not claim 'settlement.' This meant in practice, that they had no claim on the poor rates of Brough. These fairs were held at Martinmas and at Whitsuntide. Before these took place, the chief constable of the ward directed the village constables to hold sittings at which names of those to be set "at liberty" were taken. These servants were given a ticket for which they had to pay 2*d*. If a servant was not to be set free, then the constable had to check that he was being paid at the standard rate.

In the 1870s, according to Canon Simpson, good men could expect £18-£20 all found for half a year, while a good dairy maid could get £11-£12 and a young girl, £7-£8 for a half year.[297] There were also the hay hirings in midsummer, when men from a distance came seeking work. Twenty years earlier they could

The original lower Market Cross. Photograph by kind permission of John Walton.

Note 297: Simpson, J. p44.

175

get £3 for the month, in the 1860s it was double that, but the new mowing machines were just creeping in.

A tithe survey was made for Market and Church Brough, in 1841. This was where the better land lay.[298] Even so a field known as "Three day bog" shows the difficulties. Meadow and pasture predominated. The arable land was mainly under oats, but barley was still relatively important for the local brewery. Wheat had never been a reliable crop because of the climate, but when successful, it commanded high prices.

The other aspect of employment in the mid-century was the mining. In 1841 there were around 40 lead miners in Brough parish, often working in family groups, like the Powleys and Whitfields. There were about the same number of coal miners, with the Dents, the Birkbecks and the Bousfields the most numerous. By 1851, there were only six lead miners listed, and the family groups had moved elsewhere. The coal mining numbers had increased to just under 50, but these numbers were tiny compared with those employed on the Durham coalfield.

The changes recorded by 1881

By the last quarter of the nineteenth century the economy of Brough had slumped and it is worth using the 1881 census to judge the situation, as this registers the problems already discussed. First the area had been by-passed by the railways, secondly, its mineral wealth was no longer significant when compared with other parts of Britain, and thirdly, large quantities of cheap food stuffs, both cereals and meat were being imported into England from many parts of the Empire and the Americas. This third reason was the problem which struck at the heart of the economy of the area. The results can be seen in the number of empty houses and the absence of a youthful workforce in the parish. People had to move out to get jobs.

The population of Helbeck had nearly halved and William Rudd from Low Mill had become a miller in Stockton, County Durham. In Brough, part of the George Inn was untenanted, while the Oddfellows Yard had lost the Yares and Bells Yard had four empty houses. The outward migration left many households depleted. In Market Brough for example, there were only three large families recorded, the Kilvingtons, the Yares, and the Hiltons. The others had few family members in their teens or in their twenties at home. The young had had to seek work outside the area.

The 1881 census shows that of the 489 Brough-born migrants to neighbouring counties, 55% were living in county Durham. Another 29% were in Yorkshire, many just over the county border, working farms in Teesdale and

---

Note 298: CRO(K), WDRC/8, 76 Tithe map and schedule. Surveyed 1841 by James Hay.

The George Inn and the view up Brough's Main Street. Photograph by kind permission of John Walton.

Swaledale. Few had moved to Cumberland for there were similar problems there. Durham County was a good choice; it was near and could offer a variety of jobs. In particular, around Crook, Shildon and Darlington, there were jobs in mining, in the coke plants, on the railways, in the engineering works and as general labourers. Trained men, like masons, joiners and smiths, were able to get jobs in areas where new housing was growing rapidly alongside the factories and mines. Very few went into farming.

Families and neighbours from Brough, moved close to each other. The Smiths, for example, went to Crook. John Smith, a mason aged 61, and his three sons plus other branches of the family found jobs as miners or masons, and only one, Thomas, a recent migrant had a different type of job - he was a grocer. Two generations of Beckwiths, who had been coal miners on Stainmore, had also moved to Crook. One was a small farmer, but the rest were miners and labourers. The Dents, another set of Brough born householders, were in their 50s and 60s, and living in Shildon, with sons working in the mines or on the railways. Only John, in his late 60s, was an agricultural labourer. Nearby were the Yares and the Gowlings, who had been neighbours in Brough. The Yares who had migrated were in their 30s in 1881, and had, like the others found jobs in the mines and on the railways. Thomas Gowling, born in Brough in 1820, had moved his family in steps, first to Barnard Castle and then to Darlington before he had settled in Shildon in 1856. Thomas worked on the railways, as did one of his sons,

177

another was a blacksmith and another worked as an engine fitter in a factory. His brother Isaac was a labourer on Teeside.

The birth years of the children of these migrants indicates that there had been movement out of Brough from at least the mid-century, linked possibly with the closure of the mines on Stainmore. Some of the Smiths, the Gowlings and the Beckwiths had been there over 25 years, and the Dents and Yares between fifteen and ten years. Moreover new migrants, often single men, continued to arrive: men in their twenties in 1881, like Thomas Yare and Thomas Smith, had married once they had settled. Harrison Gowling, another recent arrival, from Roan Tree farm on Stainmore, was working as a railway shunter. He had found lodgings in a household where the wife had been born in Brough.

One or two lead miners, like John Shaw, had moved to Teesdale by 1881, and a few other Stainmore men had gone to the iron mines in the North York Moors, but most had moved to the Durham coalfield. Some had to take any job going. Working in the coke plant at Tudhoe at the age of 56, was Richard Steele, who had been an innkeeper in Church Brough in 1851.

Brough in 1881: a village description
Using both the 1881 census and the earliest six inch map, published in the 1860s, Church Brough is seen to have changed little in area since the seventeenth century. The castle site had been incorporated into a 120 acre farm owned by the Bainbridges, and Thomas Waller had one of 62 acres nearby. There was a cluster of cottages around the green occupied by small families of farm labourers, masons or retired people, and the Packhorse Inn was no longer there. The vicarage was one of the largest houses, and the vicar, the Rev. William Lyde, a teacher of Classics, had five male boarders. Tofts, the farm beyond the vicarage, was large, over 300 acres in size, and part of the landholdings of George Bailey, whose family had served as bailiffs and other village officials. He had two sons and two daughters and a farm servant. He also owned Belah Farm nearby.

On the road into Market Brough, across the Augill Beck bridge, lay the Low Mill, a corn mill worked by the Clarks, a father and son. Opposite was the Bridge Inn, whose owner also farmed 28 acres. Although the house of William Rudd, a miller, was empty, another Rudd worked the smithy and there was a bakery and several small cottages one of which was occupied by James Brogden, who had previously run the Brough Sowerby mill. The first edition Ordnance Survey map shows a tiny Primitive Methodist chapel lying just to the south of the Augill Beck behind the Bridge Inn. Later editions show it was rebuilt and enlarged. In Church Brough, there were eight unoccupied houses.

Market Brough

This village, in both shape and layout, was almost the same as the linear village of the mediaeval period. It lay along the wide main through road, with back lanes on either side of the buildings. Bridge Street, with the bridges at both ends across the Swindale was the link to Church Brough; there was no New Road.

Near the entrance to Market Brough was Row Bank, on the eastern side of the stream, the site of Fawcett's tallow works. This was an old established family firm which had once been located at the slaughter house near to the brewery, and now employed two men. Three retired carriers in their 70s, lived nearby, and along the Back Lane were farm workers. In Bridge Street there was a variety of occupations, with Thomas Bell's grocer's shop on the corner by Main Street.

The Castle Inn, still owned by the Cleasbys, was the most impressive building on the main street. It had sixteen bedrooms for guests and stabling for twenty horses, along with a twenty acre farm. The inn yard contained cowsheds and pig sties as well as barns. Its farm lands were south of the Baptist Chapel and stretched to Musgrave Lane. William Kilvington, a widower, occupied it with his five children and his mother. He was an innkeeper, an auctioneer and a farmer, employing four servants. In the days before estate agents were set up, it was common to find inn keepers acting as auctioneers. Mr. Bousfield at the George Inn was also an auctioneer.

Bridge Street, with 'T. D. Wilkinson's & Sons, Tailors, Drapers and General Outfitters' on the corner. Photograph by kind permission of John Walton.

Opposite was the Golden Fleece. This was also an inn and a farm, with a number of stables, and the barns in its yard. It stretched back from the main road to the bridge of Swindale Beck and a number of cottages in Bridge Street were part of its estate. It was run by Sarah Dent, a widow and her four children. When the inn was offered for sale four years later, it was as part of a group of buildings, shops and cottages, along with Bridge End House, and three closes, all belonging to the Wilkinson family, who had the tailor's shop at the corner of Bridge Street.[299]

Both sides of the main street were tightly packed with buildings of different ages and styles. When more space was needed, it had been common to build a 'yard' of close packed houses on what had been the garden or garth behind a house, leaving a narrow entrance on to the street. There were at least eight of these yards in 1881, named after the householders, or in the case of the Oddfellows, after the hall built for that friendly society. In these yards were small terraced houses, often occupied by widows, and single women who were employed in such casual and poorly paid work as charwomen and laundresses. One was occupied by a lodging house keeper. On the main street, interspersed between houses were general shops, mercers and grocers, tailors, dress makers and clog makers. There were also bacon factors, ironmongers and smithies. In addition, there was a builder's yard and a number of joiners' workshops. The inns on the south side had courtyards leading out to the back lane and they were all run in conjunction with small farms.

There were farm houses in the Main Street, like Old Hall on the south side and Balmer's House on the north. A number of houses on the main street were occupied by farm labourers who, although they did not own land, rented some of the long narrow fields which came up to the edge of the village on both sides of the roads. Here they could keep a few sheep or a cow and calf. The impression is of an ageing population on the Main Street, where 40 per cent of the householders were over 60; the farmers at Balmer's House, for example, were aged 78 and 81. Most families had shrunk as the young had left home. As in Church Brough, there were a number of empty houses. In all there were 22 uninhabited houses in Market Brough with only one new one being built.

The public buildings included the Wesleyan and the Baptist chapels, and the church. The Oddfellows Hall belonged to a Friendly Society, which provided help in time of trouble and a social life at other times. The original grammar school site had a derelict building at Gibgarth but the new building was in Church Brough. There was a post office near to the Fleece,

---

Note 299: CRO(K), WD/HH bundle, three posters.

The view up Brough's Main Street from the lower Market Cross. Photograph by kind permission of John Walton.

alongside a carrier's yard belonging to the Yares. A temperance café was opposite, next to the Castle Hotel. At Pump Square, at the road end to Helbeck there was a police house.

Helbeck Hall was a 200 acre farm in the hands of John Wearmouth. When it was advertised for sale in 1852, it had included 3,000 acres of common, said to be abounding in lead, coal and limestone. It had also 900 acres of farmland, and a moor capable of carrying four guns.[300] The other householders nearby were farmers or gamekeepers. Yosgill Mill had been turned into a corn mill according to the 1860s map, but had disappeared by the 1881 census.

Outside Market Brough an impressive country residence had been built in the early 1840s. It had a massive dining room (36 feet by 21 feet), a drawing room of similar size, large bedrooms, and cloisters containing a fernery. There was an inner courtyard, terraces, ornamental gardens, kitchen gardens, stables and a coach house. This was Augill Castle. This was occupied in the first decade of the twentieth century by Dr Abercrombie, a Fellow of the Royal Society of Medicine who worked at the Charing Cross Hospital, and the Foundling Hospital but who was known locally as Queen Victoria's private surgeon. Despite working in London, he managed to do a lot of voluntary work in Brough, and died in 1914, after a short retirement.

Note 300: CRO(K), WD/HH bundle 3. The 1910 rate survey shows Helbeck Moor assessed for shooting.

The mill zone

Behind the Main Street and northwards along the Swindale Beck, was the group of buildings known as Helbeck Mill, or sometimes, Indigo Mill. There was no longer indigo processing on the site. Here, in 1881, there was a saw mill, worked by John Longstaff, a carpenter, and a corn mill run by Margaret Thompson a recently widowed young woman with four children. The leat feeding the mill wheel is still visible beyond the buildings where the mill wheel used to be.

Further along the beck lay High Mill, an impressive collection of houses, and substantial barns and stables around a large yard. This was a corn mill run by Joseph Allison a widower, with ten children aged between 21 and three years of age. The mill building was three storeys high and the over-shot wheel was fed by a long leat which came in from the north and then dropped to the mill. Next door to the corn mill was a brewery, and the leads, vats and cisterns have been found over the years, around the site. A brewer lived in part of the building. The wheel could be adapted to run a saw mill, and there is still a saw pit at the end of the building. In the 1880s there was still no direct connection with the road out of Brough.[301] High Mill was really the last set of buildings in Brough village. Beyond were the large farms of Lane Head and Swindale Head.

Postscript[302]

In 1910, a comprehensive, nationwide rate assessment survey was made of all the properties. This shows that Brough High Mill was still a corn mill. Along Brewery Lane there was a tallow works run by Bill Hutchinson and a slaughter house occupied by Bainbridge and Allison. At Helbeck Mill a number of buildings still occupied the site. Indigo Mill was a house, and there was a saw mill, with outbuildings occupied by John Storey, plus a corn mill occupied by William Coates. All these were owned by the Barytes Company of Newcastle. One independent dwelling was occupied by John Goulding, a descendant of John Pattinson, the dyer. In Church Brough, Low Mill, on Victoria Road, was run by Henry Allison.

At the unveiling of the Clock Tower in 1912, one of the speakers, Mr J. Nanson, spoke of his boyhood memories of Brough. He recalled a silent village: the main street, green because of the grass growing through, and many houses empty and to let.[303] A sorry sight indeed, but it does pinpoint one positive characteristic of the community. When local jobs disappeared,

Note 301: Chris Dent, farmer at High Mill, Mill walk, with John Walton, Ann Sandell, Stephen Walker, March 2010.
Note 302: CRO(K) WT/DV/2/11.
Note 303: Newspaper cutting from 1912, scrapbook of John Walton.

and the economy slumped, many youngsters and families had the initiative to move away in search of work. Many did not go far, and often the family ties continued to be strong. Any reading of the newspaper accounts of village celebrations shows family members arriving from all over the north of England. After all, Musgrave Station was within easy walking distance of Brough, as was Barras for Stainmore.

To finish, it is proposed to look at a sample of families living in Brough in the nineteenth century, representing some of the typical occupations and interests: millers and miners, carriers, shopkeepers and innkeepers as well as the vicar. These accounts have been collected from the families concerned, and in the case of the Allison family, written by one of its members. Permission to publish has been given by all concerned.

CHAPTER 17

Living History: Brough Families

The Waltons

The owners of Borrowdale coalmine and Augill Smelt mill in the second half of the nineteenth century were the Walton family. Thomas Walton in a directory of 1858 was listed as the owner of Aisgill colliery, (a mis-print, according to the family, for Augill mine.) Some Waltons had been considerable landowners in the Helbeck region in the early part of the century, but as yet no definite connection has been established between them and the mine owners. The 1841 census lists Jacob Walton as a landowner on Stainmore. He came from Alston and had large scale mining interests in Weardale. The Thomas Walton, mentioned in the Brough directory came from Stanhope, where his family were connected with lead smelting. His father John and his brother Robert were part of a large family which included Joseph, later Sir Joseph Walton, a Liberal MP for Barnsley and Jacob Walton of Alston.

The family had business connections in coal and lead mines, coke works and lime kilns in an area stretching from Alston to Stanhope, and offices in Darlington and Middlesborough. Thomas was sent by his father to sort out problems in the area, where the lead mine at Augill had petered out. He settled in Brough, where he married a member of the Bailey family, who were farmers on a substantial scale. George Henry Bailey was, in essence, the main administrator of the village. He was the registrar for the district, post master, clerk of the school board and at times bailiff for the estate. It was thanks to him that when the railway was being built, a station was put in at Musgrave. Thomas Walton made some innovations at Augill, altering the smelter to deal with iron nodules found nearby. He also took over the Borrowdale coalmine on Stainmore, which remained in the family until it closed in the twentieth century.

Thomas' son, John B. Walton became a solicitor, having read classics at Durham University. Although he died at the age of 50, his achievements were considerable. He worked in London for fourteen years but kept his Brough connections. Described as a mine owner in his obituary, he was much more. He was a great supporter of the church, and for twenty years he was the Brough representative on Westmorland County Council, and a highly active worker within the village; on the committees of the Reading Room, the Oddfellows, the Masons, the Electricity company, and that of the

Agricultural Show. His sister Mary and his London born wife (he married in 1900) were also active in village institutions, supporting Brough Choral Society, the Brass band, and helping with the Belgium refugees in the first World War. In 1929 their only son, a research chemist, married the daughter of Revd. Edward Sugden, who built St Michael's church hall. He too worked in the London area but remained involved in the activities of Brough and retired there, as have his twin sons today.

It is clear that by the end of the century, the younger generation who needed to live in the London region or elsewhere for their highly specialised careers, kept their ties with the area, served it in many voluntary organisations, and eventually retired to it.

Unveiling of the Clock Tower, with part of the old Market Cross on top. Photograph by kind permission of John Walton.

The Vicar

Rev. Canon Lyde, vicar of Brough died at the age of 84 in 1914. He was remarkable for two things; he had been the vicar of Brough for 44 years and in 1906 he fell under a train and survived. In the 1881 census, when he was a widower with three daughters at home, and three servants, he gave his occupation as vicar and teacher of classics. He was running a 'crammer' for university and army entrants. His five boarders were all students from outside Westmorland: from London, Lancashire and Cumberland.

He gave much of his time to public service and over the years he became chairman of the East Ward Poor-law Guardians, Brough parish councillor, a district councillor and Brough representative on Westmorland County Council. He lost his seat on the latter in 1893 to a "young but able man," who was a Liberal, John B. Walton. The local newspaper reported that it was a spirited election with complaints from the Conservatives that they had not expected to fight the election. The newspaper concluded that it was not a personal vote against the vicar, but a general protest against clerics holding too many secular offices.[304]

His second claim to fame was the train accident, which happened at Tebay. Having caught a train at Oxenholme, the vicar, who had to clamber over other passengers to get out, slipped, and fell between the platform and the rail, as the train continued to move slowly into the station. He kept still and the train passed over him. A porter and four others helped him onto the platform. He wrote to the newspaper the following week to say that apart from losing his hat and having a great smear on his face, he was fine and he had been able to keep his umbrella by his side all the time.[305]

By the time he retired he was too old to leave the vicarage and he was helped by a very energetic curate, who founded a Boys' Scout troop and other similar community organisations.

The Yares

A more typical family were the Yares. When they celebrated their Golden Wedding in 1923, there was a full newspaper report. John Yare was a carrier, who for 40 years had been operating between Musgrave and Warcop stations. At the age of 83 he was still doing the daily run from Brough to Musgrave to pick up the papers. Yare was a very common surname in Brough: they were all inter-related. Parts of the family were joiners but John came from the shoemaking branch. His father worked in this trade, and in the 1851 census, his brother William was an apprentice to Tallentire, the shoemaker who also ran the Black Bull inn on the Main Street.

His teenage sister, typical of the period, was a servant. She worked for the local tallow chandler. By then, their mother was a widow, living with John in the house of his older sister Mary, who had married a lead miner from outside the county. Thirty years on, in the 1881 census, John was shown as married, working as a carrier and supporting the family with a smallholding of seventeen acres. His wife was Margaret, daughter of Abraham Hilton, a shopkeeper in Brough and a carrier who served Barnard Castle and Appleby.

Meanwhile, Mary, his sister had been widowed and by 1858 she had married her next door neighbour, John Gowling, also the son of a shoemaker. His father had died very young in 1834, leaving his mother, the daughter of John Pattinson the dyer, with two small sons. She had to work as a

---

Note 304: 16 March 1893 newspaper report. Lyde 59 votes, Walton 133, from John Walton's scrapbook.

Note 305: 4 January 1906 newspaper cutting from John Walton's scrapbook.

labourer to support the family according to the 1841 census. By the 1851 census, John and his brother Harrison were old enough to become farm servants, and Ann Gowling, their mother had married James Parkin, a miller in Church Brough. John became a letter deliverer after marrying Mary (née Yare) and Harrison became a farmer. Both these Yares and the Gowlings brought up families in Brough but their children did not stay. They went to Sunderland, to Liverpool and to Dewsbury. Even when one of the Gowling daughters married a neighbour, Fred Harrison, they set up business not in Brough, but in Manchester. The only one to remain was Bessie Gowling who was the housekeeper at Augill Castle. Many of the Yares went to County Durham as described in the previous chapter.

These families illustrate some typical features of life in a rural community. For the first part of the century, many villagers married and obtained jobs within the small community, often within the family. Because houses were normally rented, there was considerable movement of households but generally only within the local villages. The death of a parent meant that children were boarded out with other relatives, like Betsy Pattinson living with her grandmother in 1841, or those with widowed mothers working long hours, like the Gowlings, were generally still within reach of other members of their families.

However, by the late nineteenth century, the local economy was in decline and young people could get better money and more regulated employment elsewhere. They therefore moved away from home. Yet looking at the reports of village events in the newspapers, these migrants seem to have kept up their links with their families.

The Bell family
(information from Mr Alan Bell, Nateby)
In 1820 the Bell family moved into Brough, where the father probably worked as an agricultural labourer. The family set up a grocer's shop in Church Brough, at Raine Hill. In 1841 Richard Bell was listed as a carrier, with seven children; the eldest was Andrew, aged twenty. Ten years later Richard Bell, aged 61 was described as a farmer and carrier, with five of his children living at home. His grocery business was already established but not mentioned in the census. His sons, Edward and John, both in their late teens were probably working for him. Two other children, Elizabeth aged sixteen, and William aged fourteen, were working as servants at nearby Tofts farm.

Andrew his son, (aged 29, born in Brough) was in Durham City, running a grocery shop on the Sunderland Road, with his brother James as his apprentice. Andrew stayed in Durham, but his son, Hutchinson, was recorded in Brough in 1881. The original grocery business was moved to Market Brough, to a shop opposite Wilkinsons the tailors, next to the Golden Fleece and on the corner of Bridge Street. In 1885 when these premises were up for sale, Thomas Bell was described as the occupier, and Wilkinson the owner. In 1881, further along the south side of the Main Street, there was Bell's Yard, the yard already described with four empty houses in 1881. Further evidence from the same census suggests that some of the Bells had gone to the ironstone mines of North Yorkshire, while others went to County Durham as coal miners.

The old Bells Yard was at Gibgarth, (the Village Store of today) and it became Bell's grocery shop: next door was Gowlings Yard. The name Bells Yard was later transferred across the road when the family re-built some of the properties around Lambert's Joinery business. In 1873, Richard Bell was still advertising his business, but in that year the name of Edward Bell, a grocer and carrier, also appeared in the directories. He lived in Main Street, near to the George, in 1881, with Hutchinson Bell and Mary Yare, nephew and niece, working for him.

The Bells ran a carriers' business to Durham throughout most of the nineteenth century, and an early photograph of Edward Bell, the uncle of Hutchinson Bell, shows him sitting on his covered cart. The main grocery store became Hutchinson Bell's business. It was then passed on to Thomas his son and, when he died it was sold to Peter Foxton of Appleby. At that time, Bell's grocery business had been in the hands of the same family for over a century. Alan, a son of Thomas, chose to spend his working life in farming, just outside Nateby.

The Allison Family: Millers, and Innkeepers
by Patricia Smith (née Allison)

The Allison family came to Brough in about 1865 from Grassholme in Lunedale. There were Allisons in Brough before that but it is not known if they were related.

The earliest family member traced is Henry Allison, born 1800 in Birkdale, near Langdon Beck, Teesdale. He married Margaret Watson and was the miller at Grassholme Mill, Lunedale. They had six children and when Henry died in 1855, the eldest, another Henry, took over the mill. Another son, Joseph Watson Allison, also a miller, married Mary Ann Parkin. They had ten children, Henry, William and Mary (known as Polly) born in Grassholme and after moving to Brough, John, Joseph, James, Margaret, Isabella, Thomas and Sarah were born.

Grassholme Mill, where several generations of Allisons had lived is now under the water of Grassholme reservoir which was built in the early 1900s.

William Allison (born 1862) driving a carriage in a funeral procession up the hill to Church Brough, 1920. Photograph by kind permission of Pat Smith.

Joseph Watson Allison became the miller and farmer at High Mill, now Swindale Grange, using the water of Swindale Beck to power the mill. There was also a brewery there which served Brough's many inns and public houses. Brough had been an important staging post on the Great North Road between London and Glasgow and where, according to legend, travellers were served by nearly twenty inns and lodging houses. The brewery was worked as a separate business and it had ceased to function by the 1890s, although the attached slaughter house and tallow works on the mill site were still in operation. The large family of Allisons lived there till about 1890. Mary Ann had died in 1880 and Joseph had married Elizabeth Bentham and had two more children, Watson Edward and Frederick.

The family seems to have had a hard time in the 1890s as Isabella died in 1893. Henry, the eldest son, in 1897, Sarah in August 1898, and her father, Joseph Watson Allison died in September the same year. John seems to have left to find his fortune in America. Joseph headed south and said he was going to Canada. James left for Liverpool.

Of the survivors of the ten Allison children of the first marriage, Polly, who married Robert Thompson, was an active member of the Methodist church and a keen supporter of both the temperance movement, and the Liberal party. She had six children who mostly left Brough. Her descendants are scattered far and wide, including in Australia and South Africa. Margaret married Dick Hird and they had children. Thomas was a grocer's porter and spent his retirement days in Church Brough, with his wife, Jane Ann Simpson, whose sisters, Esther and Nellie had a sweet shop near the top of the High Street, near the small cross. Their father, John Simpson, had been a butcher. Their mother was killed in an accident with a horse and cart at Grains o'Beck, on the Middleton road when accompanying Polly to collect lemonade. (This is mentioned in the obituary of Polly Thompson.)

William, the eldest surviving son, didn't take over the mill but went into the hotel business. He married Annie Buck, the daughter of the landlord of the Castle Hotel and they set up business at the George Hotel.

Joseph Watson Allison's widow moved to Charles Yard off the High Street with her two boys, Watson Edward aged fifteen and Fred aged ten. Fred married Eleanor Huddert and lived in Kirkby Stephen with their two children. Watson was the head of two families: one with Mary Elizabeth Sayer. Their son, Watson Edward Sayer developed the quarry at Helbeck and was the head of a large family in Kirkby Stephen. There was still a Sayer managing the quarry in 1963, at the time of the closure of the Stainmore railway. Watson Edward Allison married Martha Abram and took over the Low Mill, opposite Brough School, to continue the family milling tradition. Low Mill had previously been operated by Watson's cousin, Henry Allison, who had come from Grassholme with his uncle, Joseph. Watson Allison was known to be very good with horses; he brought horses from Ireland. He had a gypsy-style caravan outside the farmhouse for many years. Watson and Martha had four boys and descendants of their son, John (Jack) still live at Low Mill, though it is no longer a mill.

William Allison and Annie Buck, at the George Hotel, developed a very successful business. The hotel was usually full of visitors and travellers and they also operated a transport business, with horse-drawn vehicles for every purpose. They kept up to fourteen horses for hire. They had carts for haulage, charabancs for outings, traps and landaus for personal transport and the village hearse. They did outside catering, such as for Brough Hill Fair and later for Brough Agricultural Show. They had seven children, two of whom died in infancy. The other five, when young, were expected to help with the hotel and carriage business.

The eldest, Jessie, married Tom Bousfield and had two children, Chris and Ann, who, with their families, still live in and around Brough. Jessie took over the George Hotel after her parents died in 1926 and 1931. Her husband had previously been a farmer at Park Houses, Brough, and when they took over the George Hotel, he continued to keep livestock on nearby fields, so providing milk, butter and cheese for the business, while his wife was a bread baker. She was able to take over the inn because Frank, the eldest son of William and Annie, was more interested in motor cars than hotels. He had started by driving donkey carts and the horse-drawn funeral hearse, as part of the family concern but he wanted to set up a motor business. His father gave him a small sum of money and the use of a barn, which happened to be on the main road adjacent to the hotel. Here he established his business in about 1920, when he was eighteen. Hotel and motor business were mutually supportive.

Frank's brother, Gilbert (Gilly) was also interested in cars and particularly motorbikes. The two of them competed in grass-track races all over the north of England, with a fair amount of success. Gilly worked in a garage in Malton, Yorkshire, married Mary Bell (of the family that owned Bell's grocery shop) and had a daughter, Gillian, whose family grew up in York.

Frank's sister, Rachael, married Tommy Collinson, a butcher in Middleton-in-Teesdale, and had two daughters, Ray and Sheila. Brother Harry married May Harris, from Bolton, and had two children, Bill and Ann. Harry worked for his brother, Frank, delivering bottled gas all round the area and he set up a grocery shop in Brough Main Street. Eventually all Harry's family emigrated to Australia.

Frank Allison married Mabel Wilson, a school teacher from the Lakes whom he met at a dance in Brough and they lived at Swindale Cottage where their son, Clifford was born in 1932. They moved to Grove Cottage in the High Street where Patricia was born in 1938. The family moved to Banks Gate, Stainmore in 1942, where they ran a filling station and later, Banks Gate farm. Cliff followed his father into his very successful motor business which had a Vauxhall dealership in Brough and branches in Appleby and Sedbergh, and received encouragement from his father when he wanted to try his hand at motor racing.

Cliff Allison started with a second-hand 500cc Formula 3 car in 1952 and raced mostly in the north of England and Scotland. He was asked to join the embryo Lotus team in 1956 and was soon travelling all over Europe and North America with Formula 1 and sports cars. He was the first

Formula 1 Team Lotus driver, and the first to gain world championship points - for sixth place in the Monaco Grand prix in 1958. He joined the Ferrari team in 1959 and had successes in early 1960; then he had a serious accident in practice for the Monaco Grand Prix which put him out of the sport for the rest of the year. After joining the British Racing Partnership in 1961 he had another accident, at Spa, Belgium, which ended his motor-racing career. A recent book: *From the Fells to Ferrari*, by Graham Gauld, tells his story. Cliff died in 2005. His sister, Pat, married with three daughters, now lives in Scotland.

Cliff Allison's daughter, Christine, is married and lives at Bowes. His three sons, Frank, Gillie and Michael, run the family business, now called Grand Prix Services, which has changed in nature to suit changing transport needs. Their mother, Mabel, lives in Church Brough.

All the Allison family went to Brough school. Frank (born 1902) and his brothers were taught by Mr Hook who was very strict but he had to allow them home when Bill Allison, from the George Hotel, came to take them out to do some work for him. Frank left school aged about twelve but never stopped studying and became a Member of the Institute of Mechanical Engineers and the representative for Cumberland and Westmorland of the Motor Agents Association, with regular journeys to London for meetings. Cliff and Pat and their cousins were taught by Miss Georgina Atkinson, now Mrs Wren (aged 93 in 2010). School milk was delivered in churns from their great-uncle's farm across the road.

Oral Tradition

These family memories cover a range of activities throughout the period of change which marked the Victorian era. Oral tradition, however, can go further back. No book about Brough can be complete without a mention of two folk legends, one based on events in the sixteenth century; the other possibly much older. This latter is the carrying of the holly tree mentioned in the 1851 directory as an ancient custom taking place on Twelfth Night. This, according to the writer, was originally a religious ceremony, intended to represent the star which guided the wise men to Christ's manger, but "it had been perverted, and the tree is now carried from one public house to the next, until it is nearly consumed, and a pulling match ensues. ...many a competitor comes off minus his coat and hat and the affair ends in drunkenness and immorality." There is an illustration of the event dated 1838, in the *Everyday Book and Table Book or Everlasting calendar* ...by William Hone, which shows a very well controlled crowd, with smartly dressed bandsmen and a flaming tree.[306]

Note 306: Thanks to Marion Williams for this reference.

Carrying the " Holly Tree " at Brough, Westmoreland.

A detailed description is given in a book, *Bygone Cumberland and Westmorland,* published in 1899, by Daniel Scott. He described the tree, with every branch lit with torches of greased reeds. This was carried in procession up and down the town accompanied by a band. Then the tree was flung down and the rival teams from three different inns would fight for it. Both winners and losers would celebrate throughout the rest of the night with ale and dancing. However, by the time he was writing, the custom had long since died out.

The other notable event in folk memory, was the donation of four bells to Brough church; the subject of a poem written in 1828 by the poet, Robert Southey for his friend, Dr John Rumney of Brough. It runs to 29 verses, but only an extract will be printed here:

> *On Stainmore side one summer night*
> *John Brunskill sat to see*
> *His herds in yonder Borrowdale*
> *Come winding up the lea.*

Behind them on the lowlands verge
In evening light serene
Brough's silent tower, then newly built
By Blenkinsop was seen

So while the merry Bells of Brough
For many an age ring on
John Brunskill will remembered be
When he is dead and gone.

As one who in his latter years
Contented with enough
Gave freely what he well could spare
To buy the bells of Brough

Thus it has proved three hundred years
Since then have passed away
And Brunskill's is a living name
Among us to this day.
Source: the *Kirkby Stephen Messenger* of May 1892.

Southey, as a visitor to the district, had become familiar with the history and landscape of the area. In contrast to his previous work on major events like the Battle of Blenheim and the Death of Nelson, he selected a small incident based in a relatively unknown village; an incident which had never been forgotten by local people. Local newspapers and guide books, in the late nineteenth century, continued to keep these memories alive.

Oral tradition is important and perhaps a future writer will be able to build on recent memories as well as contemporary documents to give details of the changes in the twentieth century already hinted at in Pat Smith's article above. How did Brough, for example, adjust to the age of motor transport?

Conclusion

Looking back over past history, the remarkable point is that Brough still survives, unlike some other villages built around a castle. The village itself is quiet, because a modern by-pass takes the "Great Highway" away from the houses, yet this main road still lies within easy reach of the village and could provide the impetus for future development.

It can be argued that the history of Brough illustrates a number of important features common to other upland rural communities in the North of

England. Supported throughout by the farming in the locality, it developed from a defensive settlement to become an administrative centre for the colonising of difficult hill country. In more settled times its market served the trade along the main road, and the road improvements of the eighteenth century supported an increase in the exploitation of local minerals. However, the isolation of the region remained a handicap and its remoteness from the major urban areas was further emphasised when the railway builders avoided it. What of its future?

History and tradition have played a vital role in the building of the present community. However small the settlement is, the past should not be ignored.

Brough Castle, 2010, by kind permission of David Yeadell.

Bibliography

Documents

Regnal Years: These began either around the date of the accession or on the date of the coronation of each monarch. [It varied through time]. Thus I Edward II was July 1307-July 1308. This system of dating was used in the Inquisitions Post Mortem listed below.

Old Calendar: The Julian calendar, with 25 March the first day of the new year, was in use in England until 1752 when the Gregorian calendar was adopted so that 1st January became the first day of the year, and in the course of that year, the 2nd September was immediately followed by 14th September. [C. R. Cheney, *Handbook of Dates*]

Note: Spellings are retained as shown in the documents.

Records

National Archives at Kew:
PRO/WO/30/48 Abstract of inn and Alehouses.
PRO/Ass/1/44/13 Assize records
PRO/ E/ 179/ 195/17-19. Poll Tax returns for Brough

Cumbrian Record Office: Kendal CRO(K)
Register of Baptisms of Brough Primitive Methodist Circuit 1844-1885.
Brough under Stainmore parish registers:
Burial register WPR 23A/19
Baptismal register WPR 23A/8
Church wardens' accounts WPR/23 A/B

Hothfield Records, CRO(K):
WD /Hoth/ 10 vol 3. Great Booke of Records - Lady Anne Clifford
WD /Hoth box 45. Steward's accounts.
WD/Hoth box 25, 30 and 34 Leases.
WD/Hoth box 34, D1, D2, Manor survey and manor rental 1604/5.
WD/ Cat/ 9177 Brough manor survey

Heelis deposits, CRO(K):
WD/HH/198/193/200 Turnpike Toll gates.
WD/HH Bundle 3 sales details.

Other deposits, CRO(K):
WD/O/3 Magistrates order book.
WQ/SR Quarter Sessions
WQ/I Appleby Indictment book
WST2(1-9) Turnpike details.
WDX 341/1 Jonathan Alderson's notebook
WPC/33 Account book of Brough Poor law Guardians
WPR/ 23a/b Stainmore boundaries for the Tithes.
WD/RG Vaux Brewery
WD/RC/8/76 Tithe map and Schedule 1841
WD/DV/2/11 Survey of 1910 for rates
WDX/ 341/3/4 Deeds
WDB/ 35 O.S. Survey book 1861.
WSMB/A Appleby borough books, vol.1-2
WCC/OL/743 Cotton mill
WD/MM/box 60

Cumbria Record Office: Carlisle, CRO(C)
Please note new citation for Carlisle Record Office. It is now CACC:
D&C Machell papers vol. 3
D&C Wills and inventories
C/ Q/11 Quarter Sessions

Lonsdale Papers, also CRO(C), now CACC:
D/Lons/3/158.
D/Lons/L/12/3/12/7 Lime accounts
D/Lons/ 12/3/10/10 lead.
D/Lons/ 10/3-10 coal etc.
D/Lons/ Li/ 4/1/28 Lady Ann's letter.
D/Lons/ L/ 12/3/9/27-31 Yosgill.
D/Lons/L/Carleton/10/1 A
D/Lons/ L/12/3/19/14

Kendal Local History Library:
Census: 1841, 1851, 1881, Westmorland, Microfilm
1820 and 1832 *The Register of voters for the Shire of Westmorland*, 1820,
        compiled by William Kaye, published 1820, Ditto 1832.
Kirkby Stephen and District Messenger, Microfilm 1890-2. [Incomplete]

Maps:
Ordnance Survey [OS]. Kindly loaned by Mr Chris Dent of Brough
25 inches to the mile, 1st Edition surveyed 1858, published 1860.
2nd edition, part surveyed 1897, published 1898.
Saxton, C. 1596, Westmorland [copied by Speed and others]
Jefferys, T. Historical Map of Westmorland, 1770, fac. CWAA 2001.

State Papers, all HMSO, London:
  Calendar, Inquisitions Post Mortem. [IPM]
  9 Ed II, 1314-1315.
  13 Rich, II
  15 Rich. II
  10 Hen V
  2 Hen VI.
  Calendar, Close Rolls: 9 Ed. II
  Calendar, Patent Rolls: Hen. III
  Calendar of Pipe Rolls: 34 ED III, 12 R II.
  Calendar of Committee of Compounding, 1650
  Calendar of Letters and Papers, Foreign and Domestic, of the reign of Henry VIII.

Oral history Sources:
  Mrs Anne Birkbeck
  Mrs Pat Smith
  Thomas Raine
  Chris Dent
  Alan Bell
  John Walton
  John Gowling

Selected Bibliography, Books and Articles:
Anon, *Report of CWAA members excursion*, 1879, TCWAA, 1st series, (1881).
Appleby, A. B., *Famine in Tudor and Stuart England*, LUP (1978).
Ashcroft, I., *Vital Statistics, Westmorland census 1787*, Kendal: Curwen Trust, (1992).
Ashcroft, L. ed.,*Vital Statistics; the Westmorland Census 1787*, Curwen Archive Texts, (1992).
Bailey, R. and Crump, R., *Corpus of Anglo-Saxon stone sculptures in Anglo-Saxon and pre-Norman Stones*, OUP, (1998).
Barfoot, P. & Wilkes, J., *Universal British Directory of Trades*, 1790/1794, London
Bailey, J. & Culley, G. [Pringle. A. on Westmorland], *Agriculture of Northumberland, Cumberland and Westmorland 1794*, Scolar Press facsimile:York, (1972).
Beresford, M., *New Towns of the Middle Ages*, London: Lutterworth, (1967).
Birley, E., *Roman Fort at Brough,* TCWAA, LVIII 1959, and 1958.
Breay, J., *Light in the Dales*, Canterbury Press, Norwich (1996).
Brewer, J. E., Gairdner, J., Brodie, R. H. eds., *Calendar of Letters and papers, Foreign and Domestic of the reign of Henry VIII*, HMSO.
Brierley, H., ed., *Registers of Brough under Stainmore*, Kendal (1923).
Bulmer, T. E., *Topography and directory of Westmorland,* 1885, Manchester, (1885)
Burgess, I. G., and Holliday, D. W., *Geology of the country around Brough under Stainmore*, Institute of Geological Sciences, HMSO (1979).
Calendar of Committee of Compounding, HMSO (1889-92).

Charlton, J., *Brough Castle*, English Heritage, (undated).

Clifford, D. H. J., ed, *Diaries of Lady Ann Clifford*, Sutton, (2003).

Curwen Records of North Westmorland, Kendal, CWAA (Record) VIII, Kendal (1932).

Davies-Shiel, M., *Watermills of Cumbria*, Dalesman, (1978).

Dyer, P. and Palliser, D. M. eds., *Diocesan Population returns in 1563, and 1601*, Records of Economic and Social History, OUP (2005).

Fenwick, C. C., *Poll Taxes of 1377, 1379 and 1381*, Oxford, (1998), Vol 1.

Fleming Papers, CWAA (record) vol XIII.

Fleming, D. S., ed. Sir G. F. Duckett, *Description of Cumberland and Westmorland, AD 1671*, CWAA (Record) Kendal, (1882).

Fraser, C. M., *Cumberland and Westmorland Lay Subsidies 1332*, TWCAA (1996).

Fraser, E. M. ed., *Northern Petitions*, Surtees Soc., Vol. 194 (1981).

Glascock, R. G., *Lay Subsidy of 1334*, Records of Economic and Social History, OUP (1975).

Harrison, S. M., *Pilgrimage of Grace in the Lake Counties, 1536-7*, RHS, London (1981).

Harrison, W. ed., Edelen, G., *Description of England*, Facsimile, New York, Cornell U.P., (1968).

Holdgate, M., *Story of Appleby in Westmorland*, Cumbria: Hayloft, (2006).

Hutchinson, W., History of Cumberland, Carlisle (1794).

Jones, M. J. et al, *Archaeological work at Brough under Stainmore, the Roman discoveries*, TCWAA (1977).

Jones, M. J. et al, *Archaeological work at Brough under Stainmore: the medieval and later settlements*, (1989) TCWAA.

Kaye, W., *Poll for Knights of the Shire to represent the County of Westmorland*, March 1820, Kendal.

Kaye, W., *List of persons entitled to vote in the election of the Knights of the Shire, Westmorland*, Appleby, (1832).

Kelly's *Directory of Cumberland and Westmorland*, 1905, London (1905)

Lathamire, *Revised Medieval Latin Word List with Fascicules*, London (1965)

Leland, *Itinerary in England and Wales 1539-45*, fac. Centaur Press, London (1964).

McKay, B. and Wilson, C., *Kirkby Stephen at Work, A Historic Directory of Trades*, Appleby, (1997).

Markham, G., ed. Best, M., *English Housewife*, McGill, Queens (1994).

Mitchell, W. R. and Joy, D., *Settle to Carlisle Railway*, Lancaster: Dalesman, (1967).

Moorhouse, G., *Pilgrimage of Grace*, Weidenfeld and Nicolson (2002).

Nicolson, J. and Burn, R. *History and Antiquities of the Counties of Westmorland and Cumberland*, London (1777).

Parson and White, *History Directory and Gazetteer of Cumberland and Westmorland, 1829*, fac. Whitehaven (1976).

Perriman, D., and Robinson, J., *Mediaeval Fortified Buildings of Cumbria*, CWAA (extra) (1998).

Phillips, C., Ferguson, C. and Wareham, A., eds., *Westmorland Hearth Tax,* British Record Society, CWAA, (2009)

Phythian-Adams, C., *Land of the Cumbrians; a study in British Provincial Origins,* Scolar Press (1996).

Richmond, I. G., *Roman leaden seals from Brough under Stainmore,* TCWAA, NS XXXVI, (1936).

Robertson, D., *The Plains of Heaven,* Casdec Ltd., (1989).

Royal Commission on Historical Monuments, *An Inventory of the Historical Monuments of Westmorland,* HMSO (1936)

Scott, D., *Recent discoveries in the Muniment rooms at Appleby and Skipton castles,* TCWAA, (1917-18).

Scott, D., *Bygone Cumberland and Westmorland,* London (1899)

Sharpe, J., *John Metcalfe Carleton, Georgian Rake of the Eden Valley,* (undated).

Shepherd, M. E., *From Hellgill to Bridge End, Aspects of econominc and social change in the Upper Eden Valley, 1840-95.* Hatfield: University Of Herts., (2004).

Shotter, D., *Romans and Britains in North West England,* NWCRS (2004).

Simmons, J. ed., *Rail 150 Years: the Stockton and Darlington Railway,* London: Methuen, (1975).

Simpson, J. Canon, *Things Old and New around Kirkby Stephen, 1863-1886,* rep. UEHS, (2006).

Simpson, W. D., *Brough under Stainmore: the castle and the church,* TCWAA, XIII, NS, (1946).

Smith, A. H., ed., *Place names of Westmorland,* XLII, EPNS, CUP (1967).

Smyth, A. P., *Warlords and Holy Men.*

Storey, R. L., *Register of Bishop Gilbert Welton* (1999); *Register of Thomas de Appleby,* 1363-95 (2006); *Register of John de Kirkby* (1993), Canterbury and York Soc.

Storey, R. L., *Chantries of Cumberland and Westmorland, 1546: Brough,* TCWAA, (1962)

Tait J., *Medieval English Boroughs,* Manchester Univ. Press, (1936, reprint 1999).

Todd, J., *Lanercost Cartulary,* CWAA (Record) XI (1997).

Walton, P., *Stainmore and Eden Valley Railways,* Oxford, (1992).

Whyte, I., *Transforming Fell and Valley,* Lancaster: University centre for North-West Studies, (2003).

Willan, T. S., *An eighteenth century shopkeeper: Abraham Dent of Kirkby Stephen,* Kelly, N. York., (1979).

Williams, E. N., *Documentary history of England,* vol 1 & 2, Penguin.

Williams, L. A., *Road Transport in Cumbria in the 19th century,* London: Allen & Unwin, (1975).

Williamson, G. C., *Lady Anne Clifford's account book, 1665, 1667-8,* TCWAA XXIII, (1923).

Winchester, A. J. L. and Wane, M. eds., *Thomas Denton, a perambulation of Cumberland in 1687-8,* Surtees Society, vol 207, (2003).

Winder, F. A., *Royalists of Westmorland,* transcriptions from Royal Composition papers, Westmorland Notebook, (1889), Kendal.

Appendices

Appendix I: Place names and a glossary

This work covers a period when there was no standardised spelling. Among the many variations for local place names are:

The Roman Fort: Verterae, Verteris.
Brough: Burgus subtus Staynesmore, Bourghe, Burgh, Vill et Burgus cum
Stainmore.
Church Brough: Burgh Supra, Over Burgh, Castle Brough.
Market Brough: Lower Brough, Nether Brough, Street Brough.
Brough Sowerby: Soureby juxta Brough.
Helbeck: Hellbeck, Hillbeck, Hilbeck.

There are a number of common names in various parts of Cumbria, of which Brough is but one example. The Borrowdale referred to in the text is on Stainmore.

Family names and farm names are also found with different spellings, often within the same document, e.g. Palliard, Palliards, and Cumpstone, Cumstune, or Gowling, Gouling, Gooling, and Goulding. Local dialect and colloquial spelling are to be found in the local papers. In general the spelling of surnames has been used as shown in the document referred to in an effort to avoid personal interpretation by the writer. The names are grouped together in the index to show these variations

Glossary:

Whies/quy	calf or young cow
Stirk	young beast
Kye/kine	cattle usually milk cows
Stag	young horse
Stottes	young male cattle
Nag	small riding horse
Black Beasts	black cattle , usually brought into the area by Scottish drovers
Load horse/Galloway	fell pony used as a packhorse
Cattle gait/gate	a stint or grazing rights on the common
Yowes	ewes
Hog	a young sheep which has not been shorn
Vaccary	large cattle farm
Turbary	peat cutting rights
Desmesne	land worked for the lord of the manor

Bigge/byge	barley
Ottes/haver	oats
Haber	hay
Barke	bark for tanning
Line	flax
Cards and combs	for wool preparation.
Harden	coarse cloth or sacking
Heckle	comb for flax
Swinglesticks	for beating the retted [soaked] flax
Webb	a length of material usually still on the loom
Fustian	coarse cloth
Lead	ale brewing tank
Messfat	malt vat
Pudor/puder	pewter

Abbreviations:

EPNS	English Place Name Society
IPM	Inquisition Post Mortem
N&B	Nicolson and Burn
OS	Ordnance Survey

Appendix II: Westmorland Weights, Measures and Money

At the end of the eighteenth century, the Board of Agriculture's survey comments on the great diversity of the measurements and gives the following information:

Weight:
The pound can be 12, 16, 18 or 21 ounces.
A stone may be 14, 16 or 20lbs. A stone of tallow, wool, yarn or hay = 16lb
A Winchester bushel, as used elsewhere in parts of England was 32 quarts.
A customary or Westmorland bushel was three times that of a Winchester one, but in the Appleby area "a bushel of potatoes is two bushels for potatoes." [sic]

Acreage:
A statute acre is 4,840 square yards but a Westmorland acre is 6,760 square yards, from A. Pringle in Bailey and Culley, *Agriculture of Westmorland*.

Money:
Until the late thirteenth century, the only coin actually minted was the silver penny (1*d.*); 240 of these weighed one pound (lb). Thus 240*d.* became £1 currency. Later subdivisions included the shilling (1*s.* or 12*d.*) and the Mark (160*d.*, or 13*s.* 4*d.*) The Half Mark or Noble (6*s.* 8*d.*) was issued in 1344 and in 1351 the Groat (4*d.*) became legal currency, from Lionel Munby, *How much is that worth?*

British Association for Local History.

The early accounts in this book are written in roman numerals, with either upper case or lower case letters for the first figure and if there are a number of minims (iii) the last is generally written as a j. The totals are often left in shillings, rather than being converted into pounds.

Xls = 40 shillings	viijd = 8*d.* or eight old pennies
Xxs = 20 shillings	vid = 6*d.*
Xs = 10 shillings	iiijd = 4*d.* or a groat
Vs = 5 shillings	ijd = 2*d.*
js = 1 shilling	

Old currency:

£1 = 20 shillings = 240*d.* = £1 decimal currency or 100 new pence.

Old currency:	In Decimal currency
10 shillings	50 new pence
5 shillings	25 new pence
1 shilling	5 new pence
6 pence	2½ new pence

Appendix III: Brough Market Charter, 1330

Edwardus dei gratia Rex Anglie Dominus Hibernie et Dux Aquit' Archiepiscopis Episcopis Abbatibus Prioribus Comitibus Baronibus Justiciariis Vicecomitibus Prepositis Ministris et omnibus Ballivis et fidelibus suis, Salutem. Sciatis nos de gratia nostra speciali concessisse et hac carta nostra confirmasse dilecto et fideli nostro Roberto de Clifford, quod ipse et heredes sui imperpetuum habeant unum mercatum singulis septimanis per diem Jovis apud Manerium suum de Burgh subtus Staynmore in Comitatu Westmerl' et unam feriam ibidem per quattuor dies duraturam, videlicet per duas dies proximos ante festum Sancti Matthei Apostoli, et, in eodem festo sancti Matthei per unum diem sequentem, nisi mercatum illud et feria illa sint ad nocumentum vicinorum mercatorum et vicinarum feriarum. Quare volumus et firmiter precipimus pro nobis et heredibus nostris, quod predictus Robertus et heredes sui imperpetuum habeant predicta mercatum et feriam apud manerium suum predictum cum omnibus libertatibus et liberis consuetudinibus ad huius modi mercatum et feriam pertinentibus nisi mercatum illud et feria illa sint ad nocumentum vicinorum mercatorum et vicinarum feriarum sicut predictum est. His Testibus venerabilibus patribus, H. Lincoln Episcopo Cancellario nostro, R Episcopo Sarum, Johanne de Eltham, Comite Cornub' fratre nostro carissime, Rogero de Mortuo Mari Comite Marchie, Willelmo de Monte Acuto, Olivero de Ingham Hugone de Turpliton Senescallo Hospicij nostri et aliis. Datum per manum nostrum apud Norhampton secundo die Augusti anno regni nostri quarto.

Per breve de private sigillo

Edward, by the grace of God, King of England, Lord of Ireland, and Duke of Acquitaine, to the archbishops, bishops, abbots, priors, counts, barons, justices, viscounts, stewards, ministers and all bailiffs and those faithful to him, greetings, Know that we of our special grace have granted and by this our charter confirmed to our beloved and faithful Robert de Clifford, that he and his heirs forever may have a market once a week on Thursdays in his manor of Burgh under Staynmore [1] in the county of Westmerland and one fair there lasting four days, that is on the two days immediately preceding the feast of St Matthew, the Apostle, and for one day following the same feast of St Matthew, unless that market and fair should harm neighbouring markets and neighbouring fairs. Therefore we wish and firmly require, for us and for our successors, that the said Robert and his heirs have the aforesaid market and fair in perpetuity in their said manor with all the liberties and free customs relevant to such markets and fairs insofar as that market and fair are not to the detriment of neighbouring markets and fairsas aforesaid.

With these as witnesses, the venerable fathers, H, bishop of Lincoln, our chancellor, R bishop of Salisbury, John of Eltham, Duke of Cornwall, our dearest brother, Roger of Mortuo Mari [2], Marcher Lord, William of Mont Aigu [3], Oliver of Ingham, Hugo of Turpliton, Seneschall of our Household, and others. Given at our hand at Norhampton [4] the second day of August in the fourth year of our reign.

By list of the privy seal

[1] Brough under Stainmore, anglice Borough under Stainmore
[2] Anglice Mortimer
[3] Anglice Montague
[4] Northampton

Source ref: CRO(K) HMC, 1330/31, CRO[K] WD/Hoth Box 45, Market Charter.

Appendix IV: 1379 Poll Tax: Brough and District

transcribed by John Gowling

NB Questionable readings are italicised. When no tax paid is shown that is because that part was illegible or damaged. Forenames have been modernised; surnames are as written. *Manservant* and *maidservant* are used to translate *serviens* and *ancilla*. The tax payable was four old pence, that is one groat for single taxpayers and for a married couple. Craftsmen (artificers) paid six pence. Further details in chapter 7.

<u>Villa de Nether Burgh cum Staynesmore</u> (i.e. Market Brough)
NB Much of this part is torn and faded.

1) William Fayrher and his wife
2) William att Milne and his wife
3) William Smyth, artificer, and his wife

4) John *Gower,* artificer, and his wife
5) John Thomson and his wife
6) John Illegible
7) ??? [Ma?land]
8) *Thomas Coler*, artificer, and his wife
9) *Richard Cader*
10) John del *Bakhous, artificer*
11) Robert Symson and his wife
12) Thomas Symson and his wife
13) Robert son of Thomas Symson
14) John Robynson and his wife
15) John del *Sagh* and his wife
16) Thomas Sanderson and his wife
17) Thomas *Thomasman Robynson*
18) *Richard* Colyer and his wife
19) Illegible
20) William de *Awgles* and his wife
21) Ralph *de Pennston* and his wife
22) Robert Webster and his wife
23) Joanna *Jakdoghter*
24) John Jenkinson *Smyth* and his wife
25) Illegible
26) Illegible and his wife
27) ??? *Symson*
28) ??? de Skelton
29) Isabella *Pensul*
30) John Thomson de *Bolton*
31) Margaria maidservant of *Henry* Smyth
32) *Thomas* de Bolton
33) Joanna maidservant of Thomas Chapman
34) John son of *Adam* del Milne
35) Thomas manservant of William Smyth
36) *Anna* maidservant of the same William
37) Elena maidservant of John del *Syke*
38) Mapota maidservant of John del Bakhous
39) Thomas ??? Shephird
40) *Alice* maidservant of William Lathe
41) Alice de ???
42) Thomas ???, artificer, and his wife
43) John Colynson de Staynesmore and his wife
44) Agnes *Wyhedynge*
45) *John …ynson* and his wife
46) Illegible …ynson and his wife
47) Illegible and his wife
48) Illegible and his wife

49) Illegible and his wife
50) Illegible and his wife
51) *Thomas del Dene* and his wife
52) *Geoffrey* Nicolson and his wife
53) Thomas del *Ffell* and his wife
54) John de Quynfell* and his wife
55) William *Luaresdale* and his wife
56) Thomas Colynson and his wife
57) *Walter* Symson and his wife
58) Geoffrey *Devyas* and his wife
59) William *Ffayrer* and his wife
60) *William de Dentt*
61) William *Shacelson* and his wife
62) Thomas de *Lalin*??? and his wife
63) Henry de *Tybay*** and his wife
64) Illegible son of the same Henry
65) Thomas Wilson de *Dene*
66) Agnes maidservant of Thomas de *lalin*
67) Elena maidservant of William *Shacelson*
68) Illegible
69) Illegible
70) Illegible
71) Illegible
72) Illegible
73) Illegible

Nether Brough had 110 adults, plus children.

<u>Villa de Burgh cum Staynesmore</u> (i.e. Church Brough)

1) Emma Sabdoghter
2) Richard Clark and his wife
3) Illegible *and his wife*
4) *Adam Smyth and his wife*
5) William Illegible *and his wife*
6) John *Spenser and his wife*
7) Robert *Wilson* and his wife
8) John son of *Robert* Wilson
9) Margaria daughter of *Robert* Wilson
10) John Robynson and his wife
11) Willam *le* Wryght, artificer, and his wife, vjd
12) Roger Mason, artificer, and his wife, iiijd

Notes:
* No 54 Old spelling of Whinfell.
** No 63 Probably Tebay

13) Robert de Dowglas and his wife
14) Elena maidservant of John de ???, iiijd
15) Michael fforester *and his wife*, iiijd
16) John *Horne*???? and his wife, iiijd
17) Anabell daughter of Roger, iiijd
18) Alice Addydoghter, iiijd
19) Jacob Cock, iiijd
20) John the servant of the vicar of Brough, iiijd
21) Adam the servant of the same vicar, iiijd
22) *Elena Goldynge*, iiijd
23) Isabella daughter of the same *Elena,* iiijd
24) Alan *Wryght* ???, iiijd
25) John Illegible, iiijd
26) Illegible *Glenton,* iiijd
27) Illegible
28) Hugh *Ladyman* and his wife, iiijd
29) Roger the servant of *Henry*, iiijd
30) *Roger Smyth* artificer and his wife, iiijd
31) Thomas Robynson and his wife, iiijd
32) William Bakster and his wife, iiijd
33) William Illegible and his wife, iiijd
34) Thomas *Broun* and his wife, iiijd
35) Richard *Waller* and his wife, iiijd
36) *Richard* Waller, artificer, iiijd
37) William Waller, artificer, and his wife, iiijd
38) Thomas ffrenke, artificer, and his wife, vjd
39) *Reginald* Bakster and his wife, iiijd
40) Hugh Smyth, artificer, and his wife, iiijd
41) Mapota de Goldyng*ton,* iiijd
42) John *Slynch*, artificer, and his wife, *vjd*
43) John *Paton* and his wife, iiijd
44) Illegible *Bret* de Illegible
45) Thomas *Chapman* and his wife, iiijd
46) Stephen *H*??*thyngton*, iiijd

Church Brough may have had 26 married couples and 20 single people. The text is too faded for certainty. If the presumed figures are accurate the adult population was over 70, to which children should be added. Clergy were taxed separately, so the vicar would be excluded from this list.

Villa de Helbek

1) Thomas de Blenkansopp, Esquier, *Vjs viij*d
2) Thomas Walker, artificer, and his wife, vjd
3) John *Michelson* and his wife, iiijd
4) Adam Colyer and his wife, iiijd

5) Robert *Bleg* and his wife, iiijd
6) John Jakson and his wife, iiijd
7) *William Toser* and his wife, iiijd
8) John *Deare* and his wife, iiijd
9) John *Ba.....an* and his wife, iiijd
NB The remainder is illegible.

This incomplete list suggests a population of at least seventeen adults, to which children must be added. Thomas de Blenkansopp's tax is difficult to read but half a mark seems to have been standard for people of his rank.

Villa de Sourby iuxta Burgh (Brough Sowerby)
1) Adam de Soulby and his wife, iiijd
2) John de Bernes and his wife, iiijd
3) John Webster, artificer, and his wife, iiijd
4) William de Soulby and his wife, iiijd
5) Robert Huchinson and his wife
6) Adam *..adsman* and his wife
7) William Shephird and his wife
8) *John* de Glenton and his wife
9) Geoffrey Wacher and his wife
10) Robert *Halvathson* and his wife
11) John Wilkynson and his wife
12) William Johanson and his wife
13) Thomas Colyer and his wife, iiijd
14) John Wacher and his wife, iiijd
15) Thomas Shepherdson, iiijd
16) William del Bernes, iiijd
17) Thomas Wildyng, iiijd
18) Agnes Shephird, iiijd
19) Agnes de Graystok, iiijd
20) John de Glenton junior, iiijd
21) Robert Wacher
22) *Thomas Barker*
23) Agnes Robyn *mayden*
24) *Cecilia* Wacher
25) Thomas de *Old*burgh
26) Johanna Shephirddoghter
27) Margaria *Gly*ndoghter
28) Emma Cok

Summa   Xs iiijd

Brough Sowerby contained 42 adults plus an unknown number of children. There was one possible weaver, one shepherd and possibly his son, one collier and three watchers. These latter may have been guardians of the nearby Forest of Stainmore or of one of the local deer parks. The woman called *Shephirddoghter* is interesting; was she perhaps also a shepherd?

Appendix V: Personal names mentioned at Brough and Brough Sowerby in the 1425 accounts

NB: Damage to the document has limited reading to some extent.

Bernes William - had a tenement and land at Brough Sowerby, at a rent of seven-pence for half a year. Also had, at Brough Sowerby, a cottage holding at a rent of two shillings.*

Blaymyre William - an estate official, probably not from Brough.

Bousfell Thomas - had an '*approviamentum*', i.e. improved land, which might also be an enclosure somewhere on Stainmoor.

Bucell Nicholas - renting cottage holding in Lower Brough at twelve pence per annum.

Bukell (first name uncertain but possibly *Thomas*) – had one unidentifiable holding on Stainmoor, and a second called Cragslettel.

Bukles Thomas** - renting Castle Close, called Castle Park, at fifty four shillings and fourpence, the Brough water mill at five pounds six and eightpence, one cottage holding in Upper Brough at three shillings and an acre of land 'near the Tofts' at twelve pence. He also had an official position in relation to *cheminagium* (Way penny)

Calshird Agnes - renting a cottage holding in Lower Brough at two shillings.

Calshird Mapota - had previously had a cottage holding, now decayed, valued at two shillings in Lower Brough.

Clerk Richard (previous reeve)

Clerk Robert - renting two bovates in Upper Brough at ten shillings.

Crag Robert - present reeve and renting two bovates in Upper Brough at ten shillings.

Crakanthorpe William - senior Manor official, perhaps one of the Newbiggin family, who 'received' or handled the estate money

Crakanthorp John - had one (illegible) holding, a second called, perhaps, *Stannedyke*, and pasture land called Blechefeld at, probably, ten shillings, whereas earlier it had been worth twenty shillings, all on Stainmoor

Cumston Robert - had a fishery, presumably in Brough Sowerby, paying four pounds and ten shillings, together with John Glenton, junior, John Ladyman, William Johnson, John Halgarth and John Glenton, senior. The total rent was four pounds ten shillings, with each paying eleven shillings and threepence, which does not add up correctly. Possibly Cumston, as leading name here, was paying the balance. Cumston also had a croft (*husbandum*) at Brough Sowerby, at a rent of twenty shillings.

Notes:

* Cottagium/cottage holding. This probably meant an established small holding, possibly with a cottage on it.

** Bukles was apparently also handling the market tolls.

Dent Robert - nothing known.

Dentt John - held a vaccary called Hesil Bank at a reduced rent, below the previous rent of forty shillings.

Devyas John - had an 'improved' holding, somewhere near Heggerscale, written as *Egilscale.*

Doge Thomas - otherwise unknown but apparently a Carlisle-based seneschal of the estate

Douglass Robert - renting a 'garden', which might be a garden or an orchard, at one penny. The reading of this surname is doubtful.

Drax Richard - Clerk, possibly a clergyman. He probably wrote the account.

Emond John - renting a parcel of land called Ploghstanecroft in Upper Brough, outside the enclosed area of meadow there, at sixpence.

Ewbank John - had some holding on Stainmoor.

Ewmonde Robert - renting a cottage holding in Upper Brough at three shillings.

Ewmondson Robert - his name also appears as *Emondson.* He was renting two bovates in Upper Brough at ten shillings. He had been the bailiff at Brough.

Frankys John - Possibly the gaoler at Appleby.

Glenton John, senior - John Glenton, unspecified, had a croft (*husbandum*) probably at Brough Sowerby, at a rent of sixteen shillings. Glenton senior also had a cottage holding at Brough Sowerby, at a rent of three shillings. He was the collector, with Thomas Skayfe, for Brough Sowerby. See also the entry for Robert Cumston on the Brough Sowerby fishery.

Glenton John, junior - see also entry for Robert Cumston on the Brough Sowerby fishery. Also had a croft (*husbandum*) at Brough Sowerby, at a rent of twenty shillings.

Godfray John - had a tenement, probably at Brough Sowerby, at a rent of five shillings.

Halgarth John - see entry for Robert Cumston on the Brough Sowerby fishery. Also had a cottage holding, probably at Brough Sowerby, at a rent of five shillings.

Johnson William - see entry for Robert Cumston on the Brough Sowerby fishery. Also had a croft (*husbandum*) at Brough Sowerby, at a rent of twenty shillings.

Ladyman John - see entry for Robert Cumston on the Brough Sowerby fishery. He also had a croft (*husbandum*) at Brough Sowerby, at a rent of eighteen shillings, down from an earlier valuation of twenty shillings. Ladyman may well be the John Letheman listed below.

Lambard Adam - renting a cottage holding in Upper Brough at twelve pence. He had previously one, now decayed, at twelve pence in Upper Brough.

Lambe John - he had a role in a vaccary, probably on Stainmoor, but the text is damaged

Letheman John - renting the barley kiln in Lower Brough at twelve pence. Also a grange (*Grangia*) in Lower Brough at twelve pence and a 'parcel' of land 'above the Tofts' at fourteen pence.

Lonnesdale Thomas - renting a cottage holding in Lower Brough at five shillings.

Lonesdale Mapot*a* - renting four bovates in Upper Brough at twenty shillings.

Maltby John - seems to have had some share with Thomas Ubank and Thomas Bukle in the Brough water mill and, possibly, in the market returns.

Neville Richard - Marcher Lord (West March), from Raby, responsible for the Clifford estates during the minority of the heir.

Nicholson John - had some unspecified holding on Stainmoor.

Nicholson William - occupying a *'purprestura'*, i.e. encroachment, towards Kaber.

Olyver Thomas - renting two bovates in Upper Brough at ten shillings.

Richardson William - renting two bovates in Upper Brough at ten shillings and a cottage holding in Upper Brough at twelve pence.

Robynson John - renting two bovates in Upper Brough at ten shillings and a cottage holding in Upper Brough at twelve pence. He was the bailiff and collector at Brough.

Robynson (first name illegible) - had some holding on Stainmoor.

Salkeld Hugh - Seneschall, probably not local.

Sandreson John - renting a cottage holding at four shillings and a parcel of land at two pence, both in Lower Brough.

Sayfe Thomas - probably a misspelling of Skayfe.

Scardale John - he was the previous reeve for Brough Sowerby.

Skayfe Henry - held foreland, i.e. newly reclaimed land, at Brough Sowerby at a rent of four pence.

Skayfe John - had a holding on Stainmoor called either *Stendyckis* or *Stonedyke*, adjacent to Redgateclose. This may have been shared with John Crakanthorpe.

Skayfe Thomas - renting pasturage with associates on Sowerby moor at four pounds and the newly enclosed Sowerby moor. In addition he had a holding in Lower Brough at twelve pence, a barn at twelve pence. He may have had a holding also on Stainmoor. In addition he was reeve for Brough Sowerby, where he had a croft (*husbandum*) at a rent of twenty shillings. He was, with John Glenton senior, collector at Brough Sowerby, and was responsible for Stainmoor *cheminagium* (Way Penny).

Slegill William - renting a cottage holding in Lower Brough at twelve pence and a parcel of land 'above the Tofts', at fourteen pence.

Smyth Stephen - had held the recently built forge in the upper part of Lower Brough.

Smyth Thomas - paying half a pound of cumin to the value of two pence for the lands he held in Lower Brough; the cumin was apparently sold on.

Spenser William - renting, with associates, the residual unenclosed land from the demesne area of seventy five acres (see John Wardale) on Sowerby moor at fourteen shillings, together with thirty nine acres of land in Lower Brough at forty shillings. He was also renting a cottage holding in Upper Brough at twelve shillings.

Talbot Richard - he had held the 'pig house' but not in the current year.

Thursk William - surname appears also as 'Thirsk'. Clifford estate official; probably not local to Brough.

Ubank Thomas - see also under John Maltby.

Ubank William - he had some holding on Stainmoor. The placename ended in '…thwaite'

Walker John - renting two bovates in Upper Brough at ten shillings.

Walker Thomas - shared a vaccary with John Whithede - see below.

Wardale John - renting, with associates, a close called Wateflatt in Upper Brough at fifty shillings. This was from a recently enclosed area of seventy five acres of demesne land. He had also, on his own, a croft (*husbandum*) at probably Brough Sowerby at a rent of twenty shillings.

Wardale Thomas - had a cottage holding at Brough Sowerby, at, probably, ten shillings rent.

Wardale William - had a cottage holding at Brough Sowerby, at a rent of five shillings.

Watchett Geoffrey - held foreland, i.e. newly reclaimed, for a tenement at Brough Sowerby at a rent of eleven shillings and fourpence. He also had two tenements at Brough Sowerby at a rent of nine shillings.

Watchett Thomas - had a croft ('*husbandum'*) possibly at Brough Sowerby, at a rent of twenty shillings.

Whithede John - shared a vaccary called *Thornhowscale,* probably the modern Thornyscale, with Thomas Walker, at a rent of forty shillings. In addition, the Vicar of Brough, whose name is not given here, rented a cottage holding in Upper Brough at two shillings.

Appendix VI: Place names in this area

The reading of place names from the 1425 accounts is limited because of damage to the document.

VERSION in DOCUMENT	LIKELY LOCATION or NAME(if known)
Appuby	Appleby
Aqua de Swyndale	Swindale Beck
Aseby Cotesford	Probably Great Asby
Asseby Garrard	Probably Little Asby
Blechefeld/Blachefeld	On Stainmore
Burgh subtus Staynmore	Brough under Stainmore
Castrum de Burgh	Brough Castle
(Le) Castelpark	Castle Park
Egilscale	Heggerscales
Elvearke/Elleark	Probably an eel trap near the Sowerby vaccary
Flattenge/Floteenge	Unidentified but near the castle
Forestija de Staynemore	Stainmore Forest
Grismenlandi	Unidentified, probably in Brough Sowerby
Hertlay	Hartley

Hesil Bank	On Stainmore
Kabergh	Kaber
Karliola	Probably Carlisle
Musgrefe in le Mire	Little Musgrave
Musgreve upon the hill	Great Musgrave
Nethirburgh	Lower Brough, i.e. Market Brough
Overburgh	Upper Brough, i.e. Church Brough
Penreth	Penrith
Ploghstanecroft	In Upper Brough
Redegateclose	Redgate Close
Rogyflatt	Unidentified, possibly in Upper Brough
Rukeby	Rookby
Sloghperpont	Unidentified
Sourebymore	Sowerby Moor
Soureby iuxta Burgh	Brough Sowerby
Stannedyke/Stendyckis/Stonedyke	On Stainmore
Staynesmore	Stainmore
Thornhowscale	Probably Thornyscale
(Les) Toftes	Knocking Tofts?
Warcop	Warcop
Wateflatt	Possibly in Upper Brough
Wynton	Winton

Appendix VII: **Yosgill Mill, employees in its later period**

NB: Italics indicate doubtful readings
* All names marked with an asterisk coincide with entries in the Brough parish register or other records, so these may well have been local people. These lists may not be complete.

A: Employees identified in July, 1784

Matthew Gill*,	Thomas Gill*,
John Todd*,	Sarah Pearson*,
Ann Dockery*.	

B: Employees identified in September/October, 1787

Charles Alderson,	James Black,
John Brown,	William Brown,
Thomas Bushby*,	J Cleasby*,
William Darby*,	J Dent,
John Elwood,	Henry Faudr,
Arthur Gibson,	Matthew Gill,
'Graham's girl',	Richard Johnson,

William Lamb*,
Thomas Lawson,
S Longstaff,
Thomas Marr,
Margaret Nicholson*,
'Old' Nicholl*,
Sarah Pearson,
Susan Pluis* (or Plews),
Robert Smith,
George Stephenson,
John Thompson,
John Todd's 'girl',
William Turner*,
'Young Turner and his wife,
John Wrightson.
(Total 47)

'Lancaster' Tom,
Ann Layton,
"Longstaff's girl",
John Newton,
Thomas Nicholson* and his son,
'Young' Nicholl*,
Thomas Pearson,
John Shield and his 'girl',
Thomas Smith,
Charles Taylor,
John Todd* and his son,
Mary Todd,
J Tonson (maybe Townson),
Robert Williams,

C: Children listed circa 1789

NB: first name is the parent

Agnes Lawson*	one girl	age 13
Thomas Wilson*	one girl	age 9
Mary Allison*	one girl, one boy	ages 14 & 8
John Allison*	two girls, one boy	ages 14, 7, 10
Nan Diton	two girls	ages 10, 17
Hendry Hewatson*	one girl	age 12
Jean Graham	one boy	age 9
Ann Wharton*	two boys, one girl	ages 12, 13, 6
Ann Louthan	one boy	age 8
Peggy Monkhouse	one boy	age 10
Simion Longsaff*	two girls, one boy	ages 12, 8, 10
John Gill*	one girl	age 16
Ann Floyd*	one girl	age 12
William Fedon*	one boy	age 9
Ann Dockrey*	one girl	age 13
Thomas Birkbeck*	two boys	age 10, 9
Jonathan Sawrs*	one boy, one girl	ages 12, 16
Mary Bird*	one boy, one girl	ages 14, 11
Ann Rickaby*	one boy	age 11
Matthew Bell*	one girl	age 14
Robert Ewbanks*	one boy	age 12
(Total 32)		

D: All identified cotton mill employees listed alphabetically

Surname	Forename	Employment date and job in the mill and any other reference
Alderson*	Charles	1787
Alderson*	*Christopher*	1788 a collier
Allinson	Dinah	1790 roving winder
Allinson*	Henry	
Allinson*	Mary	
Allinson*	Matthew	
Allinson*	Sarah	1790 spinner
Allinson	Thomas	1790 spinning master
Armstrong	Jenny	1791 spinner
Bainbridge*	Elizabeth	
Bainbridge*	Mary	carder
Birbeck*	John	
Birbeck*	Thompson	1805 collier
Black Jack	? Jas Black?	1787
Bland	Thomas	1791 picker, 1805 collier
Bowman	Jenny	1791 spinner
Brown	Edward	1791 spinner
Brown	Frank	1792 overlooker
Brown*	John	
Brown*	William	
Brunskill*	nk	
Brunskill*	Hannah	
Bushby*	Thomas	
Cail*	John	spinner
Cail*	Joseph	
Caile*	*Josuha*	
Caille*	Sarah	1790 spinner, 1792 weaving dept.
Catterall	Anne	1790 reeler
Catterall	Jane	cotton picker/ reeler
Catterall	Jenny	reeler
Catterall	Thomas	spinning master
Cleasby*	J.	
Collison*	Agness	
Collison*	Elizabeth	
Compstone	George	1791 cotton picker
Compstone	Nancy	1791 roving winder

Comstone	Isobel	1790 carder
Cumpston*	Bella	
Cumpston*	Mary	1790 spinner
Darby*	William	1787
Davis	'his boy'	1792 rover
Deighton	Nancy	1790 reeler
Dent*	John	
Dent*	*Wind??*	1787
Dockery*	Ann	
Dougy	Jane	reeler
Ellwood*	Elizabeth	cotton picker
Ellwood*	Jane	
Ellwood*	John	1787 picker, 1792 oiler
Ellwood*	Mary	spinner
Ellwood*	William	1790
*Faudr**	Henry	1787
Floyd*	Ann	
Furnass*	The elder	1792 overlooker
Furnass*	The younger - Michael	1790 reeler
Garner*	Elizabeth	
Garnett*	Agnes	1790 spinner
Gibson*	Arthur	1787
Gill*	Margaret	spinner
Gill*	Matthew	roving winder/ drawer 1776
Gill*	Thomas	1792 picker up
Glover	Mary	1791 spinner and washer
Glover	William	1791 spinner
Graham*	Ann	waste picker
Graham*	Jane	reeler
Graham*	John	
Graham*	Mable	spinner 1790 rover
Graham*	Richard	1790 spinner
Graham	Thomas	1790 spinning master
Hague	John	1776
Harrison	'his girl'	1792 spool winder (poss. poor law ref)
Hodgson*	Ann	
Hodgson*	Ann	
Hopes*	Mary	waste picker (poss. poor law ref.)

Hutchinson*	Mary	
Irwin	Hanah	
Irwin	Elkanah	
Jeffry	'his lass'	
Johnson*	Elizabeth	1792 reeler probably
Johnson*	Richard	1787
Lamb*	William	1787
Lancaster Tom	nk	1787
Langstaff*	John	spinner
Langstaff*	Ann	
Langstaff*	Elizabeth	
Langstaff*	Simon	
Lawson	Thomas	1787
Layton*	Ann	
Ley	Roger	1791 weaver
Longstaff	S.	1787
Longstaff's girl	nk	1787
Lothian	John	spinner
Lothian	Thomas	spinner
Lowson	Jenny	1790 *rover*
Lupton	Mary	1790 drawer
McCallum	Ann	1790 roving winder, 1792 weaver
McCallum	I.	1790 spinning, 1792 weaving
McCallum	C.	1792 picker up
McCallum	E.	1792 weaving dept.
McCallum	R.	1792 weaving dept.
McCallum	William	1791 spinner
Marr	Thomas	1787
Maugham	Hannah	1792 rover
Metcalf*	Ann	drawer/spinner
Metcalf	Elizabeth	1790 spinner
Metcalf	Jenny	1791 cotton picker
Metcalf*	Mary	1790 spinner
Metcalf*	Nelly	1790 roving winder/spinner
Metcalf*	William	1796 cotton picker, 1792 blacksmith, 1802 collier.
Moncaster	Margaret	single mother
Muncaster	John	
Monkhouse*	Mary	

Munkhouse*	*Joshua*	
Munkhouse	Sally	1790 carding, 1791 drawer
Newton	John	1787
Nicholl	The elder	1787
Nicholl	The younger	1787
Nicholson*	Jenny	roving winder
Nicholson*	*Leonard*	
Nicholson*	Margaret	1787 spinner and cotton picker
Nicholson*	Mary	spinner
Nicholson*	Thomas	1787
Nicholson*	son of Thomas	1787
Nixon	Jenny	1791 cotton picker
Nixon	Rachel	1791 roving winder
Nixon*	Richard	cotton picker
Nixon*	Robert	1776 cotton picker, 1791 overlooker
Noonhouse	Joseph	1792 reeler
Ollivant	Nelly	
Pearson*	Mary	1790 carder, 1792 rover
Pearson*	Sarah	1787 cotton picker
Pearson*	Sarah - her daughter	
Pearson*	Thomas	1787 drawer
Plews (Pluis)*	John	roving winder (see also coal list)
Plews (Pluis)*	Susan	1787
Plews (Pluis)*	Thomas	1790 spinner
Railton	Mary	1791 carder
Rain*	Joshua	
Rain's wife		
Sanderson*	Thomas	
Sanderson*	T. (his man)	
Sayer	Elizabeth	1791 spinner
Sayer* (or Sagar)	William	1792 spool winder
Shields	John	1786 day labourer
Shields	'his girl'	1787
Simon's wife		
Smith*	Robert	1787
Smith*	Thomas	1787
Stephenson*	George	1787
Swales*	his daughter	
Taylor*	Charles	1787

Tedding	nk	1792 spool winder
Thompson	Fanny	1792 reeler
Thompson*	John	1787
Thompson*	Margaret	cotton picker
Thwaites	Molly	1791 waste worker (poss. poor law)
Todd*	John	1787
Todd*	his son	1787
Todd*	Mary	1787
Todd*	John's girl	1787
Todd*	widow	
Tonson	J.	1787
Turner*	Christopher	1790 spinner
Turner*	John	spinner
Turner	Thomas	1790 roving, 1791 spinner
Turner*	William	1787
Turner*	his wife, possibly Sally	1787 picker
Turner*	his boy	1789 possibly also a waller
Walton*	William, junior	
Ward*	Ann	waste picker
Weightman*	John	1806 husbandman
Wharton*	Ann	cotton picker (poss. poor law)
Wharton*	Bella	
Wharton*	Elizabeth	1790 spinner
Wilkinson	Bella	overlooker
Wilkinson*	George	1792 cleaner
Williams	Robert	1787
Wilson*	Elizabeth	1790 roving winder
Wilson*	*James*	spinner
Wilson*	John	drawer/rover
Wilson*	Nancy	spinner
Wilson	Thomas	1791 spinner
Wilson*	William	1790 spinner
Wilson	Mary	1790 spinning
Woods	Mary	1790 carder
Wrightson	John	1787

Appendix VIII: Mine workers and residence if known

NK means no other information found.

Described as Coal Miners:

1777	Isaac Topping	Tarnhouse, Hillbeck.
1801	Richard Bousfield	Market Brough

Described as Miners:

1790	Christopher Brown	Market Brough
1801	Joseph Rain	Hillbeck
1808	William Metcalf	Dumma Crag (described as a 'collier' in 1802)
1808	Obadiah Miller	Market Brough

Described as Colliers:

1771	Jonas Ward	Penystone Green
1772	John Robinson	High Eubanke
1774	William Hodgson	Church Brough
1775	George Pearson	(residence not stated; he died in an accident at Hillbeck Fell colliery)
1775	Richard Brunskill	Kingspitt House, Yorkshire
1776	John Alderson	High Eubanke
1776	Joseph Saunders	Penystone Green
1777	Joseph Loader	Market Brough
1777	Christopher Smith	Stainmore Dale
1778	Anthony Beckwith	Stainmore, (1784 at Windmore End, 'Rawntree Force', 1805 Stainmore)
1781	Joshua Dolphin	Penystone Green
1781	Thomas Birbeck	Market Brough (but later at Church Brough)
1784	James Metcalfe	Church Brough.
1784	James Bennett	Little Thwaite (1790, Light Trees; Loadman's, 1789)
1784	John Brunskill	Market Brough.
1784	Thomas Bird	'from the Mill'
1786	Anthony Emmerson	Dumay Crag
1786	Simon Bulman	'killed in Coal Pit', location unknown
1787	John Simpson	Park House (1792, Market Brough, worked at Loadman's, 1789)
1787	William Bland	Market Brough, worked at Loadman's, 1789
1787	James Beckwith	Dumma Crag, 1794, Stainmore
1788	Christopher Alderson	Windmore End, Stainmore in 1790, and Gray Lodge in 1797
1787	Henry Cowton	Stainmore
1787	Richard Alderson	High Ewbank, Tanhill pits
1787	Simon Alderson	High Ewbank, Tanhill pits
1787	Matthew Oyston	High Ewbank, Tanhill pits

1787	John Oyston	High Ewbank, Tanhill pits
1787	Thomas Holiday	High Ewbank, Tanhill pits
1787	John Preston	High Ewbank, Tanhill pits
1787	John Moore	High Ewbank, Tanhill pits
1787	George Megson	Low Pits
1787	John Metcalf	Low Pits
1787	James Metcalf	Low Pits
1787	Isaac Simpson	Park Houses
1787	Henry Longridge	Park Houses
1787	Christopher Brown	Newton
1788	Joseph Birbeck	Windmore End
1788	James Anderson	Market Brough
1789	John Beckwith	Church Brough, worked at Loadman's
1789	John Youdale	nk
1789	Robert Thompson	Market Brough
1789	William Todd	Church Brough, 1792 at Market Brough, 1789 worked at Loadman's
1791	John Shield	Long Cragg End
1794	John Anderson	Market Brough
1794	Matthew Bell	nk
1794	Thomas Simpson	Market Brough
1794	Thomas Coulson	nk
1794	Richard Johnson	nk
1795	William Balderstone	Stainmore
1796	Jonathan Birbeck	Lanehead, 1805 at Swindale Head
1796	Henry Coulton	Stainmore
1797	William Hopes	Market Brough (see also Poor Law records)
1798	Nicholas Furnas	Market Brough, Church Brough in 1800
1798	John Birkbeck	Todd House, Dumma Crag in 1804, Stainmore 1811
1798	George Graham	Market Brough
1799	Ralph Woodward	Stainmore
1799	Richard Bousfield	Dumma Crag and Market Brough in 1801
1802	Richard Birkbeck	Gibson Lane Head
1802	William Metcalf	Dumma Crag
1803	John Hopes	Market Brough (see also Poor Law records)
1803	James Staceye (later Stacey)	Plaintree Hall, Dumma Crag
1804	Thomas Pluis	Market Brough (name appears in Yosgill records)
1805	Thomas Bland	Market Brough
1805	Thomas Smith	The Warehouse, Stainmore
1805	Anthony Dent	Church Brough
1805	Edward Bousfield	Cooper House
1805	Thompson Birkbeck	Market Brough and Church Brough in 1811
1805	David Crass	Stainmore
1806	George Birkbeck	Gibson Lane Head

1807	William Coats	Long Crag
1807	George Dent	Blackmore Gate
1807	John Coulton	Dumma Crag
1808	Robert Birkbeck	Gibson Lane Head
1808	James Birkbeck	Church Brough
1808	Thomas Bousfield	Slape Stones
1808	George Emmerson	Bleath Gill
1809	John Coulstone	Cumpstone Lane Head
1811	Thomas Anderson	Market Brough
1811	Simon Anderson	Gibson Lane Head
1811	Thomas Brunskill	Market Brough
1811	John Alderson	Long Cragg
1812	John Bragg	Strice Gill
1812	William Rane	Stainmore
1829	John Moffitt	Market Brough
1829	Robert Buckle	Hag Gap and Hillbeck

Other names

1829 Brougham, Whitelock, Gibson & Robinson – owners Low Pits and Light Trees collieries – Mousgill Row

1829 John Gibson, Mousgill Row, superintendent to above collieries

Appendix IX: List of tenants of the Earl of Thanet in Brough in the late eighteenth century

These people held houses or land, some having several holdings, under various leases and at various times. Therefore the numbers refer to holdings, not to population. The specific locations are not known. Some holdings may have been for mining, rather than farming or houses.

A: East Stainmore, circa 1775

No.	Surname	First name	Other references
1	Sayer	Henry	
2	Ewbanke	Jonathan	
3	Nichelson	Robert	
4	Sayers	Christopher	
5	Nicholson	John	
6	Nicholson	Thomas	
7	Shaw	Jeffrey	
8	Shaw	Francis	
9	Sanderson	Thomas	
10	Cleasby	Stephen	
11	Waller	Jane	Daughter of Edward

References CRO(K) WD/HH/8, CRO(K) WD/HH/9 and D Lons L/12/3/7

12	Waller	William	
13	Wheatley	nk	
14	Bonson	John	A coal carrier
15	Nicholson	Eliz	Wife of John
16	Pearson	Francis	
17	Sanderson	Charles	
18	Nanson	William	A butcher
19	Jackson	Isabell	Spinster
20	Monkhouse	Miles	Gentleman
21	Rudd	William	
22	Wilkin	William	
23	Rudd	Thomas	
24	Wilkinson	Adam	
25	Fawcett	James	Gentleman
26	Waistell	Lancelot	
27	Monkhouse	Myles	

At Mousgill Row within East Stainmore

28	Nicholson	Eliz	
29	Ewbanke	Joshua	The elder
30	Ewbanke	Jonathan	
31	Hilton	John	
32	Nicholson	Jonathan	
33	Brunskill	Michael	
34	Johnson	James	The younger
35	Mason	John	
36	Sanderson	Thomas	
37	Hilton	George	
38	Nicholson John and Johnson James		
39	Milner	Joseph	
40	Johnson	James	The younger
41	Johnson	Henry	
42	Shaw	William	
43	Nicholson	Abraham	
44	Brunskill	John	Clerk
45	Brunskill	Richard	
46	Waistell	Michael	
47	Waistell	Jeffry	
48	Baxter	Richard	The younger
49	Davis	Charles	An innkeeper
50	Holiday	Christopher	
51	Cleasby James, Harrison Edward and Longstaff John		
52	Longstaff	John	
53	Harrison	Edward	
54	Harrison	Edward	

55	Atkinson	George	
56	Brunskill	William	Also held Taw & Whins; closes at High Intake & Low Intake
57	Dickinson	William	
58	Brunskill	Michael	Clerk: north side of east Stainmore
59	Dickinson, Arthur Hilton and Wilkinson, John		
60	Varty	Frances	Awgill Bridge
61	Loadman	John	
62	Loadman	John	
63	Shaw	Thomas	
64	Johnson	Robert	
65	Smith	Robert	The elder
66	Harrison	Lancelot	
67	Cleasby	Thomas	
68	Smith	Matthew	
69	Bland	Thomas	
70	Bird	Hugh	
71	Bainbridge	William	
72	Whelpdale	Thomas	
73	Davis	Charles	
74	Ellwood	John	
75	Weightman	John	
76	Johnson	Thomas	
77	Holiday	Edward	
78	Wright	Thomas	
79	Thompson	Jonathan	
80	Whelpdale	Thomas	
81	Scott	John	An infant
82	Walton	Rowland	
83	Shield	John	
84	Robinson	George	
85	Hodgson	Thomas	
86	Blacklaw	Adam	
87	Scott	Anna	Wife of Patrick
88	nk	Nancy	Wife of Norman
89	Thompson	Ian	
90	Brunskill	John	
91	Alderson	Christopher	Clerk
92	Cleasby	James	
93	Moss	Robert	
94	Hastwell	Michael	
95	Hastwell	William	
96	Munkhouse	Mary and Thomas	
97	Smith	John	In right of his wife

At South Stainmore

98	Morland	John and Michael
99	Bousfield	Robert
100	Morland, John and Harrison, Richard and Morland, Michael	

At Brough Sowerby (circa 1780)

101	Robinson	John	Esquire
102	Alderson	*Joan*	
103	Langstaff	Thomas	
104	Middleton	Isabele	
105	Wilkin	William	Mister
106	Rudd	William	
107	Cawthropp	nk	
108	Cumstone	Robert	The elder
109	Waistell	Lancelot	
110	Waistell	John	
111	Waistell	Ann	An infant
112	Rudd	William	
113	Middleton	Isabele	
114	Waistell	Lancelot	
115	Waistell	John	
116	Waistell	John	
117	Kipling	nk (?John)	
118	Waistell	John	The son
119	Cumpston	Robert	
120	Cumpstone	Robert	
121	Campbell	Margaret	
122	Scott	Margaret	
123	Cumstone	Robert	
124	Rudd	Robert	
125	Wilkins	William	Mister
126	Alderson	Jonathan	
127	Munkhouse	Richard	Clerk and Mister
128	Munkhouse	Thomas	
129	Grainger	John	
130	Grainger	John	The younger
131	Campbell	Sarah	
132	Cumpstone	Isabele	
133	Cumpstone	Robert	The younger
134	Bell	nk (?Lancelot)	The Reverend Mister
135	Dickinson	John	
136	Monkhouse	Myles	Mister
137	Monkhouse	Miles	
138	Monkhouse	Miles	
139	Nicholson	Elizabeth	4 cattlegates in Brough Sowerby intack

140	Nicholson	Elizabeth	
141	Coultherd	James	
142	Brunskill	nk	An infant
143	Rudd	Thomas	
144	Langstaff	Thomas	
145	Bell	Lancelot	Sold to: Clerk
146	Highmore	Ann	Wife of James
147	Rudd	Thomas	
148	Dixon	Bartholomew	Esquire
149	Wheatley	nk	
150	Dickinson	William	
151	Harrison	nk	Possibly a widow
152	Atkinson John and Dickinson William		
153	Nicholson	John	
154	Wilkinson	Adam	
155	Baxter	Richard	
156	Cleasby	Stephen	
157	Monkhouse	Miles	
158	Longstaff, Robert and Morland, Mary		
159	Coulthard	Jane	Wife of Thomas
160	Walter	Jane	Daughter of Edward; three cattlegates in Brough Sowerby intack

At Heggerscales, 1780

161	Williamson	John	
162	Gorst	Gilpin	Clerk:
	and Barnet	Richard	Barnet held in right of his wife
163	Hodgson	Agnes	An infant
	and Hodgson	Elizabeth	
164	Cleasby	John	

Tenants at Church Brough, circa 1797

165	Hodgson	Thomas	
166	Wilson	Elizabeth	Wife of John Wilson
167	Bellas	nk	Reverend Mister
168	Hodgson	Thomas	
169	Trout	Thomas	
170	Bird	John	
171	Kirk	David	
172	Hodgson	Thomas	The younger
173	Jackson	William	
174	Salkeld	John	
175	Todd	John	
176	Rudd	Thomas	

177	Hindson	John	
178	Allison	Thomas	
179	Grainger	Thomas	
180	Bellas	Lancelot	Reverend Mister
181	Rowe	nk	
182	Nanson	Thomas	WTWN p8
183	Middleton	George	Possibly a shopkeeper
184	Wilson	nk	Reverend Mister
185	Rudd	John	
186	Richardson	nk	Possibly a JP
187	Gawthrop	Mary	Wife of William
188	Bowe	Thomas	
189	*Morron*	David	
190	Wilson	John	
191	Bird	James	
192	Fawcett	John Davis	
193	Bowe	Michael	
194	Davis	John	
195	Harrison	John	
196	Rudd	John	An infant
197	Rudd	George	
198	Elliott	William	

At Market Brough

199	Simpson	Elizabeth	Miss
200	Rudd	Thomas	
201	Asbridge	William	
202	Bell	Christopher	
203	Lamb	Margaret	
204	Richardson	Francis	
205	Kirk	David	
206	Nanson	John	
207	Scott	nk	Mrs
208	*Bird*(or *Hird*)	Sarah	Wife of James
209	Hutchinson	William	
210	Ellwood	Elizabeth	
211	Sayers	Christopher	
212	Thwaites	Robert	
213	Towenson	Thomas	
214	Towenson	Agnes	
215	Page	Mary	
216	Johnson	Isaac	
217	Normand	nk	Mrs
218	Hodgson	Thomas	
219	Hird	Sarah	Wife of *James*

220	Wright	Frances	
221	Hodgson	Sarah	
222	Spencer	Richard	
223	Horn	Michael	
224	Robinson	John	Esquire
225	Graham	George	
226	Smith	Mary	
227	Smith	Ester	
228	Wilson	John	High Bank
229	Bailes	John	

Free rents in Brough

230	Hodgson	Thomas	
231	Jackson	William	
232	Longstaff	Elizabeth	
233	Bird	John	
234	Bowe	Michael	
235	Bailes	John	
236	Lamb	nk	Mrs
237	Hodgson	Thomas	The elder
238	Nicholson	John	
239	Hutchinson	nk	Mister
240	Richardson	Frances	
241	Shaw	nk	Reverend Mister,
242	Rudd	Robert	
243	Petty	Isabella	
244	Munkhouse	Sarah	
245	Normand	nk	Mrs
246	Bird	James	
247	Allison	Thomas	
248	Hodgson	Thomas	The younger

Burrels Fell rents

249	Sayer	Christopher	
250	Rowe	Robert	
251	Rowe	Thomas	

Freeholders

252	Carlton	John Metcalf	Esquire
253	Thompson	nk	Miss
254	Shaw	Henry	Clerk
255	Bayles	John	
256	Highmore	Ann	
257	Hodgson	Thomas	

258	Middleton	Isabell	
259	Hodgson	Thomas	Gentleman
260	Musgrave	Philip	Sir
261	Rudd	Thomas	
262	Davis	Joseph	
263	Richardson	Francis	
264	Thanet		Earl of
265	Norman	Nancy	Wife of Martin
266	Bowe	Michael	
267	Thwaites	Robert	
268	Petty	John	
269	Sayer	Christopher	
270	Jackson	William	
271	Bird	Hugh	
272	Fowler	John	
273	Munkhouse	Thomas	Esquire
274	Maugham	John	
275	Munkhouse	Sarah	
276	Gorst	Gilpin	Clerk
277	Mason Fenton	John	Clerk
278	Harrison	John	

Index

Note: As Brough is mentioned frequently only major references to it are indexed. References to Church Brough, Market Brough and Brough Sowerby are under those names. See these headings for variants on the names. The appendices are not indexed.

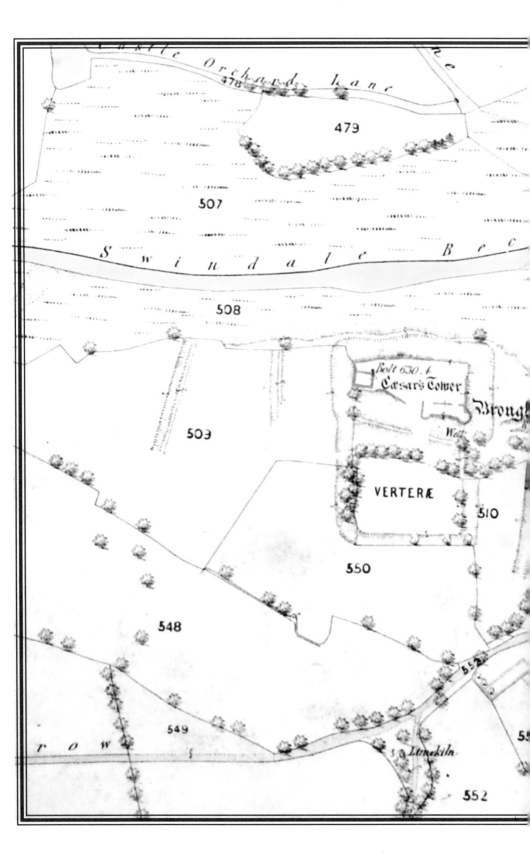